# Contents

Acknowledgments ............................................................................ v

Introduction: Assessing the Multiple Intelligences
        *Bruce Torff* .................................................................... vii

Section 1:  Multiple Intelligences and Assessment: The View from
        Project Zero  ...................................................................... 1

    If Binet Had Looked Beyond the Classroom: The Assessment
    of Multiple Intelligences
        *Thomas Hatch and Howard Gardner* ............................ 5

    Alternative Assessment from a Multiple Intelligences
    Perspective
        *Jie-Qi Chen and Howard Gardner* ............................... 27

    From Research to Reform: Finding Better Ways to
    Put Theory into Practice
        *Thomas Hatch* .............................................................. 55

Section 2:  Portfolios and Projects: Assessment in the
        Classroom  ........................................................................ 67

    Portfolios Invite Reflection—From Students *and* Staff
        *Elizabeth A. Hebert* ...................................................... 69

The Power in Portfolios: "A Way for Sitting Beside" Each
Learner
        *Evangeline Harris Stefanakis* ........................................... 79

Domain Projects as Assessment Vehicles in a Computer-
Rich Environment
        *Joseph Walters and Howard Gardner* ........................... 85

**Section 3: Alternative Assessments and Educational Practices .. 109**

Giftedness, Diversity, and Problem Solving
        *C. June Maker, Aleene B. Nielson, and*
        *Judith A. Rogers* ........................................................... 111

Authentic Assessment of Problem Solving and Giftedness in
Secondary School Students
        *C. June Maker* ............................................................... 133

Assessment in Context: The Alternative to Standardized
Testing
        *Howard Gardner* .......................................................... 153

**Authors** ................................................................................. 209

**Acknowledgments** ............................................................... 211

**Index** ..................................................................................... 213

# Multiple Intelligences and Assessment

$cx/cx$

## A Collection of Articles

Edited by
Bruce Torff

TRAINING AND PUBLISHING, INC.

Arlington Heights, Illinois

**Multiple Intelligences and Assessment: A Collection of Articles**

Published by IRI/SkyLight Training and Publishing, Inc.
2626 S. Clearbrook Dr., Arlington Heights, IL 60005
800-348-4474 or 847-290-6600
Fax 847-290-6609
info@iriskylight.com
http://www.iriskylight.com

Creative Director: Robin Fogarty
Managing Editor: T. B. Zaban
Editor: Edward Roberts
Proofreader: Jennifer Gillis
Researcher: Marilyn Foley
Type Compositor: Donna Ramirez, Christina Georgi
Formatter: Donna Ramirez
Illustration and Cover Designer: David Stockman
Book Designer: Heidi Ray
Production Supervisor: Bob Crump

ISBN 1-57517-065-5
LCCCN: 96-77781

1856C-4-98 PG
Item number 1451

06 05 04 03 02 01 00 99 98      15 14 13 12 11 10 9 8 7 6 5 4 3

# Acknowledgments

The Editor would like to thank several people for their assistance with this book and related projects: Lisa Bromer, Laura Deeds, Robin Fogarty, Thomas Hatch, Mindy Kornhaber, Mara Krechevsky, Julia Noblitt, Edward Roberts, Julie Viens, and Edward Warburton. I would especially like to thank Howard Gardner for his helpful comments on the introductory chapter.

# Introduction

# Assessing the Multiple Intelligences

Since *Frames of Mind* appeared on bookstore shelves in 1983, Howard Gardner's theory of multiple intelligences (MI) has attracted widespread interest among educators (Kornhaber and Krechevsky 1994). Schools have moved to organize curricula around Gardner's list of intelligences. Networks of schools focused on MI have been formed. Numerous publications and videotapes explore the educational implications of MI theory, and professional development activities based on MI are common.

MI has sounded a resonant chord in the educational community, for at least three reasons. First, the basic message of MI is straightforward and plausible—the child has several intellectual potentials, not just one, and these potentials are defined, shaped, and combined by the surrounding culture (Gardner 1983, 1993). To many educators, the notion of multiple intelligences simply makes more sense than a single "general" intelligence. Second, MI is seen as child-centered. Educators are encouraged that MI speaks to the diverse gifts of individual children. Unlike other models of intelligence, MI seems to focus on children instead of tests. Finally, MI appeals to multicultural sensibilities. Educators have applauded MI's emphasis on accounting for the diverse instantiations of "intelligence" in different cultures around the world—not just for performances on the sit-down tests favored in Western society. MI is viewed as a theory of intelligence that counters Western biases. In essence, MI is a plausible notion about the human being's intellectual endowment, a notion that appeals to educators' views about children and cultures.

Gardner (1983, 1993) has stressed that MI is a psychological theory—a notion about the structure of human intellect—not an educational strategy. At the same time, Gardner and colleagues at Project Zero have conducted a variety of research projects exploring the educational implications of MI (see the articles in this volume). Project Zero is an educational research organization co-directed by Gardner and David Perkins at the Harvard Graduate School of Education. Researchers at Project Zero work on a variety of grant-funded research initiatives, not all of which are concerned with MI theory, but all of which aim to improve educational practices through systematic studies of thinking, learning, and teaching. Whereas Gardner and colleagues have built a research base on the educational implications of MI, they make no attempt to fashion an exhaustive "MI method" (Hatch 1993). Researchers at Project Zero make suggestions for applying MI to education but encourage educators to develop their own ideas as well.

> **MI is a response to our society's heavy emphasis on standardized testing.**

To date, many of these educational efforts have focused on MI as a vehicle for curriculum and instruction. Much of the literature on MI is designed to help teachers create and teach MI-infused lessons. Far less ink has been spilled in applying MI to the issues of *assessment* (that is, how educators and learners take stock of progress made and ground yet to cover).

This attention to assessment is surprising in light of the detailed treatment given the topic in *Frames of Mind*. In particular, MI is a response to our society's heavy emphasis on standardized testing—the practice of employing examinations (e.g., the Scholastic Aptitude Test) to capture the intellectual achievement of the individual and compare it to the norms set by the peer group. Standardized tests play a prominent role in our society's educational practices—just ask any high school student sweating out the SAT.

Prevalent as standardized tests may be, they have come under increasing attack in recent years. Many psychologists and educators have questioned the extent to which standardized tests measure behavior as it occurs in the real world (Cole et al. 1978; Gardner 1983,

1993). This "ecological validity" issue is a vexing one: to what extent do tests really reflect the intellectual achievements of the individual? How well do standardized tests predict adult success (e.g., job performance)?

Remarkably poorly, it turns out. On average, cognitive ability tests account for only 4% of the variance in job performance (Wigdor and Garner 1982). Only 4%! Ninety-six percent of what makes a person good on the job is attributable to factors that do not show up on tests. Tests do a somewhat better job of predicting school performance; after all, schoolwork and tests share many attributes (Gardner 1983, 1993; Sternberg et al. 1995). It is striking, though, that tests predict job performance so poorly. The results suggest that there is much more operating in real life than the skills captured on standardized tests.

> How well do standardized tests predict adult success? Remarkably poorly, it turns out.

The weak performance of standardized tests is not surprising, Gardner (1983, 1993) suggests, for two reasons. First, standardized tests sample too narrow a range. They place a heavy premium on two sets of skills (linguistic and logical-mathematical) and pay too little attention to a variety of other human intelligences (spatial, musical, bodily-kinesthetic, interpersonal, intrapersonal, and naturalist). Second, in many cases standardized tests are quite remote from the real-world contexts in which knowledge is acquired and used (that is, problem-solving on tests is typically "decontextualized"). Indeed, tests typically consist of pencil-and-paper activities performed in a short time period without help or tools. Real-world uses of many skills are quite the opposite: they require physical performances and other actions not adaptable to desk-top formats; they involve collaborations with other people; they rely on tool use; and they occupy extended time periods.

The MI-driven critique of standardized testing raises some pressing assessment questions. If the child has multiple intelligences, how should educators go about assessing them? What are the alternatives to standardized tests? MI, a theory of human intellect turned educational tool, calls for assessment procedures that veer away sharply from contemporary assessment practices centering on standardized tests. The chapters in this book describe alternative assessments that capture the range of intelligences, allow the intelligences to be given something closer to equal weight, employ intelligence-fair assessment formats, and focus on student performances in authentic contexts. Here are bold steps toward the development of assessment procedures for the multiple intelligences.

## REFERENCES

Cole, M., M. Hood, and R. McDermott. 1978. Concepts of ecological validity. *The Quarterly Newsletter of the Institute for Comparative Human Development* 2: 34–37.

Gardner, H. 1983. *Frames of mind.* New York: Basic Books.

———. 1993. *Multiple intelligences: The theory into practice.* New York: Basic Books.

Hatch, T. 1993. From research to reform. *Educational Horizons* 197: 197–203.

Kornhaber, M. and M. Krechevsky. 1994. Expanding definitions of teaching and learning: Notes from the MI underground. In *Creating school policy: Trends, dilemmas, and prospects,* edited by P. Cookson. New York: Garland Press.

Sternberg, R., R. Wagner, W. Williams, and J. Horvath. 1995. Testing common sense. *American Psychologist* 50 (11): 912–27.

Wigdor, A., and W. Garner, eds. 1982. *Ability testing: Uses, consequences, and controversies.* Washington, DC: National Academy Press.

# Section 1

# Multiple Intelligences and Assessment: The View from Project Zero

The first section provides an overview of MI and describes research projects conducted at Project Zero on alternative assessments in variety of settings. Hatch and Gardner set the stage by describing and critiquing the traditional model of intelligence, paying particular attention to the decontextualized assessment procedures spawned by that model. The authors introduce two research projects conducted at Project Zero. They start with Arts PROPEL, which focused on alternative assessments in three art forms (imaginative writing, music, and visual arts) at the middle and secondary levels (Gardner 1989; Zessoules, Wolf, and Gardner 1988). The authors then outline Project Spectrum, which focused on diversifying assessment practices in preschool and elementary settings (Krechevsky and Gardner 1990).

Project Spectrum receives detailed treatment in the chapter by Chen and Gardner. The authors make the case for alternative assessments that capture the intellectual competences in a wide range of domains, employ media appropriate to the domain, engage the learner in meaningful activities, and involve assessment that is ongoing (as opposed to the "one-shot" variety).

The chapter by Hatch points the way from educational theory and research to classroom change. He discusses two Project Zero research efforts in this direction, beginning with the Mather Project,

which investigated alternative assessments in an after-school program. Hatch then presents the ATLAS project, an educational reform
effort conducted collaboratively by Gardner and colleagues at Project
Zero, Ted Sizer and colleagues at the Coalition for Essential Schools,
James Comer and colleagues at the School Development Program,
and researchers at the Education Development Center. ATLAS is an
acronym for Alternative Teaching, Learning, and Assessment for
Schools (see *Educational Leadership,* February 1994). Among other
things, ATLAS draws together several strands of Project Zero theory
and research, including MI and more recent work on the acquisition
of deep understanding of the concepts in a domain (Gardner 1991;
Gardner and Boix-Mansilla 1994).

These introductory chapters set out twin themes for alternative
assessments developed by Gardner and colleagues at Project Zero.
First, "intelligence-fair" assessments are needed that allow students
to solve problems or create products using the materials of the intellectual medium—not by filtering knowledge to be assessed through
the intelligences used in test-taking (linguistic and logical/math-
ematical, for the most part). Second, the authors call for "assessment
in context" that engages learners not with the decontextualized
problems found on standardized tests but with familiar and ecologi-
cally-valid tasks and settings. These themes yield the conclusion that
direct assessment of the intelligences can be problematic (Gardner,
personal communication 1996):

> Increasingly, I find it unproductive to assess intelligences per se. I
> doubt that one could do it and if one could, it would probably yield
> just the labeling that we don't want. Instead, I talk about assessing val-
> ued competences and skills. These may—presumably do—involve tar-
> geted intelligences, though whether a particular intelligence or set of
> intelligences happen to be involved is always an inference. If we talk
> about assessing reading a map or finding [one's] way around an unfa-
> miliar neighborhood, these are important competences. They may re-
> veal something about spatial intelligence, but perhaps not; I don't use
> much spatial intelligence in my own navigation, for example. What is
> important from my MI perspective is that the person can accomplish
> important tasks, and not which particular one or two intelligences are
> at work. It is the use of tasks that sample a wide range of intelligences
> which is key to Spectrum and other MI-inspired assessment efforts.
>
> Having expressed my own reservations, I do not mean to con-
> demn all efforts to measure the intelligences, some of which have been
> carried out at Project Zero. Specific instruments have been created for

specific purposes, and they should be evaluated in terms of the extent to which they achieve the purposes. However, it is my belief that anyone who devises an instrument to measure human competences has a special obligation to make sure it is not abused. I went on television in Australia to condemn an application of MI theory which seemed to be a perversion of that theory; and I hope the devisors of so-called MI tests will be prepared to do the same, if the need arises.

## REFERENCES

Gardner, H. 1989. Zero-based arts education: An introduction to arts PROPEL. *Studies in Art Education: A Journal of Issues and Research* 30 (2): 71–83.

————. 1991. *The unschooled mind.* New York: Basic Books.

Gardner, H., and V. Boix-Mansilla, eds. 1994. Teaching for understanding in the disciplines and beyond. *Teachers College Record* 96 (2): 198–218.

Krechevsky, M., and H. Gardner. 1990. The emergence and nurturance of multiple intelligences: The Project spectrum approach. In *Encouraging the development of exceptional skills and talents,* edited by M. J. A. Howe. Leicester, England: The British Psychological Society.

Zessoules, R., D. Wolf, and H. Gardner. 1988. A better balance: Arts PROPEL as an alternative to discipline-based arts education. In *Beyond DBAE: The case for multiple visions of art education,* edited by J. Barton, A. Lederman, and P. London. North Dartmouth, MA: University Council on Art Education.

# If Binet Had Looked Beyond the Classroom: The Assessment of Multiple Intelligences

by Thomas Hatch and Howard Gardner

## INTRODUCTION

If some of the great figures of the modern era were gathered together, we would find among them Albert Einstein, Virginia Woolf, Martha Graham, Mahatma Gandhi, Pablo Picasso, Sigmund Freud, and Igor Stravinsky. We also might discover Alfred Binet, the originator of perhaps the first intelligence tests and a major influence on psychology and education today. Armed with his test, Binet might be trying to predict which of his colleagues would achieve success in school. This is similar, in fact, to the task that was set for him by the Parisian government at the turn of the century. If, however, Binet was instructed to try to predict who would achieve success in fields ranging from painting to politics, it is not clear how he would proceed. How would he assess skills? Would he choose to focus all, or even the majority, of his resources on standardized tests? Would psychologists who analyzed performances on the these tests conclude that thinking was essentially a process of "general" problem solving?

In this chapter, we will present a new approach to educational curriculum and assessment which may help us to address these questions. This approach, based on the Theory of Multiple Intelligences (Gardner 1983), suggests that we need to take a broader view of thinking processes and human achievement as they are realized in different domains of accomplishment. In order to take this broader perspective, we need to construct contextualized assessments which engage the distinct abilities of a number of intelligences. Through

From *International Journal of Educational Research*, vol. 14, no. 5, 415–29. © 1990 by Thomas Hatch and Howard Gardner. Reprinted with permission.

this process, we seek to make assessment a regular part of learning, to recognize abilities not covered on standardized tests, and to give teachers a greater role in the assessment process. Such an approach can shift the focus from ranking students to helping them build on their own intellectual capacities and take optimal advantage of the educational resources around them.

## BACKGROUND

In the past twenty years, traditional notions of intelligence and standardized tests like the IQ have been scrutinized from a number of perspectives (see for example Block and Dworkin 1976; Ceci and Liker 1987; Gould 1981; Sternberg 1985). Gardner (1983) has drawn on findings in the fields of developmental psychology and neuropsychology to call into question the narrow focus on linguistic and logical-mathematic skills in traditional tests and theories of intelligence.

### The Breakdown of the Universal View of Development

In the 1960s a certain synthesis in developmental psychology, due primarily to the pathbreaking work of Piaget, held sway. According to this view of "universal development," all normal children passed through stages of development at the same pace in all domains. By the 1970s, Piaget's version of universal development was being questioned by many in the field. Numerous studies found that a child's level of development in one domain failed to predict that child's level of development in other domains (see Gelman 1978 for a useful summary). At Project Zero, Gardner and a number of colleagues in the Piagetian tradition focused on development in a number of artistic domains. Those domains included music, drawing, expressive language, and three-dimensional representation. They found that, with age controlled, the achievement of developmental milestones in one domain was largely independent of development in the other domains (Gardner and Wolf 1983).

In addition to this line of psychological investigation, research on the abilities of people who had suffered damage to the brain also contradicted Piaget's basic intuition. Studies indicated that functioning in the domain of language, for example, could be severely impaired while functioning in other areas remained largely unaffected (Gardner 1975). These selective deficits indicated that different parts of the brain subserve different functions; this finding, in turn, supported the notion that these functions could develop independently.

As the universal account of development began to unravel, investigations of development in individual domains became more crucial. As long as it was believed that ability was the same across domains, it did not matter greatly which domain was chosen for measurement. Assessing ability in language or math should yield similar results to assessments in other domains. However, for those, like Gardner, who came to believe that abilities functioned and developed independently, focusing on a restricted set of domains resulted in a severely distorted view of an individual's competence.

> **Thinking in different domains cannot be attributed to a general problem solving capacity.**

### The Theory of Multiple Intelligences

These theoretical and practical concerns contributed to the positing of a more pluralistic view of intellect. In the book *Frames of Mind* (1983), Gardner defined a human intelligence as "the capacity to solve problems or fashion products which are valued in one or more cultural settings." From this Multiple Intelligences perspective (hereafter MI), intelligence is displayed, discovered, and developed within the context of meaningful, culturally significant activities. This theory emphasizes that there is no general problem solving ability, highlights the roles and achievements valued in a wide variety of cultures, and challenges the belief that intelligence(s) can be adequately assessed through standardized paper and pencil tests.

Imagine again, some of the great figures of the modern era, but this time picture them at work: Einstein carrying out a thought experiment, Woolf writing in her notebook, Graham dancing on a stage, Gandhi addressing a crowd, Picasso painting a canvas, Freud analyzing a patient, and Stravinsky composing at the piano. From a Multiple Intelligences standpoint, these figures are not simply working, or painting, or dancing; they are *thinking*—finding and solving problems or creating products—in radically different media.

The work of individuals like these strongly suggests that thinking in different domains cannot be attributed to a general problem solving capacity. For instance if Graham, Woolf, and Einstein were all interested in trying to express how it feels to be on the moon, each one might take a different approach. Graham might address the problem from a bodily-kinesthetic angle. By moving her body (or those of other dancers) and trying out different steps, she might be able to imagine or recreate the giant leap of the first small steps on the moon. Albert Einstein on the other hand might remain rooted in his chair, imagine how the body moves, and visualize the gravitational forces that act upon it. Woolf might animate some celestial object, use a metaphor to make a connection to a more common experience, or engage in stream of consciousness about lunar themes. Each one is at work on the same general problem, but the materials, strategies, and specific tasks are different in each case. The distinct processes of thinking that each goes through cannot be confused.

Extending the definition of intelligence to encompass such a wide range of abilities highlights the finding of problems and the creation of culturally valued products as central aspects of intelligence. While "problem solving" may be an apt description of Einstein at work on a mathematical equation, it ignores how he conceived of new questions and how he created a new theoretical framework; it also fails to capture Picasso's task as he painted a canvas and cannot explain Stravinsky's efforts to compose a symphony. "Problem solving" implies that a task has been defined and that all the intelligent individual has to do is solve it. In their longitudinal study of artists, Getzels and Csikszentmihalyi (1976) provide evidence to counter this view by demonstrating the important role of finding, manipulating, and defining problems in the work of artists. Indeed, they showed that the artists' skill in "problem finding" was related to ratings of the quality of the works and to the levels of artistic success they achieved later in their careers.

The creation of valued products and the importance of problem-finding is not restricted to artistic domains. Architects, mechanical engineers, and scientists are at work building office towers, turbo engines, psychological theories and other products. Intellectual biographies of such individuals as Darwin (Gruber 1974) and studies of creativity in a number of fields (Csikszentmihalyi 1989) highlight that finding the right problem plays a  crucial role in all kinds of creative achievement. Increasingly, psychologists are emphasizing that even in standard psychological tasks, successful performance—especially for young children and individuals from other cultures—rests on the ability to find the "right" problem within the welter of unfamiliar stimuli (Rogoff, Guavain, and Gardner 1987; Deloache and Brown 1987). But as most theories of intelligence ignore these product creating and problem-finding aspects of cognition, they are not represented in assessment of either intelligence or achievement.

Part of the difficulty in problem-finding is to uncover the problems that are appropriate and valued within a specific culture. Achievement does not mean the same thing all over the world. If a young Freud or Woolf were transplanted to another culture, they might find it necessary to develop other aspects of their abilities in order to achieve the same success and acclaim they earned in the West. While linguistic intelligence like that of Woolf and Freud is of paramount importance in societies where success depends on literacy, spatial and bodily kinesthetic abilities are of central importance in other cultures. For example, among the Anang of Nigeria, these intelligences must be developed in order to become a master carver; in the Puluwat islands, a small handful of individuals can achieve eminence as master navigators.

> MI theory argues that distinct measures are needed to assess the unique capacities of each intelligence.

Because it emphasizes that the different intelligences are used in conjunction with different tasks and media, MI theory argues that distinct measures are needed to assess the unique capacities of each intelligence. These distinct domains and symbol systems require different kinds of sensory processing and present unique constraints and problems. As a consequence, paper and pencil tests which ignore the unique aspects of symbol systems such as music or the specific demands involved in interpersonal or bodily-kinesthetic tasks cannot adequately address a person's Multiple Intelligences.

## The Determination of Intelligences

On the basis of a review of the literature in a number of areas and the development of specific criteria, Gardner (1983) posited the existence of seven distinct intelligences (see Table 1). Selection of an intelligence was based on eight different criteria including the potential of isolation by brain damage, the existence of exceptional populations, a distinct developmental history, and evidence from psychological tasks.

Each of the seven intelligences is characterized by a set of core components. These core components are basic information-processing mechanisms which can deal with specific kinds of input. In the case of music, these components include the abilities to produce and appreciate rhythm, pitch, timbre, and the forms of musical expressiveness. For Stravinsky, these abilities were evident at a young age in

---

## Table 1
## The Seven Intelligences and the Core Components

| | |
|---|---|
| Logical-mathematical | sensitivity to patterns, orderliness, and systematicity; ability to handle long chains of reasoning. |
| Linguistic | sensitivity to the sounds, rhythms, and meanings of words; sensitivity to the different functions of language. |
| Musical | abilities to produce and appreciate rhythm, pitch, and timbre; appreciation of the forms of musical expressiveness. |
| Spatial | capacities to perceive the spatial world accurately, to perform transformations on one's initial perceptions, and to re-create aspects of one's visual experience. |
| Bodily-kinesthetic | abilities to control one's body movements and to handle objects skillfully. |
| Inter-personal | capacities to discern and respond appropriately to the moods, temperaments, motivations and desires of other people. |
| Intrapersonal | access to one's own feelings, the ability to discriminate among them and draw upon them to guide behavior. |

---

his capacities to perceive and reproduce melodies and intervals; as an adult, his compositions showed his command of the expressive potential of music.

The varied pursuits of Picasso and Einstein illustrate that the core components of an intelligence can serve widely different purposes. Picasso utilized an uncanny ability to perceive and depict forms and images in painting while Einstein manipulated mental images to tackle some of the fundamental questions of physics. Individuals like Einstein and Woolf also show that it is unusual to find a person who relies entirely on one intelligence. Einstein clearly had advanced spatial and logical-mathematical intelligences; Woolf's writing often combined her linguistic skills with deep reflections on her own thoughts and feelings.

## MI THEORY AND ASSESSMENT

Armed with the knowledge that people have a range of intelligences, the educator is immediately faced with two questions. Is it possible to assess these intelligences appropriately? And what difference might it make educationally? In the rest of this chapter, we will out-line an alternative view of assessment, illustrate how it can be applied in several educational projects, and present some preliminary find-ings from one of our projects.

### Intelligence-Fair Assessment

Consider again our seven figures; this time they are gathered in a classroom. We can imagine each one seated behind a desk, pencil in hand, poring over a test. While we might gain some information about their abilities and their academic progress in this fashion, it would make little sense to attempt to detect their diverse talents in this manner. Even Einstein, who was clearly gifted in the areas of logic and math, failed his entrance exams to the Polytechnic Institute in Zurich. Only after this failure, when he attended a school which highlighted visual understanding, did Einstein begin to blossom (Holton 1978). Before that time, Einstein's spatial abilities had gone largely unrecognized or undervalued in school.

Intelligence-fair assessments are a useful alternative to paper and pencil tests. Intelligence-fair assessments engage the core com-ponents (separately or in consort) of particular intelligences. The idea is to create rich, affordance-loaded circumstances which invite individuals to deploy specific intelligences without the necessity of invoking linguistic or logical intelligences en route. For example, in contrast to a word problem, a drawing or painting task would be an "intelligence-fair" assessment of Picasso's spatial skills. In order to assess Martha Graham's bodily-kinesthetic abilities, she would have to be allowed to leave her desk and dance; in order to consider Gandhi's interpersonal abilities, it would be necessary to see the ef-fects and influence he had directly on other people.

Compare several hypothetical assessments of musical intelli-gence. On the one hand, a rhythm might be played and students could be asked to write out the beat and the appropriate time signa-ture. On the other hand, students could be asked to demonstrate their mastery of the same rhythm by clapping or drumming it back. Similarly, part of a piece might be played and students could be asked to name it or students could be asked to play or sing the next line and create a variation based upon it. In both examples, the second, "intelligence-fair" alternative diminishes the need for logical and linguistic abilities and directly engages the central musical abilities to produce and perceive rhythm and pitch.

> There is evidence that tests which are releated to success in school fail to inform instructional practice directly.

For the most part, the necessity for "intelligence-fair" assessments has been recognized within the disciplines of the arts. Evaluations of achievement and skill in music, such as auditions for Julliard and recital competitions like the Van Cliburn, are based on musical performance; in the visual arts, assessments often depend upon the analysis of an artist's portfolio of works. Such assessments can accommodate the efforts of people from a wide range of ages and developmental levels. For music, the difficulty of the piece to be performed can be chosen to meet the skills of the performer. In the visual arts, the works in the portfolio can be selected to show both the progress an individual has made and the range of techniques and styles that have been mastered.

### Assessment in Context
In addition to ignoring the unique capacities of many of the intelligences, current tests are often composed of abstract, decontextualized problems. Rather than tapping abilities while individuals are involved in meaningful tasks like reading a book or balancing a budget, common test items like analogies and definitions have little value outside of school. Such items are often unfamiliar and bear little relation to the tasks that a composer, a psychoanalyst, and many other productive individuals face.

Several studies have documented the limited value of standardized tests for identifying and nurturing talented individuals (see for example Wing and Wallach 1971). In addition to having little relation to valued tasks and performances outside of school, Curtis and Glaser (1984) show that there is even evidence that tests which are related to success in school fail to inform instructional practice directly. For example, while scores on vocabulary tests are related to scholastic performance, raising those scores does not necessarily lead to better performance in critical instructional tasks like reading comprehension. With such evidence, it is questionable whether current tests would be of any use in helping a young Freud or Stravinsky develop his own unique abilities.

MI Theory's contention that intelligence is best displayed while people are involved in meaningful activities suggests that assessments should involve tasks that are familiar and valued within a culture. The work of Cole and his colleagues has demonstrated that when standardized tests and Western psychological tasks are administered in other cultures, individuals from non-Western societies perform much more poorly than their counterparts in the West (Laboratory of Comparative Human Cognition 1982). However, when these tests and tasks are adjusted or introduced in a way which makes the tasks more meaningful for the members of other societies, performances of the non-Western subjects improves dramatically.

While being "culture-fair" is a first step, assessments should also be "context-appropriate." Rather than being decontextualized, assessments should be familiar and ecologically valid; as nearly as possible, they should use familiar tasks in typical settings. Recent research in a variety of settings has shown that the skills that people display in their everyday occupations may be underestimated in more formal tests (Lave 1980; Rogoff 1982; Scribner 1986). Thus, while a vocabulary or comprehension test may tell us something about Woolf's linguistic competence, an assessment of her ability to produce a story provides a far better and more valid indication of how she can use that competence to carry out a highly valued activity within Western culture.

Employing meaningful and valued tasks in assessments has the added benefit that feedback, criticism, and assistance can be directed at precisely those activities in which an individual participates. For Woolf, evaluations based on most vocabulary or comprehension tests would be of little value; they would yield scores, but few concrete suggestions for improvement. An assessment of her writing, on the other hand, provides the opportunity to analyze her use of voice, to examine how she develops characters, and to make recommendations which will be of direct benefit in her next literary effort.

## PUTTING TESTING IN ITS PLACE

In the fifties, most individuals took a few tests in school, but now most will have taken thirty standardized tests before they reach college (Haney and Madaus 1989). Nonetheless, it is generally agreed that this progress in testing has not been followed by commensurate improvements in education. At present, the results and feedback from most assessments are dwarfed in importance and emotional significance by scores from standardized tests. The enormous implications of many of these tests for the life of individuals and the solvency of schools can overshadow immediate educational goals and place a stranglehold on the educational process.

**Progress in testing has not been followed by commensurate improvements in education.**

Standardized tests promote a "wall-chart" mentality in which the achievement of scores is more important than the acquisition of knowledge. Courses, both within school and out, have been developed to teach students how to take tests; yet once the classroom has been left behind, those test-taking skills will find little use in a world that requires the abilities needed to write reports, deal with computers, and get along with fellow workers.

The concentration on testing is especially dubious in the U.S. today because it sends the wrong message to teachers. It can lead teachers to focus on the material that may be covered on a standardized test while ignoring other tasks and information that they think may be interesting and important for their students. For example, Neill and Medina (1989) report that districts in thirteen different states have attempted to "align" their curricula so that students will not spend study time on materials on which they will never be tested. This is particularly disturbing given the fact that most tests are intended to measure general changes in academic performance and are not designed to guide or facilitate instruction (Glaser 1985).

In order to make testing more useful for teachers and students, tests must be developed which are based on the curriculum and provide regular feedback to inform instruction (Gardner 1991; Glaser 1985). One way to accomplish this goal is to take advantage of the information that is yielded naturally in the course of learning. Assessment in apprenticeships is accomplished in just such an unobtrusive fashion. The master supplies tasks of gradually increasing difficulty while monitoring, from a distance, the student's progress in those tasks that are central to learning. There is no interruption, the work is its own test, with feedback supplied where necessary to help the apprentice to complete the task satisfactorily.

Several researchers have pointed out the value of apprenticeships for education both in school and out (Collins, Brown, and
Newman 1989; Moore 1986). For example,
Resnick (1987) reports that one of the key
features of successful "thinking skills" programs was the incorporation of elements of
apprenticeship. While current educational
approaches cannot be scrapped and simply
replaced by an apprenticeship system, we can
strive to develop alternative assessments
which are based on meaningful instructional
tasks. Such alternative assessments can take
the emphasis off testing and put it back on
learning.

> While current educa-
> tional approaches
> cannot be scrapped
> and replaced by an
> apprenticeship
> system, we can strive
> to develop alternative
> assessments.

## ALTERNATIVE MODELS OF ASSESSMENT

At Harvard Project Zero, programs that integrate "intelligence-fair"
assessments into the curriculum are being developed at a variety of
age levels. These programs illustrate some of the ways in which regular feedback can be supplied throughout the learning process and
how teachers and students can be given more control over the assessments. In addition, while each of these projects is a response to local
conditions with assessments done in context on site, efforts are being
made to ensure that some aspects of the assessments can be compared to sites elsewhere in the nation.

### Arts PROPEL

A collaborative project with the Educational Testing Service and the
Pittsburgh Public School System, Arts PROPEL assesses growth and
learning at the middle and high school level in areas not covered by
most standard aptitude or achievement measures (for further details,
see Gardner 1989a; Zessoules, Wolf, and Gardner 1988). This goal is
accomplished through the use of curriculum-compatible "domain
projects," and the collection of students' works in portfolios.

The domain projects focus on a central issue or theme (such as
composition in graphic arts and voice in expressive writing), contain
time for production, perception, and reflection, and present multiple
opportunities for student and teacher assessment. For example, in
the musical performance project, musical abilities are developed and

assessed as an ensemble of students practice or perform. In a typical session, the practice of a piece is recorded and students are asked to analyze their own performance and that of the ensemble in terms of rhythm and harmony; then the piece is played and recorded again. The recorded performances and the reflections are collected in a portfolio and can be scored by the teacher. While linguistic intelligence is certainly involved in this process, the student's *musical* abilities to perceive and produce rhythm and pitch are central to the project.

By collecting works from the regular instructional activities in portfolios, PROPEL enables teachers and students to control the assessment process. In addition to producing the works, students help in the assessment by reviewing their own portfolios, selecting the works that will serve as the basis for more formal assessments, and reflecting on their progress. Teachers review the portfolios to see how students are responding to instruction and feedback. PROPEL is currently at work developing guidelines and scoring systems which the teachers and other observers can use to reliably evaluate the portfolios. This should make it possible to compare works of students from different schools.

> Students help in the assessment by reviewing their own portfolios and reflecting on their progress.

### The Key School

The Key School, an elementary school in Indianapolis, uses video portfolios based on student projects to document and assess development (for further information on the Key School see Olson 1988). Several times during the year, students create projects on a school-wide theme, such as "Man and his Environment" or "Patterns." Students present the projects, giving background and goals, and answering questions from their classmates. Each student's presentations along with interviews at the beginning and end of each year are videotaped and collected throughout a child's tenure at the Key School.

We are currently engaged in devising a set of criteria along which these rich projects can be assessed. Among the dimensions that we are considering are the following: (1) how the student conceptualizes the project and its relation to the school theme; (2) how the student presents the project to the class; (3) how competent is the project in terms of accuracy, technical execution, aesthetic appeal, and originality; (4) to what extent does the project reveal something individual about the child today, in the past, and in future lines of growth; (5) what evidence is provided of cooperation in the preparation of the project. Complementing or even replacing the role of the standardized test, this approach should provide invaluable information about the growth of the child's thinking within various media of expression and communication. Conceivably, such information could eventually be included in student report cards.

> Checklists to document children's interest and progress help teachers take advantage of the useful information that is generated.

### Project Spectrum

Project Spectrum, co-directed by David Feldman of Tufts University and Howard Gardner of Harvard University, is designed to determine if children as young as four and five have distinct profiles of ability. While assessments were originally planned to cover only the seven intelligences discussed in *Frames of Mind*, it soon became clear that a larger number of capacities needed to be examined. At present, Project Spectrum draws from fifteen different assessments to determine children's intellectual strengths and weaknesses. These assessments can be employed over the course of a year as part of the regular preschool curriculum (for further information see Hatch and Gardner 1986; Krechevsky and Gardner 1990; Malkus, Feldman, and Gardner 1988; Ramos-Ford and Gardner 1991; Wexler-Sherman, Feldman, and Gardner 1988).

In a "Spectrum" classroom children can choose from a wide variety of "intelligence-fair" materials including figures and props for telling stories, games involving numbers, musical instruments, and mechanical objects which children can take apart and reassemble to exercise their spatial skills. Also available are weekly or bi-weekly activities such as "Weekend" news which engages children's descriptive language skills and creative movement sessions which allow teachers to observe how children's bodily-kinesthetic abilities develop.

Through these activities, a wide range of abilities can be examined unobtrusively. Guidelines for observation and checklists to document children's interest and progress in these areas help teachers to take advantage of the useful information that is generated throughout the year. Many of the activities also have detailed scoring systems which the teachers can use to take an in-depth look at the intellectual profiles of individual children.

In order to help parents take advantage of the information that is yielded over the course of the year, observers working in conjunction with the Spectrum teachers have prepared "Spectrum reports." These reports supply a narrative description of a child's strengths and weaknesses which is based on the results of the informal observations and the individual assessments. Also included are suggestions for activities the child might enjoy and recommendations of resources in the community which can be used to respond to this intellectual profile.

The Spectrum approach is quite labor-intensive. As a result, efforts are currently underway to adapt seven of the activities for use in the Modified Spectrum Field Inventory which can be administered in two one-hour sessions in a home or classroom setting. While the integration of the assessments into the curriculum is lost in this approach, related activities can be introduced into the classroom to ensure that assessments are based on familiar and interesting materials.

## INITIAL FINDINGS FROM PROJECT SPECTRUM

While each of these projects has been enthusiastically received by teachers, parents, and students, data collection is not far enough advanced to judge the feasibility of these assessments. At present, preliminary data are only available from the Project Spectrum assessments. These assessments have been piloted in two different forms. In the 1987–88 academic year, twenty children in a classroom at the Eliot-Pearson Children's School in Medford, Massachusetts took part in a year-long Spectrum program. These children came from a primarily white, middle-and upper-income population, and ranged in age from 42 to 58 months at the beginning of the school year. Over the course of the year, these children were scored on ten different Spectrum activities (see Table 2) and the Stanford-Binet Intelligence Scale, Fourth Edition. In the 1988–89 academic year, the Modified Spectrum Field Inventory was used with fifteen children in a combined kindergarten and first grade classroom. These children attended a public school in a low-to-middle income district.

The analyses were primarily concerned with determining whether or not young children do exhibit a range of abilities as the

## Table 2
## Spectrum Assessments used in 1987–88

*Dinosaur Game:* the Dinosaur Game is designed as a measure of a child's understanding of number concepts, counting skills, ability to adhere to rules, and use of strategy.

*Bus Game:* the Bus Game assesses a child's ability to create a useful notation system, perform mental calculations, and organize number information for one or more variables.

*Treasure Hunt Game:* the Treasure Hunt Game assesses a child's ability to make logical inferences. The child is asked to organize information to discover the rule governing the placement of various treasures.

*Assembly Activity:* the Assembly Activity is designed to measure a child's mechanical ability. Successful completion of the activity depends on fine motor skills and visual-spatial, observational and problem-solving abilities.

*Art Portfolios:* the contents of a child's art portfolio are reviewed twice a year, and assessed on criteria that include use of lines and shapes, color, space, detail, and representation and design. Children also participate in three structured drawing activities. The drawings are assessed on criteria similar to those used in the portfolio assessment.

*Music Production Activity:* the Music Production Activity is designed to assess a child's abilities to maintain accurate pitch and rhythm while singing and to recall a song's musical properties.

*Music Perception Activity:* the music perception activity assesses a child's ability to discriminate pitch. The activity consists of song recognition, error recognition, and pitch discrimination.

*Storyboard Activity:* the Storyboard Activity measures a range of langauge skills including complexity of vocabulary and sentence structure, use of connectors, use of descriptive language and dialogue, and ability to pursue a storyline.

*Creative Movement:* the ongoing movement curriculum focuses on children's abilities in five areas of dance and creative movement—sensitivity to rhythm, expressiveness, body control, generation of movement ideas, and responsiveness to music.

*Classroom Model:* the purpose of the Classroom Model Activity is the assess a child's ability to observe and analyze social events and experiences. A model of the classroom and figures with photographs of each member of the class are used to help children describe the social interactions that take place and to reflect on the relationships that are formed within the classroom.

Theory of Multiple Intelligences suggests. In order to investigate this hypothesis, we examined: (1) whether or not young children exhibit distinct profiles of intellectual strengths and weaknesses; (2) whether or not performances on activities designed to tap different intelligences are significantly correlated; and (3) in the case of the preschool sample, whether or not children's performances on the Spectrum assessments were significantly correlated with their overall IQ. Because of the small sample sizes and the formative nature of the work on Project Spectrum, we regard these results as suggestive but not definitive.

For the preschool sample, in order to compare children's performances across the Spectrum activities, we computed standard deviations for each activity. Children who scored one standard deviation or more above the mean on a particular measure were considered to have a "strength" in that area, while those who scored one standard deviation below the mean were described as having a "weakness" in that area. This analysis suggested that these children did not perform at the same level across activities; instead, it suggested that they had particular intellectual strengths and weaknesses. Fifteen of the twenty children demonstrated a strength on at least one activity, and twelve children showed a weakness on one or more activities. Only one child was identified as having no strengths or weaknesses, although her scores ranged from –.98 to +.87 standard deviations from the mean.

These results were supported by the findings from a correlated analysis of children's performances on the different activities. Only the two number activities were significantly correlated ($r = .78$, $p < .01$). Interestingly, in the other areas where we had two measures—music and science—there were no significant, within-domain correlations. The fact that only the performances on the two number activities were significantly correlated could be due to the degree of similarity between the activities. While the music activities were singing and music perception and the science activities were hypothesis-testing and mechanical skill, both number activities involved calculation.

The comparison of the Stanford-Binet and the Spectrum assessments indicated that there was a limited overlap between children's performances on these two very different measures. The Stanford-Binet was administrated by an independent psychometrician to nineteen of the twenty children. Two of those nineteen did not complete the measure and are not included in the analysis. Scores ranged from low-average (86) to very superior (133) with a mean of 113.

A correlational analysis revealed that only the number activities were significantly correlated with the Stanford-Binet composite scores (dinosaur game $r = .69$, $p = .003$; bus game $r = .51$, $p = .04$). This is not surprising given the Stanford-Binet's focus on logical-mathematical skills. The narrative language measure, however, was not significantly correlated with the composite scores. This could be due to the fact that each measures a different kind of language skill: vocabulary and comprehension vs. narrative language. (For a more detailed discussion of the results of this study see Krechevsky and Gardner 1990.)

In the second study, eight kindergarteners (four boys and four girls) and seven first graders (five girls and two boys) were assessed on the seven activities of the Modified Spectrum Field Inventory (MSPFI). These activities are based on the assessments used in the year long Spectrum program and consist of activities in the areas of language (storyboard), number and logic (bus game), movement (creative movement), social analysis (classroom model), art (drawing), music (xylophone games), and mechanics (assembly). These assessments were administered in two one-hour sessions. These sessions were videotaped and each activity was scored by two independent observers. Spearman rank order correlations between the scores of the two observers ranged from .88 (language) to .97 (art).

As in the preschool study, strengths and weaknesses were calculated using standard deviations. Unlike the results of the first study, this analysis suggested that the children were performing at relatively comparable levels across the activities. Conceivably, individual differences in this sample may have been overshadowed by developmental and gender differences. Of the five first grade girls, all demonstrated at least one strength, and one showed a strength on six of the seven activities. Most strikingly, none of the girls had a weakness in any area. In contrast, neither of the two first grade boys showed any strengths and both displayed weaknesses in three areas. Only two kindergarteners showed any strengths, and of the other five kindergarteners, all but one demonstrated at least one weakness.

Using less stringent criteria to determine strengths and weaknesses of the kindergarteners and first graders, however, did reveal a more varied picture of children's performances across the activities. All but two children in the sample were ranked among the top five on at least one activity; fourteen of the fifteen children also ranked among the bottom five on at least one activity. In this analysis, although the first grade girls dominated the rankings, the children did demonstrate relative strengths and weaknesses. (For a further discussion of this study see Gardner and Hatch 1989.)

For the most part, these preliminary results are in the direction predicted by the Theory of Multiple Intelligences. For the younger children, performance on the different Spectrum activities appeared to be independent, relative strengths and/or weaknesses were identified, and there was limited overlap between performances on the Stanford-Binet and the Spectrum assessments. In the second study, despite the wide age range in the sample, an examination of the children's ranks on each activity revealed areas of strength and weakness for most of the children.

> **Examination of the children's ranks on each activity revealed areas of strength and weakness for most of the children.**

Further study with larger samples is required to verify these findings and establish the validity and the reliability of these instruments. This will also make it possible to establish norms and identify children's strengths and weaknesses in a more consistent manner. In the future, the impact of such factors as age, gender, social class background, and familiarity of the assessments on children's performances also should be examined.

Although the question of whether MI Theory is open to disconfirmation has been raised on several occasions, any number of findings from Project Spectrum could challenge portions of its claims; if future studies show that performances on different activities are correlated, if, after norms are established, the assessments fail to reveal strengths and weaknesses for a significant number of children, and if the scores on such measures as the Stanford-Binet explain a significant portion of the variance in performances on the Spectrum activities, the theory will be disconfirmed. Such findings, however, would not lead to the conclusion that alternative forms of assessment are not necessary or useful. Such a verdict awaits detailed analyses which focus on the educational value and the personal and social impact of such alternatives.

## CONCLUSION

Many psychologists and psychometricians have argued that there are general problem solving, achievement, and reasoning skills. From such a perspective, the reasoning processes of the composer, the politician, and the mathematician are more alike than different; tests of linguistic and logical-mathematical skill are presumed to reflect accurately the intelligence and achievement of these and most other individuals.

In contrast, the Theory of Multiple Intelligences suggests that when individuals are observed while they are involved in meaningful activities, their reasoning processes are more different than alike. The products created and the problems found and solved by composers, politicians, and mathematicians involve distinct symbol systems, operations, sense modalities, and require the use of different intelligences. The tasks are not the same for the painter or the physicist and it is unfair and misleading to try to measure their achievements on the same, "neutral," scale.

As a consequence, "intelligence-fair," contextualized assessments are required to gauge ability and document its development. Critical thinking or reasoning programs which treat thinking in a generic way, indifferent to the constraints of different media and the demands of strikingly different tasks, are taking intelligence out of context. While such programs may improve skills employed in some common tasks, they run the risk of failing to engage the very thinking processes which enabled the great figures of the era to achieve eminence and contribute to the further development of many domains.

In the view of the Theory of Multiple Intelligences and the empirical results gleaned thus far, the continued dominance of standardized tests, with their decontextualized emphasis on a small number of language and logical-mathematical skills, seems increasingly ill-founded. These tests have systematically ignored the wide range of abilities that are valued within our culture, and they are of little use in helping us to recognize and educate individuals of eminence. By constraining the curriculum and taking control of the learning process away from teachers and students, an over-reliance on standardized testing may discourage many students from discovering activities which they can enjoy and at which they can achieve some success.

Turning our attention to alternative forms of assessment might eventually increase our ability to address the strengths and weaknesses of each student. It is bracing to imagine a school that does not depend on tests, but utilizes a variety of methods to engage and assess the abilities of each individual. Such a school may help us to educate every child including those with abilities as varied as Gandhi, Graham, and Picasso.

*Acknowledgements:* The research described in this chapter has been generously supported by the Grant Foundation, the Lilly Endowment, the Markle Foundation, the Rockefeller Brothers Fund, the Rockefeller Foundation, the Spencer Foundation, the Bernard Van Leer Foundation, and the OERI Center for Technology in Education at the Bank Street College of Education. We thank our colleagues at the Eliot-Pearson Pre-School and in the Somerville Public School system for their collaboration.

## REFERENCES

Block, N., & Dworkin, G. (1976). *The IQ controversy.* New York: Pantheon.

Ceci, S. J., & Liker, J. (1987). IQ and reasoning complexity: The role of experience. *Journal of Experimental Psychology: General,* 116, 304–6.

Collins, A., Brown, J. S. & Newman, S. E. (1989). Cognitive apprenticeship: Teaching the craft of reading, writing, and mathematics. In L. Resnick (Ed.), *Cognition and instruction: Issues and agendas.* Hillsdale, NJ: L. Erlbaum.

Csikszentmihalyi, M. (1989). Motivation and creativity. *New Ideas in Psychology,* 6(2), 159–76.

Curtis, M. E., & Glaser, R. (1984). Intelligence testing, cognition, and instruction. *International Journal of Psychology,* 19, 475–97.

Deloache, J. S., & Brown, A. L. (1987). The early emergence of planning skills in children. In J. Bruner and H. Haste (Eds.), *Making sense: The child's construction of the world* (pp. 108–30). London: Methuen.

Gardner, H. (1975). *The shattered mind.* New York: Knopf.

———. (1983). *Frames of mind.* New York: Basic Books.

————. (1989a). Zero-based arts education: An introduction to ARTS PROPEL. *Studies in Art Education, 3*(2), 71–83.

————. (1989b). Assessment in context: The alternative to standardized testing. In B. Gifford (Ed.), *Report of the commission on testing and public policy.* Boston: Kluwer.

————. (1991). *The unschooled mind.* New York: Basic Books.

Gardner, H., & Hatch, T. (1989). Multiple Intelligences go to school. *Educational Researcher.* 18(8), 4–10.

Gardner, H., & Wolf, D. (1983). Waves and streams of symbolization. In D. R. Rogers & J. A. Sloboda (Eds.), *The acquisition of symbolic skills* (pp. 19–42). London: Plenum Press.

Gelman, R. (1978). Cognitive development. *Annual Review of Psychology, 29,* 297–332.

Getzels, J. W., & Csikszentmihalyi, M.(1976). *The creative vision.* New York: Wiley.

Glaser, R. (1985). Individuals and learning: The new aptitudes. *Educational Researcher,* 1(6), 5–13.

Gould, S. J. (1981). *The mismeasure of man.* New York: Norton.

Gruber, H. (1974). *Darwin on man: A psychological study of scientific creativity.* New York: Dutton.

Haney, W., & Madaus, G. (1989). Searching for alternatives to Standardized Testing: Why's, what's, and whither's. *Phi Delta Kappan,* 70(9), 683–87.

Hatch, T., & Gardner, H. (1986). From testing intelligence to assessing competences: A pluralistic view of intellect. *Roeper Review,* 8, 147–50.

Holton, G. (1978). *Scientific imagination: Case studies.* New York: Cambridge University Press.

Krechevsky, M., & Gardner, H. (1990). The emergence and nurturance of Multiple Intelligences. In M. J. A. Howe (Ed.), *Encouraging the development of exceptional abilities and talents.*

Laboratory of Comparative Human Cognition. (1982). Culture and intelligence. In R. Sternberg (Ed.), *Handbook of human intelligence* (Vol. 2, pp. 642–722). New York: Cambridge University Press.

Lave, J. (1980). What's special about experiments as contexts for thinking? *Quarterly Newsletter of the Laboratory of Comparative Human Cognition,* 2, 86–91.

Malkus, U., Feldman, D. H., & Gardner, H. (1988). Dimensions of mind in early childhood. In A. D. Pellegrini (Ed.), *Psychological bases of early education.* (pp. 25–38). New York: John Wiley & Sons.

Moore, D. T. (1986). Learning at work: Case studies in non-school education. *Anthropology and Education Quarterly,* 17, 166–84.

Neill, D. M., & Medina, N. J. (1989). Standardized Testing: Harmful to educational health. *Phi Delta Kappan,* 70, (9), 688–97.

Olson, L. (1988). Children flourish here: 8 teachers and a theory changed a school world. *Education Week,* 18(1), 18–19.

Ramos-Ford, V., & Gardner, H. (1991). Giftedness from a multiple intelligences perspective. In N. Colangelo and G. Davis (Eds.), *The handbook of gifted education.* Boston: Allyn & Bacon.

Resnick, L. (1987). The 1987 Presidential Address: Learning in school and out. *Educational Research,* 13–20.

Rogoff, B. (1982). Integrating context and cognitive development. In M. Lamb & A. Brown (Eds.), *Advances in developmental psychology,* (Vol. 2, pp. 125–170). Hillsdale, NJ: L. Erlbaum.

Rogoff, B., Guavain, M., & Gardner, W. (1987). Children's adjustment of plans to circumstances. In S. L. Friedman, E. Scholnick, & R. R. Cocking (Eds.), *Blueprints for thinking: The role of planning in cognitive development* (pp. 303–20). Cambridge: Cambridge University Press.

Scribner, S. (1986). Thinking in action: Some characteristics of practical thought. In R. Sternberg & R. K. Wagner (Eds.), *Practical intelligence.* New York: Cambridge University Press.

Sternberg, R. J. (1985). *Beyond IQ.* New York: Cambridge University Press.

Wexler-Sherman, C., Feldman, D., & Gardner, H. (1988). A pluralistic view of intellect: the Project Spectrum approach. *Theory into Practice,* 28, 77–83.

Wing, C. W., & Wallach, M. A.(1971). *College admissions and the psychology of talent.* New York: Holt, Rinehart, and Winston.

Zessoules, R., Wolf, D., & Gardner, H. (1988). A better balance: ARTS PROPEL as an alternative to discipline-based art education. In J. Burton, A. Lederman, & P. Landon (Eds.), *Beyond discipline-based art education.* University Council on Art Education.

# Alternative Assessment from a Multiple Intelligences Perspective

by Jie-Qi Chen and Howard Gardner

*H*ow smart are you? "I'm pretty smart," you may be thinking. When we ask this question at meetings and workshops, we also hear responses like, "That's not an easy question. If I compare myself to my colleagues, I'd have to say I'm about average." Or, "I'm not sure. I have a hard time with some job demands and sometimes have doubts about my competence."

Consider a second question: *How are you smart?* This question tends to elicit answers like, "I'm an articulate speaker and I enjoy writing, but I have trouble with math, especially statistics." Or, "I'm good at designing charts and other graphics, but it's hard for me to express my ideas in words." Or, "I learn to play musical instruments easily, because I have good sense of pitch."

Although both questions concern human capability or competence, they provoke different responses that reflect different models of intelligence. The underlying notion of the first question is that intelligence is a single overall property with one dimension, along which everyone can be arrayed. Moreover, this general mental ability can be measured reasonably well by a variety of standardized tests, especially by IQ tests designed specifically for this purpose (Eysenck 1979; Snyderman and Rothman 1988). In this view, IQ and scores on other standardized tests of intelligence have predictive value for many educational, economic, and social outcomes (Herrnstein and Murray 1994; Jensen 1969).

From *Beyond Traditional Intellectual Assessment: Contemporary and Emerging Theories, Tests, and Issues,* edited by D. F. Flanagan, J. L. Genshaft, and P. L. Harrison, published by Guilford Publications. Copyright © 1994 by Guilford Publications. Reprinted with permission.

In contrast, the second question suggests a theoretical view that recognizes many discrete facets of cognition and acknowledges that people have different cognitive strengths and contrasting cognitive styles. In this view, the array of intelligences cannot be assured adequately with a brief sampling of short-answer psychological tasks in a decontextualized situation. Rather, they are more validly documented by the use of contextually rich instruments and an authentic assessment approach that sample a range of discrete cognitive capacities.

In this essay, we describe the theory of multiple intelligences (Gardner 1993a, thereafter MI theory) and present it as a source of an alternative approach to assessment. We begin by reviewing the origins of the theory and its distinctive characteristics. We then chart its challenges to traditional conceptions of intelligence, particularly the psychometric view of intelligence and Piaget's theory of cognitive development. Moving from theory to practice, we identify general features of an MI style assessment, including descriptions of measures, materials, and contexts. We also describe a research project that has developed and piloted domain-specific assessment tasks and observational guidelines as an example of the application of MI theory to assessment. Finally, we report on an empirical study that offers evidence for the notion that intellect is structured in terms of specific, relatively independent abilities.

## THE THEORY OF MULTIPLE INTELLIGENCES: ITS ORIGINS AND CLAIMS

Multiple intelligences theory grew from the efforts of one of the authors of this chapter, Howard Gardner, to reconceptualize the nature of intelligence. Gardner began by considering the range of adult end states that are appreciated in diverse cultures around the world and then asking what kind of mind-brain would be needed to realize these various end states. Gardner's assumption was that *any* set of adult competence that may be valued in a culture merits consideration as a potential intelligence (Gardner 1994).

Most studies of intelligence are based on short-answer psychological tests and correlations among these tests. Gardner proceeded in a different investigative fashion. He surveyed bodies of information and knowledge that had never been considered together for the purpose of defining intelligence (Gardner 1993a). One aspect of the research focused on atypical populations, such as prodigies, idiot savants, autistic children, and children with learning disabilities. These populations tend to exhibit jagged cognitive profiles with level of performance. Such profiles are inconsistent with a unitary view of intelligence. Also scrutinized was research on patients who had suffered isolated loss of cognitive function through brain damage; the highly specific nature of their deficits provides strong evidence that humans possess discrete kinds of intelligence. Further evidence for MI theory came from studies of skill development in normal children and from investigations that evaluated the effectiveness of skill training efforts. A central question that emerged from research on skill training cannot be ignored in the study of intelligence: Does training in skill A transfer to skill B? For example, does training in mathematics enhance one's musical abilities? Finally, cross-cultural studies revealed that intelligence may be manifested differently in different cultures; a society in the South Seas may value the ability to navigate through island passages using the stars, just as the western society values the ability to write a symphony, perform open heart surgery, or carry a football across an opponent's goal line.

These diverse sources provided converging evidence that in describing intelligence, one must consider not only abstract thinking skills and problem-solving abilities but also the applications of such skills and abilities. Pursuing this line of argument, Gardner defines intelligence as "the ability to solve problems, or to create products, that are valued within one or more cultural settings" (1993a, x). With this definition of intelligence, a variety of skills valued in different cultures and historical settings become objects of study (Gardner and Hatch 1989; Walters and Gardner 1986).

As a species, human beings have evolved over the millennia to carry out several distinct, relatively independent forms of competence, geared to meet the specific demands of everyday life. Based on his study of the sources mentioned above, Gardner proposes seven different itelligences: linguistic, logical-mathematical, musical, spatial, bodily-kinesthetic, interpersonal, and intrapersonal. Though the linguistic and logical-mathematical intelligences have been emphasized in psychometric testing and school settings, the seven intelligences in the MI framework have equal claims to priority and are as equally valid and important (Gardner, 1987b, 1993a).

According to MI theory, the seven itelligences are to a significant extent independent of one another. Each exhibits particular problem-solving features, information-processing capacities, and development trajectories. As a function of this independence, the development of the intelligences may proceed at different rates and individuals can display an uneven profile of abilities across intelligences.

Although relatively autonomous, the intelligences do not work in isolation. The fact that nearly every cultural role requires a combination of intelligences suggests the importance of considering that individuals possess various aptitudes rather than a singular problem-solving faculty. With a combination of skills, an individual can become very competent in certain tasks or fields even though he or she may not be particularly gifted in any specific intelligence (Gardner 1991; Walters and Gardner 1986).

Intelligences do not function as abstract entities. Each intelligence is expressed through one or more symbol systems, such as spoken or written language, numbers, music notation, picturing, or mapping. Through symbol systems, intelligences are applied in specific *domains* or bodies of knowledge within a culture, such as mathematics, art, basketball, and medicine. An intelligence may be deployed in many domains (e.g., spatial forms of intelligence may operate in the domains of visual arts, navigation, and engineering). Similarly, performance in a domain may require the use of more than one intelligence. For example, the domain of musical performance involves bodily-kinesthetic and personal as well as musical intelligences (Gardner 1993a).

As noted, MI theory emphasizes the relative independence of the intelligences. MI theory does not question the existence, but challenges the explanatory and utility power of "g" (general intelligence). One can make "g" higher or lower by varying the kinds of tests given. Moreover, evidence for "g" is provided almost entirely by test of linguistic or logical intelligence. As such, even if "g" reflects the capacities of certain individuals as they operate in certain contexts, it unduly constricts the definition of intelligence. It treats a particular form of scholastic performance as if it encompassed the entire range of human capacities and leads to disdain for those who are not psychometrically bright (Gardner 1995b).

Consider the diverse cognitive profiles that individuals exhibit. Gardner claims that intelligences, to a great extent, are shaped by cultural influences and refined by educational process. While all humans exhibit the range of intelligences, individuals differ—

presumably for both hereditary and environmental reasons—in the extent to which these intelligences are developed in various settings. It is through the process of education that "raw" intellectual competencies are developed and individuals are prepared to assume mature cultural roles. Rich educational experiences, including the use of appropriate forms of assessment, are essential for the development of each individual's particular configuration of interests and abilities (Adams and Feldman 1993; Gardner 1991, 1993c).

> **Research on both typical and atypical populations has produced evidence inconsistent with the position of a general intelligence.**

## CHALLENGES TO TRADITIONAL CONCEPTS OF INTELLIGENCE

### Challenges to the Psychometric View of Intelligence

MI theory challenges the psychometric view of intelligence on several fronts. First, MI theory questions the conception of intelligence as a single entity which is general, stable, and representative of the entire range of cognitive behaviors (Herrnstein and Murray 1994; Snyderman and Rothman 1987; for a critical review see Gould, 1981). As previously noted, research on both typical and atypical populations has produced evidence that is inconsistent with the position of a general intelligence. MI theory argues that it is dangerous to single out one dimension and array individuals on that ability, particularly if the implication is that this rank ordering indicates how smart people are in a global sense. Such a notion gives rise to the idea of a cognitive elite and encourages the notion that some people are special from the start and that those who are not in the elite cause our social problems (Gardner 1995a; Gould 1994).

We are aware that, based on correlations among psychological tests and subjects, numerous studies support the idea of a positive manifold—the idea that there exists an underlying factor that contributes to performance of all measures of intellect. However, many of the measures used in these studies are short-answer, paper-and-pencil tests, and most of the tests measure primarily logical-mathematical and linguistic intelligences. Given that the tests measure only two intelligences and rely on the same means of measurement, it is not surprising that scores on the tests are correlated. MI theory predicts, however, that if a wide range of areas is assessed, individuals will display an uneven profile of abilities, and correlations among diverse abilities will not be high (Gardner and Walters 1993).

Noting that intelligence tests focus primarily on linguistic and logical-mathematical forms of thinking, we recognize that some current intelligence tests do measure more than two cognitive abilities. In fact, some tests measure up to seven different components, including crystallized intelligence, visual ability, auditory intelligence, short-term memory, long-term retrieval, speed of processing, and fluid intelligence (Carroll 1993; McGhee 1993; Woodcock 1990). Guilford (1967) claims that there are 120 or even 150 components of intelligence. These intelligence tests, however, are based on "horizontal" theories of intelligence. That is, mental faculties measured in these tests putatively function similarly in all content areas and operate according to one general law. MI theory is a "vertical" conceptualization of intelligence. According to MI theory, the mind is organized in terms of content areas. There is no single "horizontal" capacity, such as memory, perception, or speed of processing that cuts across domains. Accordingly, individuals can be rapid or slow learners or exhibit novel stereotypical thinking in any one of the seven intelligences without there being predictable consequences for any of the other intelligences (Gardner 1993b).

> Tests based on the psychometric view tend to exclude capacities that cannot be measured through the use of short answer questions.

With regard to how intelligence is measured, we acknowledge that there is a continuum of testing instruments from those that are mass produced, standardized, paper and pencil-based to those that feature interaction between test takers and test administrators and use a variety of materials, such as blocks, pictures, and geographic shapes. Despite this range, tests based on the psychometric view tend to be one-shot experience and exclude capacities that cannot be measured through the use of such tasks as short answer questions, block design, or picture arrangement. MI theory argues that the capacities excluded, such as artisitic ability, athletic competence, and interpersonal skills, must be measured directly. MI theory calls for measuring intelligences by asking individuals to solve problems in the contexts in which they naturally occur. This approach expands the range of what is measured and permits assessment of the intelligences as an individual applies them in meaningful ways.

Challenging the psychometric assumption regarding biological determinism or racially-based intelligence (Jensen 1969; Herrnstein and Murray 1994), MI theory argues that intelligence, or intelligences, should be viewed as an interaction between biological proclivities and the opportunities for learning that exist in a culture (Kornhaber, Krechevsky, and Gardner 1990). In MI theory, intelligences are expressed as abilities valued within a cultural setting. Thus the theory switches the focus of study away from individuals to interactions between individuals and societies. Genes regulate all human behavior, but no form of behavior will emerge without the appropriate environmental triggers or supports (Gardner 1995a).

> Logical-mathematical thinking is only one kind of intelligence, and does not reflect the core operations of other forms of intelligence.

### Challenges to Piaget's Theory of Cognitive Development

Piaget's account of cognitive development is a theoretically distinct perspective. Departing from the psychometric view, Piaget emphasizes the developmental, rather than static, nature of intelligence and the qualitatively, rather than quantitatively, different mind of the child. However, Piaget's theory is also similar to the psychometric view, in its claim that the mental structures that characterize developmental stages are best represented as a single entity or unified set of processes. In Piaget's theory, mental structures are general rather than specific and universal rather than cultural. In this limited respect, Piaget views intelligence as a single entity.

The universal or general quality of mind in Piaget's theory is defined in terms of logical-mathematical thought about the physical aspects of the world, including the understanding of causality, time, and space. However, logical-mathematical thinking is only one kind of human intelligence, and it does not reflect the core operations of other forms of intelligence. In contrast to Piaget's belief, MI theory holds that there are no general structures that are applied to every domain. Rather, what exists in the mind of the child at a moment in time is a variety of skills in a variety of domains, each skill functioning at a certain level of mastery with respect to that domain (Chen 1993; Feldman 1994; Krechevsky and Gardner 1990).

Piaget's theory assumes that cognitive development is essentially the result of the child's spontaneous tendencies to learn about the world, with the environment playing a minor role in the process. In contrast, MI theory argues that for progressive and productive change to occur in any intellectual domain, quite specific environmental conditions must be systematically presented and sustained over time. These environmental forces may be material, technological, social, or cultural in character. The role of education is not to wait passively for cognition to develop by itself, but rather to orchestrate a variety of environmental conditions that will catalyze, facilitate, and enable developmental progress in diverse intellect domains (Feldman 1994; Gardner 1993d).

## ASSESSMENT FROM A MULTIPLE INTELLIGENCES PERSPECTIVE

MI theory calls for a significant departure from traditional concepts of intelligences. Although not its initial intention, MI theory has also led to the development of alternative forms of assessment. A risk to any innovation is the danger that it will be assimilated into traditional forms and distorted in the process (Adams and Feldman 1993). And in fact, there have been repeated requests for standardized, paper-and-pencil MI tests (Gardner 1993b). To avoid inadvertently producing another psychometrically-inspired tracking approach, in the section that follows, we will describe the central features of an MI approach to assessment, including measures, instruments, materials, context, and purposes.

### Measures: Valuing Intellectual Capacities in a Wide Range of Domains

As described earlier, MI theory maintains that human intelligence is pluralistic, each intelligence is relatively autonomous, and all of the intelligences are of potentially equal import. Assessment based on MI theory incorporates a range of measures designed to tap the different facets of each intellectual capacity.

In emphasizing the measurement of intellectual capacities in a wide range of domains, it is important to note that we do not deny the existence of some correlation among cognitive abilities, nor do we propose that standard psychometric measures be abolished overnight. Instead, we advocate the investigation of alternative methods of assessment as well as the assessment of a broader range of skills and abilities. MI approach to assessment recognizes those students who excel in linguistic and logical pursuits as well as those students who have cognitive and personal strengths in other intelligences. By virtue of the wider range it measures, MI types of assessment identify more students who are "smart," albeit in different ways (Gardner 1984; 1986; 1993c).

It has been documented that students who have trouble with some academic subjects, such as reading or math, are not necessarily inadequate in all areas (Chen 1993; Levin 1990). The challenge is to provide comparable opportunities for these students to demonstrate their strengths and interests. When the students recognize that they are good at something, and when this accomplishment is acknowledged by teachers and classmates, the students experience success and feel valued. In some instances, the sense of success in one area may make the students more likely to engage in areas where they feel less comfortable. At that point, the use of multiple measures goes beyond its initial purpose of identifying diverse cognitive abilities and begins to serve as a means of bridging a student's strengths in one area to other areas of learning (Chen 1993).

> MI theory argues that "intelligence-fair" instruments are needed to assess the unique capacities of each intelligence.

### Instruments: Using Media Appropriate to the Domain

Because it emphasizes that each intelligence exhibits particular problem-solving features and operational mechanism, MI theory argues that "intelligence-fair" instruments are needed in order to assess the unique capacities of each intelligence. "Intelligence-fair" instruments engage the key abilities of particular intelligences, allowing one to look directly at the functioning of each intellectual capacity, rather than forcing the individual to reveal his or her intelligence through the customary lens of a linguistic or logical instrument.

For example, bodily intelligence can be assessed by recording how a person learns and remembers a new dance or physical exercise. To consider a person's interpersonal intelligence, it would be necessary to observe how he or she interacts with and influences others in different social situations. It is important to note that what is being assessed here is not intelligence in pure form. Intelligences are always expressed in the context of specific tasks, domains, and disciplines. For example, there is no "pure" spatial intelligence, instead, there is spatial intelligence as expressed in a child's puzzle solution, route finding, blocking building, or basketball passing (Gardner 1993a).

Unfortunately, until now nearly all intelligence assessment has depended directly or indirectly on the measurement of linguistic and logical mathematical abilities. This kind of test ignores that distinct domains and symbol systems require different kinds of sensory processing and present unique constraints and problems. As a consequence, if students are not strong in linguistic-logical areas, their abilities in other areas would be more likely obscured. However, if we can assess an individual's ability to solve problems or create products using the materials of the domain, we are confident that many students will reveal their strengths in different areas, and the notion of general brightness will become greatly attenuated (Gardner 1987a, 1993c).

## Materials: Engaging Children in Meaningful Activities and Learning

The design of MI types of assessment is responsive to the fact that children have had different environmental and educational experiences. Considering that each intelligence is an expression of the interplay among genetic and environmental factors, children's prior experience with assessment materials directly affects their performance on tasks. For example, children who have little experience with blocks are less likely to do well in a block design task. Similarly, it would be unfair to assess a child's musical ability by asking her to play a xylophone if she has never seen such a musical instrument. In recognition of the role that experience plays, MI approach to assessment aims to provide materials with which children are familiar. To the extent that children are not familiar with materials, they are given ample opportunities to explore the materials prior to the assessment.

Many current intelligences tests use blocks, pictures, and geometric shapes. These materials are familiar to most children in industrial societies. Yet they provide little intrinsic incentive for children to engage in the activity, and they have little meaning to children's daily lives. For assessment to be meaningful for students and instructive for teachers, it should occur in the context of students working on problems and projects that genuinely engage them and that hold their interest and motivate them to do well. Such assessments may not be as easy to design as the standard multiple choice test, but they are more likely to elicit a student's full repertoire of skills and to yield information that is useful for subsequent learning and instruction (Gardner 1993c).

### Context: Assessment as an Ongoing Process

Learning is not a one-shot experience. Assessment should not be either; instead, it should be an ongoing process fully integrated into the natural learning environment. When a child's ability is measured through a one-shot experience, the child's profile is often incomplete and possibly distorted. In contrast, when assessment is naturally embedded in the learning environment, it allows teachers to observe children's performances in various situations over time. Such observations make it possible to gain multiple samples of a child's ability, document the dynamics and variation of the child's performances within a domain and across domains, and therefore more accurately portray the child's intellectual profile.

> Assessment naturally embedded in the learning environment more accurately portrays the child's intellectual profile.

MI types of assessment emphasize blurring the traditional distinction between assessment and instruction. A teacher uses the results of assessment to plan instruction; as instruction proceeds, the teacher has new opportunities to assess a child's developing competence. In this process, assessment and instruction inform and enhance each other. Initially, methods for ongoing assessment would be introduced explicitly; but, over time, assessment would occur spontaneously with little need for explicit recognition or labeling by either the student or the teacher (Gardner 1993c).

### Purpose of Assessment: Identifying Strengths as Well as Weaknesses

The development of MI theory started with the question, "What basic cognitive abilities account for what people can do?" The question implies that intelligence should be viewed as a profile of strengths, interests, and weaknesses. As well, the question stimulates the design of assessment vehicles that simultaneously help uncover and foster an individual's competence. Further, the question suggests that human beings have unique combinations of abilities that are qualitatively different and cannot be quantitatively ranked and sorted.

Traditional tests—achievement, readiness, intelligence, and the like—are often designed to rank and sort students based on a single score. Reference to single test scores leads to an almost exclusive focus on deficits when test scores are relatively low. Consequently, psychologists often spend too much time ranking individuals and not nearly enough time helping them. And educators often focus too much on remediating student's deficits rather than bridging their strengths to other areas of learning.

Instead of ranking, sorting, and remediating, the purpose of MI types of assessment is to support students on the basis of their complete intellectual profile—strengths and weaknesses. The assessor provides feedback to the student that is helpful immediately, such as suggestions about what to study or work on, pointers on which habits are productive and which are not, as well as explanations of what can be expected in terms of assessments. It is especially important that feedback include concrete suggestions and information about which relative strengths the student should build upon, independent of their rank within a comparable group of students (Gardner 1993c).

## PROJECT SPECTRUM: DOMAIN-SPECIFIC ASSESSMENT

Armed with findings about human cognition and its development and in light of perceived need for an alternative to formal testing, Gardner and his colleagues at Harvard Project Zero began to design programs which feature new approaches to assessment. Below we describe one of these efforts, the effort of Project Spectrum to tap a wide range of cognitive abilities in young children.

Project Spectrum was a collaborative research project co-directed by Howard Gardner at Harvard Project Zero and David Feldman at Tufts University. The name of the project, Spectrum, reflects its mission to recognize diverse intellectual strengths in children. From 1984 to 1993, Spectrum researchers completed a number of programs, including the development of new means of assessing the cognitive abilities of preschool children, implementation of an intervention program for first-graders based on the Spectrum approach, and coordination of a mentorship program for inner city first and second grade students. All of these programs—whether they were done in preschools or elementary schools, or whether they involved teachers or community members—included a rich assessment component designed to identify children's areas of strengths and use them as the basis for an individualized educational program.

Over the nine years of work, Spectrum researchers developed two kinds of domain-specific assessment instruments: *Preschool Assessment Activities* and *Observational Guidelines* (Chen, Isberg, and Krechevsky 1995; Krechevsky 1994). The *Spectrum Preschool Assessment Activities* include fifteen activities in seven different domains of knowledge: language, math, music, art, social understanding, mechanical science, and movement. Rather than attempting to look at intelligences in pure form when developing assessment activities, Spectrum researchers looked at the domains that are compatible with school curricula.

The assessments are embedded in meaningful, hands-on activities that share a number of distinctive features. The activities give children inviting materials to manipulate, such as toy figures or a playdough birthday cake; they are intelligence-fair, using materials appropriate to the domain rather than relying on language and math as assessment vehicles; and they examine abilities relevant to achieving fulfilling adult roles. While Spectrum assessment activities measure skills that are valued by adult society, these skills are used in a context that is meaningful to the child. For example, to assess social understanding skills, children are encouraged to manipulate figures in a scaled-down, three-dimensional replica of their classroom; to assess math skills, children are asked to keep track of passengers getting on and off a toy bus. (For detailed descriptions of Spectrum preschool assessment activities, see Adams and Feldman 1993; Krechevsky 1994; Krechevsky and Gardner 1990).

A majority of these Spectrum assessment activities are structured tasks that can be administered in a one-on-one setting. Each task measures specific abilities, often requires particular materials, and is accompanied by written instructions for task administration. These instructions include a score sheet detailing the skills exercised in each activity and how to evaluate them, so that the child's performance on many activities is quantifiable (Krechevsky 1994).

Like the score sheets, the *Observational Guidelines* are designed to highlight the distinct skills required for achievement in different cognitive domains. Unlike the score sheets, they can be used in a

# Table 1
# Domain-Specific Observational Guidelines

## VISUAL ARTS

### Perception
- is aware of visual elements in the environment and in artwork (e.g., color, lines, shapes, patterns, detail)
- is sensitive to different artistic styles (e.g., can distinguish abstract art from realism, impressionism, etc.)

### Production
*Representation*
- is able to represent visual world accurately in two or three dimensions
- is able to create recognizable symbols for common objects (e.g., people, vegetation, houses, animals) and coordinate elements spatially into unified whole
- uses realistic proportions, detailed features, deliberate choice of color

*Artistry*
- is able to use various elements of art (e.g., line, color, shape) to depict emotions, produce certain effects, and embellish drawings or 3D work
- conveys strong mood through literal representation (e.g., smiling sun, crying face) and abstract features (e.g., dark colors or drooping lines to express sadness); produces drawings or sculptures that appear "lively," "sad," or "powerful"
- shows concern with decoration and embellishment
- produces drawings that are colorful, balanced, and/or rhythmic

*Exploration*
- is flexible and inventive in use of art materials (e.g., experiments with paint, chalk, clay)
- uses lines and shapes to generate a wide variety of forms (e.g., open and closed, explosive and controlled) in 2-D or 3-D work
- is able to execute a range of subjects or themes (e.g., people, animals, buildings, landscapes)

## MECHANICAL SCIENCE

### Visual-Spatial Abilities
- is able to construct or reconstruct physical objects and simple machines in two or three dimensions
- understands spatial relationships between parts of a mechanical object

### Problem-Solving Approach with Mechanical Objects
- uses and learns from trial-and-error approach

---

## Table 1 cont.

- uses systematic approach in solving mechanical problems
- compares and generalizes information

**Understanding of Causal and Functional Relationships**
- infers relationships based on observation
- understands relationship of parts to whole, the function of these parts, and how parts are put together

**Fine Motor Skills**
- is adept at manipulating small parts or objects
- exhibits good eye-hand coordination (e.g., hammers on head of nail rather than on fingers)

MOVEMENT

**Body Control**
- shows an awareness of and ability to isolate and use different body parts
- plans, sequences, and execute moves efficiently—movements do not seem random or disjointed
- is able to replicate one's own movements and those of others

**Sensitivity to Rhythm**
- moves in synchrony with stable or changing rhythms, particularly in music (e.g., child attempts to move with the rhythm, as opposed to being unaware of or disregarding rhythmic changes)
- is able to set a rhythm of one's own and regulate it to achieve a desired effect

**Expressivity**
- evokes moods and images through movement using gestures and body postures; stimulus can be a verbal image, a prop, or music
- is able to respond to mood or tonal quality of a instrument or music selection (e.g., uses light and fluid movements for lyrical music versus strong and staccato movements for a march)

**Generation of Movement Ideas**
- is able to invent interesting and novel movement ideas, verbally and/or physically, or offer extensions of ideas (e.g., suggesting that children raise their arms to look like clouds floating in the sky)
- responds immediately to ideas and images with original movements
- choreographs a simple dance, perhaps teaching it to others

**Responsiveness to Music**
- responds differently to different kinds of music
- shows sensitivity to rhythm and expressiveness when responding to music

## Table 1 cont.

- explores available space (vertical and horizontal) comfortably using different levels, moving easily and fluidly around the space
- anticipates others in a shared space
- experiments with her body in space—e.g., turning and spinning

### MUSIC

**Music Perception**
- is sensitive to dynamics (loud and soft)
- is sensitive to tempo and rhythmic patterns
- discriminates pitch
- identifies musical and musicians' styles
- identifies different instruments and sounds

**Music Production**
- is able to maintain accurate pitch
- is able to maintain accurate tempo and rhythmic patterns
- exhibits expressiveness when singing or playing instrument
- can recall and reproduce musical properties of songs and other compositions

**Music Composition**
- creates simple compositions with some sense of beginning, middle, and end
- creates simple notation system

### SOCIAL UNDERSTANDING

**Understanding of Self**
- identifies own abilities, skills, interests, and areas of difficulty
- reflects upon own feelings, experiences, and accomplishments
- draws upon these reflections to understand and guide own behavior
- shows insight into the factors that enable an individual to do well or have difficulty in an area

**Understanding of Others**
- demonstrates knowledge of peers and their activities
- attends closely to others
- recognizes others' thoughts, feelings, and abilities
- draws conclusions about others based on their activities

**Assumption of Distinctive Social Roles**
*Leader*
- often initiates and organizes activities
- organizes other children
- assigns roles to others
- explains how activity is carried out
- oversees and directs activities

## Table 1 cont.

*Facilitator*
- often shares ideas, information, and skills with other children
- mediates conflict
- invites other children to play
- extends and elaborates other children's ideas
- provides help when others need attention

*Caregiver/Friend*
- comforts other children when they are upset
- shows sensitivity to other children's feelings
- shows understanding of friends' likes and dislikes

### MATHEMATICS

**Numerical Reasoning**
- adept at calculations (e.g., find short-cuts)
- able to estimate
- adept at quantifying objects and information (e.g., by record keeping, creating effective notation, graphing)
- able to identify numerical relationships (e.g., probability, ratio)

**Spatial Reasoning**
- finds spatial patterns
- adept with puzzles
- uses imagery to visualize and conceptualize a problem

**Logical Problem Solving**
- focuses on relationships and overall structure of problem instead of isolated facts
- makes logical inferences
- generalizes rules
- develops and uses strategies (e.g., when playing games)

### SCIENCE

**Observation Skills**
- engages in close observation of materials to learn about their physical characteristics; uses one or more of the senses
- often notices changes in the environment (e.g., new leaves on plants, bugs on trees, subtle seasonal changes)
- shows interest in recording observations through drawings, charts, sequence cards, or other methods

**Identification of Similarities and Differences**
- likes to compare and contrast materials and/or events
- classifies materials and often notices similarities and/or differences between specimens (e.g., compares and contrasts crabs and spiders)

# Table 1 cont.

**Hypothesis Formation and Experimentation**
- makes predictions based on observations
- asks "what if" type questions and offers explanations for why things are the way they are
- conducts simple experiments or generates ideas for experiments to test own or others' hypotheses (e.g., drops large and small rocks in water to see if one size sinks faster than the other; waters plant with paint instead of water)

**Interest in/Knowledge of Nature/Scientific Phenomena**
- exhibits extensive knowledge about various scientific topics; spontaneously offers information about these topics or reports on own or others' experience with natural world
- shows interest in natural phenomena, or related materials such as natural history books, over extended periods of time
- regularly asks questions about things observed

## LANGUAGE

**Invented Narrative/Storytelling**
- uses imagination and originality in storytelling
- enjoys listening to or reading stories
- exhibits interest in plot design and development, character elaboration and motivation, descriptions of settings, scenes or moods, use of dialogue, etc.
- brings a sense of narrative to different tasks
- shows performing ability or dramatic flair, including a distinctive style, expressiveness, or an ability to play a variety of roles

**Descriptive Language/Reporting**
- provides accurate and coherent accounts of events, feelings and experiences (e.g., uses correct sequence and appropriate level of detail; distinguishes fact from fantasy)
- provides accurate labels and descriptions for things
- shows interest in explaining how things work or in describing a procedure
- engages in logical argument or inquiry

**Poetic Use of Language/Wordplay**
- enjoys and is adept at wordplay such as puns, rhymes, metaphors
- plays with word meanings and sounds
- demonstrates interest in learning new words
- uses words in a humorous fashion

range of situations and invite observers to make qualitative as well as quantitative evaluations. Created for early elementary teachers to use in their classrooms, the *Guidelines* consist of eight sets of key abilities in the domains of language, math, natural science, mechanical science, art, social understanding, music, and movement (see Table 1). Key abilities are the abilities that children need to perform tasks successfully in each domain. In the case of music, key abilities include music perception, production, and composition. Spectrum researchers further identify a set of core elements or specific cognitive skills that help children exercise and execute the designated key ability. For example, core elements for music production include the abilities to maintain accurate pitch, tempo, and rhythmic patterns; to exhibit expressiveness when singing or playing an instrument, and to recall and reproduce musical properties (Chen, Isberg, and Krechevsky 1995). By directing observations in terms of domains, key abilities, and core elements, the guidelines provide teachers with a means of organizing and recording their observations of individual children and of systematizing information they may already be gleaning in a more intuitive way.

The *Spectrum Preschool Assessment Activities* and *Observational Guidelines* are valuable additions to the classroom because they cover a wide range of intellectual domains, including areas like mechanical science, creative movement, music, and visual arts, that usually are ignored in traditional tests of intelligence. Further, in contrast to many traditional forms of assessment that are designed to identify deficits, Spectrum assessment instruments aim to identify children's strengths and interests. Spectrum's work is based on the assumption that every individual has strengths; the challenge is to sample a wide enough range of possibilities so that they can be detected (Adams and Feldman 1993).

We now have data from a number of empirical studies that grew out of the Spectrum framework. For example, when we worked with four public first grade classrooms in Somerville, Massachusetts, we identified areas of strength for thirteen of the fifteen at-risk students (about 87%) on the basis of their demonstrated competence and interest in an area. These children's strengths spanned many areas, including art, mechanical science, social understanding, math, language, science, and movement. Identification of strengths in such diverse areas would not have been possible had these children been in a classroom environment that did not provide them opportunities to explore different intellectual domains (Chen 1993).

The example cited above leads to another characteristic shared by the *Spectrum Preschool Assessment Activities* and the *Observational Guidelines*. In order to use the instruments appropriately, one must first supply opportunities for intelligences or sets of intelligences to be activated. For example, to help identify areas of strength for at-risk students in our Somerville project, teachers first introduced eight learning centers into the classroom. These learning centers were stocked with inviting materials, from dress-up clothes to magnifying glasses, that students used for structured exercises as well as open-ended play. Only after the children had ample opportunity to explore diverse areas and become immersed in their own areas of interest could we begin to assess their intellectual strengths.

> Only after the children had opportunity to explore diverse areas could we begin to assess their intellectual strengths.

Stressing the importance of learning experiences for the development of intelligences, the *Spectrum Preschool Assessment Activities* and the *Observational Guidelines* are designed to dissolve the traditional boundary between assessment and curriculum or learning. For example, teachers can use the key abilities and core elements in the *Observational Guidelines* not only to observe and identify a child's intellectual strengths, but also to generate further learning experiences and plan an individualized curriculum for that child. The *Observational Guidelines* thus can be used to help nurture, as well as identify, the child's intellectual strengths.

The Spectrum *Preschool Assessment Activities* and the *Observational Guidelines* are domain-specific assessment instruments that can be used independently. However, when used together, they provide a more comprehensive approach to assessing children's performance and documenting their performance. The *Assessment Activities* help describe the child's place in a developmental process at a particular point in time, whereas the *Guidelines* direct ongoing observations in a natural learning environment, so that a child's developmental progress can be tracked over time. Furthermore, the *Observational Guidelines* can be used to obtain a rough approximation of the ways in which children differ from one another, and to identify those children who might benefit from a structured assessment activity that more closely examines a particular domain.

---

## Table 2
## Spectrum Field Inventory

*Dinosaur Game*
    Measures understanding of number concepts and counting skills.

*Storytelling*
    Measures a range of language skills including complexity of sentence structure, use of descriptive language, use of expressive dialogue, and ability to pursue a story line.

*Art Portfolio*
    Measures representational ability, extent of exploration, and level of artistry as these abilities are expressed through the medium of drawing.

*Pretend Birthday Party (Social Analytic Task)*
    Assesses understanding of friendship, conflict situations, and others' needs and feelings.

*Singing*
    Assesses the ability to maintain accurate pitch and rhythm and recall a song's musical properties.

*Assembly*
    Measures mechanical ability which involves visual-spatial abilities as well as a range of observational and problem-solving skills.

---

## INTELLIGENCE AS DOMAIN-SPECIFIC: EVIDENCE FROM AN EMPIRICAL STUDY

MI theory has attracted much attention in the fields of cognition and education (Kornhaber and Krechevsky 1994). It is concordant with many people's implicit belief about the nature of human intelligence. From its inception MI theory has been based on massive amounts of empirical data. Gardner and his colleagues are continuing to monitor the considerable body of new data relevant to the claims of the theory. Some of the work is being done at the Harvard Project Zero (Gardner 1993b; Krechevsky 1991; Winner, Rosenblatt, Windmueller, Davidson, and Gardner 1986); some of it is being done by other researchers, either explicitly investigating MI theory (Adams 1993; Rosnow 1991; Rosnow, Skleder, Jaeger, and Rind, 1994; Rosnow, Skleder, and Rind, 1995) or implicitly touching on its claims (Rauscher, Shaw, and Ky, 1993). Adams' study (1993), briefly described below, examines the relationship among diverse cognitive abilities (for a more detailed description of the study, see Adams 1993). This study was supported by the National Institute of Child Health and Human Development and is one component of a longitudinal study being conducted by Dr. Marc Bornstein and Dr. Cathy Tamis-LeMonda.

The sample in Adams' study consisted of 42 subjects, including 22 girls and 20 boys. The subjects were predominantly white and from middle- to upper-income families. The age range of the subjects was 4.2 to 4.8 years, with a mean of 4.45 years. All subjects were seen in their homes for two one-hour sessions and completed three tasks per session. The tasks were designed to measure mathematical, linguistic, artistic, social, musical, and mechanical abilities in 4-year-olds (see Table 2). The development of the tasks were based on the early work of Project Spectrum. The set of tasks is called the Spectrum Field Inventory. The tasks were administered by a trained experimenter in a game-like atmosphere.

> Results suggest that an individual's level of performance often varies when a diverse set of abilities is measured.

The Box test (Mardia, Kent, and Bibby 1979) was used to assess the joint independence of the group scores on the six tasks. The null hypothesis that all scores were uncorrelated with one another was rejected ($F = 35.76$, $p<.01$). That is, overall, Adams found that the cognitive abilities measured were not independent of each other. The sense in which they are not independent is defined in statistical terms. Meeting the statistical criterion for independence is an either/ or proposition, yet Gardner does not claim there is no relation among the intelligences. His claim is that multiple intelligences are *relatively* independent. The Box test does not provide information about the degree of dependence in the structure of the scores that are analyzed, nor is there another multivariate technique that does yield such information (Adams 1993).

To identify possible sources of covariation that contributed to the overall result, Adams generated a Pearson correlation matrix of all possible pairings of the task scores (see Table 3). As indicated in Table 3, 10 of the 15 correlations in the matrix were not significant. This finding runs counter to the repeated reports of substantial positive correlations among IQ tests (Detterman and Daniel 1989; Gould 1981; Humphreys 1982; Sattler 1992).

## Table 3
## Correlation Matrix of Group Scores on Tasks
### Tasks

| Tasks | Story | Art | Birthday | Singing | Assembly |
|---|---|---|---|---|---|
| Dinosaur | .44** | .20 | .25 | .21 | .41** |
| Story | | .43* | .26 | -.14 | .15 |
| Art | | | .51** | -.37 | .48** |
| Birthday | | | | -.03 | .23 |
| Singing | | | | | .06 |

*p<.05.
**p<.01.

To explore further the potential specificity of intellectual abilities, Adams (1993) also analyzed each individual's levels of performance in relation to the group. Using the standard deviation as a criterion, Adams defined three levels of performance. Strong, weak, and average performances were defined as scores above +1 standard deviation, below -1 standard deviation, and between +1 and -1 standard deviations, respectively. Defining the three levels of performance in relation to the standard deviation provides a set of objective criteria for determining the degree of variability within an individual's set of scores.

Of the 42 subjects in Adams' study, three children completed fewer than half of the six tasks and were eliminated from the analysis. In the remaining 39 profiles, only four subjects (10%) exhibited the same level of performance on all tasks. Thirty-five subjects (90%) performed varying levels of tasks. Of these 35 subjects, 16 (46%) earned scores that scattered over a range of 3 to 5 standard deviations. These results suggest that an individual's level of performance often varies when a diverse set of abilities is measured (Adams 1993).

The results of the study are based on a sample of 42, drawn from a predominately white middle- to upper-income population. This limits their generalizability. Nonetheless, taken as a whole, the results of Adams' study offer some support for the position that intelligence is domain-specific.

## CONCLUDING NOTES

Assessment, as much current literature points out, provides top levers for affecting educational practice. Many people criticize current educational practices; a significant part of our educational malaise, however, lies in the instruments that are used to assess student learning and, not incidentally, to signal what learning is. This kind of instrument is often presented in a standard pencil-and-paper short-answer fashion, sampling only a small proportion of intellectual abilities and often rewarding a certain kind of decontextualized facility. In other words, it may be a better indicator of test-taking skill than understanding of central aspects of the disciplines. Because this kind of instrument systematically ignores the wide range of abilities that are valued in our culture, it does little to help us recognize and nurture individuals' potential. By constraining the curriculum and taking control of the learning process away from teachers and students, this kind of instrument in fact discourages many students from discovering activities they can enjoy and at which they can achieve some success (Hatch and Gardner 1990).

> **Based on MI theory, assessments can examine and build upon the range of an individuals' cognitive potentials or competence.**

Taking into account psychological, biological, and cultural dimensions of cognition, MI theory presents a more empirically-sensitive and scientifically-compelling understanding of human intelligences and provides an impetus for alternative assessment. Based on MI theory, assessments can be designed to examine and build upon the range of an individual's cognitive potentials or competence. This kind of assessment is sensitive to what individuals are capable of accomplishing; it also suggests alternative routes to the achievement of important educational goals (learning mathematics via spatial relations; learning music through linguistic techniques).

The ultimate goal of MI approach to assessment is to help create environments that foster individual as well as group potential.

Clearly, such assessments will require concerted efforts over a long period of time to develop quality instruments and carefully trained individuals who can administer and interpret them in a sensitive manner. However, when one ponders the enormous human potential currently wasted in our society because it labels as "intelligence" only a small subset of human talents, such as an investment seems worthwhile (Gardner 1993b).

*Acknowledgment:* Preparation of this paper was aided by grants from the MacArthur Foundation, the Rockefeller Foundation, and the Spencer Foundation. We would like to thank Margaret Adams and Emily Isberg for their helpful comments on an earlier version of the paper.

## REFERENCES

Adams, M. (1993). *An empirical investigation of domain-specific theories of preschool children's cognitive abilities.* Unpublished Doctoral dissertation, Tufts University, Medford, MA.

Adams, M., and Feldman, D. H. (1993). Project Spectrum: A theory-based approach to early education. In R. Pasnak and M. L. Howe (Eds.), *Emerging themes in cognitive development: Vol. II: Competencies* (pp. 53–76). New York: Springer-Verlag.

Carrol, J. B. (1993). *Human cognitive abilities: A survey of factor-analytic studies.* Cambridge, England: Cambridge University Press.

Chen, J. Q. (1993, April). *Building on children's strengths: Project Spectrum intervention program for students at risk for school failure.* Paper presented at biennial conference of Society for Research of Child Development, New Orleans, LA.

Chen, J. Q., Isberg, E., and Krechevsky, M. (1995). *Project Spectrum Early Learning Activities.* Cambridge, MA: Harvard Project Zero.

Detterman, D. K., and Daniel, M. H. (1989). Correlations of mental tests with each other and with cognitive variables are highest for low IQ groups. *Intelligence, 13,* 349–359.

Eysenck, H. J. (1979). *The structure and measurement of intelligence.* Berlin: Springer-Verlag.

Feldman, D. H. (1994). *Beyond universals in cognitive development* (2nd ed.). Norwood, NJ: Ablex.

Gardner, H. (1984). Assessing intelligence: A comment on "Testing intelligence without IQ test" by R. J. Sternberg. *Phi Delta Kappa, 65*(10), 699–700.

————.(1986). The waning of intelligence tests. In R. Sternberg and D. Detterman (Eds.), *The acquisition of symbolic skills* (pp. 19–42). London: Plenum Press.

————. (1987a). Beyond the IQ: Education and human development. *Harvard Educational Review, 57*, 187–193.

————. (1987b). The theory of multiple intelligences. *Annals of Dyslexia, 37*, 19–35.

————. (1991). *The unschooled mind: How children think and how schools should teach.* New York: Basic Books.

————. (1993a). *Frames of mind: The theory of multiple intelligences* (tenth anniversary ed.). New York: Basic Books.

————. (1993b). *Multiple intelligences: The theory in practice.* New York: Basic Books.

————. (1993c). Assessment in context: The alternative to standardized testing. In H. Gardner (Ed.), *Multiple intelligences: The theory in practice* (pp. 161–183). New York: Basic Books.

————. (1993d). Intelligence in seven phases. In H. Gardner (Ed.), *Multiple intelligences: The theory in practice* (pp. 213–230). New York: Basic Books.

————. (1994). Multiple intelligences theory. In R. J. Sternberg (Ed.), *Encyclopedia of human intelligence* (pp. 740–742). New York: Macmillan.

————. (1995a). Cracking open the IQ box. *The American Prospect, Winter (20),* pp. 20, 71–80.

————. (1995b). Reflections on multiple intelligences: Myths and messages. *Phi Delta Kappan* 77(3), 200–209.

Gardner, H., and Hatch, T. (1989). Multiple intelligences go to school: Educational implications of the theory of multiple intelligences. *Educational Research, 18,* 4–10.

Gardner, H., and Waters, J. M. (1993). A rounded version. In H. Gardner (Ed.), *Multiple intelligences: The theory in practice* (pp. 13–34). New York: Basic Books.

Gould, S. J. (1981). *The mismeasure of man.* New York: Norton.

————. (1994, November 28). Curveball. *The New Yorker*, pp. 139–149.

Guilford, J. P. (1967). *The nature of human intelligence.* New York: McGraw-Hill.

Hatch, T., and Gardner, H. (1990). If Binet had looked beyond the classroom: The assessment of multiple intelligences. *International Journal of Educational Research, 14*(5), 415–429.

Herrnstein, R. J., and Murray, C. (1994). *The bell curve: Intelligence and class structure in American life.* New York: Free Press.

Humphreys, L. G. (1982). The hierarchical factor model and general intelligence. In N. Hirschberg and L. G. Humphreys (Eds.), *Multivariate applications in the social sciences* (pp. 223–239). Hillsdale, NJ: Erlbaum.

Jensen, A. (1969). How much can we boost IQ and scholastic achievement? *Harvard Educational Review, 39*(1), 1–123.

Kornhaber, M., and Krechevsky, M. (1994). Expanding definition of learning and teaching: Notes from the MI underground. In P. W. Cookson (Ed.)., *Creating school policy: Trends, dilemmas, and prospects.* New York: Garland Press.

Kornhaber, M., and Krechevsky, M., and Gardner, H. (1990). Engaging intelligence. *Educational Psychologist, 25*(3–4), 177–99.

Krechevsky, M. (1991). Project Spectrum: An innovative assessment alternative. *Educational Leadership, 2,* 43–48.

———. (1994). *Project Spectrum preschool assessment handbook.* Cambridge, MA: Harvard Project Zero.

Krechevsky, M., and Gardner, H. (1990). The emergence and nurturance of multiple intelligences: The Project Spectrum approach. In M. J. Howe (Ed.), *Encouraging the development of exceptional skills and talents* (pp. 222–245). Leicester, England: British Psychological Society.

Levin, H. M. (1990). Accelerated schools: A new strategy for at-risk students. *Policy Bulletin, 6,* 1–7.

Mardia, K. V., Kent, J. T., and Bibby, J. M. (1979). *Multivariate analysis.* New York: Academic Press.

McGhee, R. (1993). Fluid and crystallized intelligence: Confirmatory factor analysis of the Differential Abilities Scale, Detroit Tests of Learning Aptitude-3, and Woodcock-Johnson Psycho-educational Battery-Revised. *Journal of Psychoeducational Assessment, WJ-R Monograph,* 20–38.

Rauscher, F., Shaw, G. L., and Ky, K. N. (1993, October 14). Music and spatial task performance. *Nature, 365*(6447), p. 611.

Rosnow, R. L. (1991). Inside rumor: A personal Journey. *American Psychologist, 46*(5), 484–496.

Rosnow, R. L., Skleder, A. A., Jaeger, M., & Rind, B. (1994). Intelligence and epistemics of interpersonal acumen: Testing some implications of Gardner's theory. *Intelligence, 19,* 93–116.

Rosnow, R. L., Skleder, A. A., and Rind, B. (1995). Reading other people: A hidden cognitive structure? *General Psychologist, 31,* 1–10.

Sattler, J. M. (1992). *Assessment of children* (4th ed.). San Diego: Sattler.

Snyderman, M., and Rothman, S. (1987). Survey of expert opinion on intelligence and aptitude testing. *American Psychologist, 42,* 137–144.

———. (1988). *The IQ controversy, the media and public policy.* New Brunswick, NJ: Transaction.

Sternberg, R. J. (1985). Cognitive approaches to intelligence. In B. B. Wolman (Ed.), *Handbook of intelligence: Theories, measurements, and application* (pp. 59–118). New York: Wiley.

Walters, J. M. and Gardner, H. (1986). The theory of multiple intelligences: Some issues and answers. In R. Sternberg and R. Wagner (Eds.), *Practical intelligences* (pp. 163–183). New York: Cambridge University Press.

Winner, E., Rosenblatt, E., Windmueller, G., Davidson, L., & Gardner, H. (1986). Children's perceptions of "aesthetic" properties of the arts: Domain specific or pan-artistic? *British Journal of Development Psychology, 4,* 149–160.

Woodcock, R. W. (1990). Theoretical foundations of the WJ-R measures of cognitive ability. *Journal of Psychoeducational Assessment, 8,* 231–258.

# From Research to Reform: Finding Better Ways to Put Theory into Practice

by Thomas Hatch

T he world is full of good ideas. Some of those ideas spawned educational movements that had substantial impacts on many individuals and some schools. But, for the most part, significant change in the educational system is extremely hard to come by.[1] Part of the problem is that theorists are very good at generating good ideas, but are not as successful at getting those ideas to work for students in schools for long periods of time.

It is not fair to suggest that somehow theorists, researchers, and other academics are responsible for this state of affairs. After all, the traditional role of universities in education is to prepare teachers to work in schools and not to change the very nature of the work of schools and school systems that are already functioning. Nor is it sensible to suggest that somehow the academic community can "rescue" the nation's schools. Recognizing the difficulty of stimulating and sustaining educational reforms, however, more and more "academics" are concerning themselves with making their ideas work "in context" and are beginning to address the problem of change directly.[2] Described here are several avenues through which the ideas of one group of educators, Howard Gardner and his colleagues at Harvard Project Zero, are making their way into schools. In conclusion, several means are outlined by which the academic community can help to increase the capacity of schools for change and thereby turn good ideas into common practice.

From *educational HORIZONS*, vol. 72, summer 1993, 197–202. Copyright © 1993 by Thomas Hatch. Reprinted with permission.

## MULTIPLE INTELLIGENCES, PROJECTS, AND ALTERNATIVE ASSESSMENT

In the field of education, there are a number of inspirational theories that capture the imagination of wide audiences. To take a recent example, Howard Gardner's Theory of Multiple Intelligences encouraged many people to rethink how schools value and support the abilities of children.[3] Gardner suggests that there has been an undue emphasis on linguistic and logical-mathematical intelligences in both schools and tests at the expense of the development of a wide range of other intelligences.

In more recent work, Gardner and his colleagues at Project Zero and elsewhere also promote the idea that both curricula and assessments need to reflect the kinds of activities—the "authentic" activities—that students are likely to experience outside of school. For example, they argue that students should be spending more time completing the kinds of projects that carpenters, artists, and historians pursue every day.[4] By receiving coaching and instruction for a variety of skills within the context of those projects, students can develop their abilities in meaningful ways. Instead of simply being tested at the end of such projects, students collect and reflect on the work they do in the course of such meaningful activities. Students thereby gain a deeper understanding of the material and have a chance to learn how to improve their products.

Over the past ten years, these ideas have found their way into schools through a number of avenues. Some schools and many individuals have taken it upon themselves to expand upon these ideas in their own classrooms. Gardner and his colleagues explored these ideas in research projects that yielded assessments, curriculum activities, and programs that can be used both inside and outside of school. Most recently, Gardner and his colleagues started collaborating with other educators to integrate these ideas into a comprehensive approach to educational reform. These efforts illustrate how powerful ideas can inspire, support, and create change in schools, but at the same time, they raise serious questions about the possibilities of sustaining reforms on a wide scale.

## INSPIRING CHANGE IN SCHOOLS

As Kornhaber and Krechevsky detail in an analysis of nine schools that put the Theory of Multiple Intelligences (hereafter MI) into practice, MI spawned a significant grass-roots effort.[5] At least in part, the popularity of MI can be attributed to the fact that many people—either as teachers, parents, or students—have seen firsthand how the conventional educational system has failed to address the diverse needs and strengths of students. As one administrator of an MI-inspired program commented:

> . . . I think teachers—good teachers anyway—have been making provisions for those kids [children weak in language and math], but feeling a great sense of guilt. If they took time away from the program to allow the youngster to do more music, to do art, to do dance, to interpret more through the non-traditional method, they had to do it with a closed door. Now they can keep the door open, now they can celebrate what youngsters can do, and I think that's why it's [MI] been so appealing to people all over. It's gotten them to open their doors, and to yell, loud and clear, "This child is special."[6]

Another interesting factor in this grass-roots movement is the fact that neither *Frames of Mind,* where Gardner originally presented the theory, nor subsequent publications, presents a specific model or even broad guidelines for implementation.[7] In fact, while a number of different projects that use the ideas have been described, there never has been an attempt to prescribe a single course of action. Instead individual schools, administrators, or teachers are left with considerable latitude in putting these ideas into practice.

According to Kornhaber and Krechevsky, this grass-roots effort contributed to two primary kinds of curricula, an increased emphasis on alternative assessments, and to some changes in organizational structures. In terms of curriculum, many of the nine schools studied instituted classes or activities focusing on the development of particular intelligences. For example, some schools instituted learning centers associated with each intelligence, some included specific instruction in central aspects of each intelligence, and many sought the involvement of experts in different domains. In addition, many of the teachers in these schools created projects or activities that drew upon a number of different intelligences. For example, in one school the computer coordinator invited students interested in technology to become managers of the computer lab. In order to perform their responsibilities, the students had to use their interpersonal, linguistic, and organizational skills among others. In other schools, students explored subjects like architecture by carrying out activities that drew on several different intelligences: writing about buildings they would like to design, sketching parts of their own school building, composing songs about architecture, and creating models of geometric shapes.

Not surprisingly, many of the schools also reexamined their systems of assessment in order to better reflect the diverse strengths and needs of their students. In one middle school, this reexamination led the teachers to visit the sixth graders from their feeder schools and to ask the students about their strengths. A seventh grade teacher reported that one girl brought her violin to this interview and explained that Itzak Perlman, whom she saw on "Sesame Street," was her idol. A boy who was described as having speech and motor difficulties talked about his love for karate and then volunteered to play his cello. The coverage, explained:

> . . . when they [the students] have that audience, when they are the experts, they really were able to totally engage us. And they knew who they were. When you give them the floor and they are the expert, they are able to define themselves. And what we saw then was their own self-esteem just starting to soar. And this tied in beautifully with our own school philosophy that says that we create an environment where every child has the opportunity to experience the dignity of their expertise.[8]

While most schools have not gone as far in developing new approaches to assessment, other schools have changed their report cards to incorporate more of the intelligences and are experimenting with innovations like portfolios.

In addition to enhancing curriculum and assessment methods, Kornhaber and Krechevsky report that MI theory is reflected in the structure and organization of the schools. Many created teacher teams and encouraged teachers with different specialties to work together. In the process, teachers started to discover their own intelligences and to call on their colleagues for help in areas where they are not as strong. In addition, in one case, assessments of the students' strengths were used to create an individualized schedule. The schedule was designed so that classes a student may find challenging were surrounded by those that correspond with their strengths and in which they were more likely to experience success.

Although these schools had to develop these ideas without substantial or consistent outside support, this independence has a number of benefits. It allows educators to develop a sense of ownership for and commitment to ideas they might not experience if a more prescriptive approach was offered. In addition, the flexibility and originality give educators a chance to tailor ideas to their situation. Not every teacher will be able—or be interested in—interviewing sixth graders from another school, but for one group of teachers at least, it may be the perfect approach. The drawback to individual schools developing their own programs is that it is an extremely long and difficult process, and only those people with the utmost energy and commitment are likely to persevere. The teachers and administrators in the schools that Kornhaber and Krechevsky described worked well beyond the normal commitments. Learning about MI and other theories, consulting with experts, and meeting with their peers and parents, often began well before school—at 6 a.m. breakfasts in one case—and lasted well into the evening. Unless a way is found to make the development and use of these ideas more manageable, it is unlikely that such grass-roots efforts can grow substantially.

> **Teachers started to discover their own intelligences and to call on their colleagues for help in areas where they are not as strong.**

## SUPPORTING CHANGE IN SCHOOLS

While no single MI approach has been prescribed, Gardner and his colleagues at Harvard Project Zero have engaged in a number of projects that explore the implications of MI theory and related ideas like project-based learning. Many of these projects began with the goal of addressing specific research questions, but they also spawned a number of ideas for curricula and assessments. More recently, these projects took as a goal the development of materials such as handbooks and videotapes, model programs, and teacher networks explicitly designed to support the spread of these ideas within schools.

The Mather After School Project serves as an example of this growing concern with the means and methods of putting theory into practice.[9] A collaborative endeavor drawing on the ideas of William Damon, Howard Gardner, David Perkins, and Allan Collins, and Michael K. Marshall, the principal of Mather School, the project is designed to meet several goals. First, the program is intended to investigate the benefits of project-based learning for the development of literacy and thinking skills. Second, it provides teachers with a comfortable setting outside the traditional pressures of standardized tests, coverage, and other administrative demands in which to try this approach.

Currently, the after school program is run by six teachers from the Mather School, a public elementary school in an urban, culturally diverse neighborhood in Boston. Each teacher leads a group of fifteen third–fifth grade students twice a week in a project such as publishing a newspaper or designing board games. Initially the goal was to create specific projects that could be used over and over again (and eventually in the regular school day). However, it was readily apparent that the most successful projects drew directly from the interests of the teachers and students and were flexible enough to respond to new ideas and interests as they arose. As a result, a process was developed that helps teachers to generate and implement their own projects. In this process, teachers are given a "guidebook" that explains the approach, attend a summer workshop in which they develop a project, carry out the project in the after school program with the guidance and support of the research staff, and reflect on the progress of their projects in bi-weekly meetings with other teachers and researchers.[10]

Through the teachers' participation in this process, they gained experience and developed strategies that helped them both in the after school program and the regular school day. In particular, the teachers felt that they were better able to respond to the interests and ideas of their students. As one of the teachers explained in an interview:

> I learned how . . . if you allow them [the students] a little bit more freedom and set reachable goals for them and yourself that it's easier on everybody and you don't feel so much pressure . . . people are more willing to do things and want to get them done, and I find that with the students that were in the group at the time, with myself and with anyone else who is working with me, where it's not "it's my way and that's the only way" but you're open to different approaches, where children feel comfortable telling you . . . giving their suggestions, and I've learned how to accept it, how to accept it as sort of a constructive criticism.

The teachers also described how they were becoming more flexible in the classroom, learning how to improvise and to act as facilitators of the students' work. As another teacher explained when describing the project approach:

> You have to be very flexible. Things may not go as you want them. You may not be able to do everything you want to do in that given day and time. And you are more of a facilitator; you're not direct teaching like what we do most of the time during the day. . . . You are not just a teacher—"Okay class, this is what we are going to learn today"— you've told them everything before they even get started, never mind their ideas. But with the project-based approach, they come up with their own ideas and that's how you elaborate or begin a project. So, it's vastly different because you are not just teaching. You're learning from them, and they're learning from each other in groups.

As this question suggests, for many of these teachers, this project development process allowed them to understand and develop learning experiences that were substantially different from what they traditionally did in the classroom.

One of the advantages of an approach like this is that it allows teachers to feel an ownership of the projects they would not feel if they were simply handed a curriculum. In contrast to the grass-roots efforts described previously, the project development process makes it possible for teachers to benefit from and to share specific expertise it might take them years to develop on their own. The approach is also quite flexible. There are not many teachers who have the time or energy to work in an after school program at the end of a long school day. However, it is possible to lessen the burden by conducting the program during the summer or by staffing an after school program with pre-service teachers. In addition, teachers can benefit simply from using the guidebook or participating in the workshops. The teachers in the after school project who benefited the most were those who spent two or three years working together intensively with a team of researchers. It is not clear at this point how much time and support will be needed to make such an approach effective on a wider scale.

## CREATING CHANGE IN SCHOOLS

In the last two years, Gardner and his colleagues from the Development Group of Project Zero also joined a larger collaboration that is intended to bring together a number of reform ideas into one comprehensive effort. ATLAS Communities is an initiative that includes the Coalition of Essential Schools chaired by Ted Sizer, the School

Development Program directed by James Comer, and the Educational Development Center headed by Janet Whitla. As one of the eleven "design teams" originally sponsored by the New American Schools Development Corporation, ATLAS Communities' goal is to create a design for a pre-K–12 "pathway" that addresses needed changes at all levels from the curricula in the classroom to the rules and regulations in the policy arena. The acronym ATLAS reflects the collaborators' commitment to "authentic teaching, learning, and assessment for all students."

In order to fulfill this commitment, the ATLAS design integrates and expands upon some of the key reform initiatives of each of the four organizations. Thus, ATLAS Communities includes supportive organizational and management structures and involve parents and the wider community as partners in the educational process—two hallmarks of the School Development Program. In addition, ATLAS Communities strives to create a "personalized" learning environment in which all students are known well and includes a curriculum that is built around essential questions—two features of the approach of the Coalition of Essential Schools. From the Educational Development Center, ATLAS draws an emphasis on active, hands-on learning and the integration of technology into the curriculum. From Project Zero, ATLAS incorporates the use of ongoing assessments such as portfolios and curricula that respond to the strengths of each student.

> **Portfolios that document each student's strengths and needs can help to create a personalized learning environment.**

By putting these elements in a single approach, ATLAS hopes to create changes in schools that reinforce each other. Thus, portfolios that document each student's strengths and needs can help to create a personalized learning environment; similarly, a supportive management structure may be more responsive to issues such as adjusting the schedule or creating teams of teachers in order to help transform the curriculum. In addition, rather than prescribing these reforms, ATLAS involves the schools and communities in shaping the process of change. Currently, this approach is being carried out in collaboration with schools from Gorham, Maine; Norfolk, Virginia; and Prince George's County, Maryland. Over time, ATLAS hopes to create a network of schools and an ATLAS faculty that can support reform on a much wider basis.

While the size and scope of an effort like this can create a fertile environment for the introduction of innovative ideas, the scale also presents a number of challenges. The initial steps of such an effort are particularly difficult. Few organizations, inside or outside education, are prepared to undergo a massive reorganization; and such a major effort can create considerable uncertainty and anxiety. Large scale initiatives also run the risk of pulling people in too many directions at once. If not managed carefully, the time and resources needed for one aspect of the initiative may undercut other aspects. Creating change across schools—from pre-K–12—also means that two or three distinct school organizations must be merged. The traditional divisions between elementary, middle, and high schools are barriers to change that are not addressed by efforts that focus solely on one school or level of schooling at a time. Nonetheless, once changes begin to occur, there may be a kind of "domino effect" in which new developments—in different aspects of the system as well as in different schools—begin to reinforce each other and smooth the way for the kinds of innovations that can change the very nature of schooling in America.

> In schools today, change is a recognized necessity, but it is not a natural part of what happens every day.

## SHARING THE BURDEN OF CHANGE IN SCHOOLS

Each one of these methods of putting ideas and theories to work in schools is better suited to some sites and situations than others. Schools that have the energy and resources to put together their own change initiatives may be better off on their own than signing up with a particular reform effort. Schools that already involve after school programs, summer schools, extra-curricular activities, or project-based curricula may benefit immediately from the approach of the Mather After School Program. Districts that have or desire closer connections across levels may be ready to become ATLAS Communities.

Despite their unique characteristics, however, these approaches have some common requirements. First, they all require special efforts. In schools today, change is a recognized necessity, but it is not a natural part of what happens every day. Teachers, administrators, and others have to spend time outside their normal working hours in order to make these initiatives work. Second, each approach draws on the help of outside experts. Schools that take on the process of changing themselves may not involve as much outside help as other efforts, but they still look to consultants and other visitors for assistance. Third, all require time for the changes to sink in and for new expectations, behaviors, and approaches to evolve.

Currently, schools are ill-equipped to deal with any of these requirements. This situation is understandable given that the traditional mission of schools is to prepare students for later life. Schools are not designed to respond to new ideas, to adopt new programs, or to change on a regular basis. Thus, in many ways, the academic community has been producing a commodity—new ideas—that our schools are not prepared to buy. It is not fair to suggest that schools do not *want* to change. Many communities, schools, teachers, and other school personnel are calling and looking for ways to improve themselves. But they lack the *capacity* for change.

Creating a capacity for change is not a simple process. But it is a process in which the academic community can play a significant role by developing better ways to share its expertise, personnel, and resources.

First of all, developing and learning about new ideas and programs should be a regular and natural part of what people do in schools. Instead of special meetings, weekend retreats, and breakfast study groups, a portion of every day should be reserved for reflecting on the current progress of students, staff, and the school and planning for the future. To allow time for these meetings, universities and research groups can help to supply the personnel needed to keep classrooms running effectively. Contributing well-supervised preservice teachers, training parents or other volunteers, or allowing and encouraging researchers to provide direct support in the classroom can provide extra help. There are already some school-university partnerships that lead in this direction. However, a broad and systematic effort to change the nature of the daily workload of school personnel is required.

Second, the distinction between "insiders" and "outsiders" must be broken down. Currently, most members of the academic community remain outside schools, serving only as visitors, consultants, or collaborators on a temporary basis. This situation creates a natural suspicion about the "outsiders'" motives and abilities by those who work in schools every day. In many cases this situation is compounded because researchers take "their" new ideas *to* schools rather than building on the strengths or responding to the problems *of* particular schools and classrooms. To correct this problem, academics and academic institutions should develop long-term relationships with schools and districts. For example, rather than carrying out disparate initiatives all over the country, academic institutions could systematically direct new initiatives, workshops, consultants, and other resources to local schools and districts. This approach would make it possible for researchers and others to come to an understanding of and begin to respond to the specific problems that plague particular schools and districts. Of course, it is still important to disseminate ideas and programs beyond the local community, but if each university or academic institution concentrated its efforts in a few easily accessible places, schools would be better served across the nation. In this manner, academic institutions could stand with their local schools and share the responsibility for improvement.

> **Educators are reinforced for having good ideas, but praise for ideas must be balanced with the resolve to make them work.**

Third, academic institutions need to change the way educators are prepared. While there have been many calls to transform education for teachers, it is time to create and support a new profession. Currently, in most schools of education, one studies to become an administrator, a teacher, a counselor, or a researcher. No one is prepared to work with school personnel to support development and change. Schools of education need to develop programs of study to help people to become agents of educational reform: to prepare them to develop collaborative relationships with teachers; to create, manage, and sustain new initiatives; and to support the reflections and progress of school personnel.

Finally, the value of the contributions of the academic community must be reconsidered. In today's society, educators are reinforced for having good ideas that can be summarized succinctly and disseminated quickly. Certainly such achievements are noteworthy and deserve support, but praise for ideas must be balanced with the resolve to make them work. Too much emphasis on the ideas themselves will result in a group without the expertise or the capacity to make and sustain change on a consistent basis. Thus, funding must be provided to establish long-term relationships between schools and academic institutions, not just short-term tests of new ideas. All must have realistic expectations about the kinds of changes that can occur quickly, and the patience to take the time for changes to evolve at a reasonable pace. Through these kinds of initiatives, instead of being the laboratories in which researchers work, schools can become the communities that they serve.

## NOTES

1.  L. Cuban, *How Teachers Taught: Constancy and Change in American Classrooms, 1890–1980* (New York: Longman, 1984); L. Cuban, "Reforming Again, Again, and Again," *Educational Researcher* (April 1990): 3–13; R. Elmore, ed., *Restructuring Schools* (San Francisco: Jossey-Bass, 1990); S. Sarason, *The Culture of the School and the Problem of Change* (Boston: Allyn-Bacon, 1971); and S. Sarason, *The Predictable Failure of Educational Reform* (San Francisco: Jossey-Bass, 1990).

2.  See for example M. Fullan and M. Miles, "Getting Reform Right: What Works and What Doesn't," *Phi Delta Kappan* 73, no. 10 (June 1992): 745–752, and M. Fullan with S. Steigelbauer, *The New Meaning of Educational Change* (New York: Teacher's College Press, 1991).

3.  H. Gardner, *Frames of Mind* (New York: Basic Books, 1983), and H. Gardner, *Multiple Intelligences: The Theory in Practice* (New York: Basic Books, 1993).

4.  H. Gardner, *The Unschooled Mind.* (New York: Basic Books, 1991).

5.  M. Korhaber and M. Krechevsky, "Expanding Definitions of Learning and Teaching: Notes from the M. I. Underground" in *Creating School Policy: Trends, Dilemmas, and Prospects,* ed. P. Cookson (New York: Garland Press, [1994]).

6.  Ibid., 9.

7.  See for example, H. Gardner and T. Hatch, "Multiple Intelligences Go to School," *Educational Researcher* 18, no. 8 (1989): 4–10.

8.  Quoted in M. Kornhaber, personal communication.

9.  T. Hatch, H. Goodrich, C. Unger, and G. Wiatrowski, "On the Edge of School: Creating a New Context for Students' Development," in *Promoting Community-Based Programs for Socialization and Learning, New Directions in Child Development* 63, 51–64.

10. H. Goodrich, T. Hatch, G. Wiatrowski, and C. Unger. *Teaching through Projects: Creating Effective Learning Environments* (San Francisco: Addison-Wesley).

# Portfolios and Projects: Assessment in the Classroom

T he second section investigates how MI relates to two key players on the educational stage—portfolio assessment and project-based curriculum. Hebert puts forth a teacher's eye view of the issues involved in implementing portfolios in elementary schools. The author suggests that portfolios are a powerful tool for taking stock of the child's multiple intelligences. Placing a strong emphasis on having students "tell their stories" about their work, Hebert asserts that portfolios have the effect of encouraging reflective thinking among teachers as well as students.

Stefanakis points to a key element in the portfolio process—the relationship between the learner and teacher. Whereas typical assessments place the examiner "across" from the learner (in the role of evaluator), portfolio assessment effectively shifts the balance of power toward the student. According to Stefanakis, the teacher that "sits beside" the learner—taking on the role of facilitator rather than evaluator—is best positioned to create a profile of the child's multiple intelligences.

Walters and Gardner explore the idea of assessment through a project-based curriculum, discussing along the way how technologies can assist alternative assessments in an MI framework. Among other topics, Walters and Gardner describe Project Catalyst, which explored computer-assisted educational strategies in subjects ranging from computer programming (Just Enough Pascal) through social studies (Immigrant 1850) to musical composition (Songsmith).

Taken together, the articles by Walters and Gardner, Stefanakis, and Hebert underscore three aspects of projects and portfolios. First, these devices capture the growth of individual students over time, instead of relying on snapshot-quick assessments designed to compare the individual's work to that of the peer group. Second, portfolios and projects work to involve the learner in the assessment process, making assessment less the exclusive province of the adult examiner. Finally, portfolios and projects encourage learners to engage in reflective thinking, turning assessment activities into fruitful incidents of learning.

# Portfolios Invite Reflection—From Students *and* Staff

by Elizabeth A. Hebert

F our years ago, Crow Island Elementary School began a project that has reaped benefits far beyond what any of us could have imagined. The focus of the project was assessment of children's learning, and the tangible product is a new reporting form augmented by student portfolios.

> **The project grew out of our dissatisfaction with mandated standardized modes of assessment.**

More important, however, has been the process of developing our thinking and teaching around new ways of looking at children's learning. In fact, this process became more valuable to us as a faculty than the assessment product, helpful as it has been.

## OUR COMMITMENT TO ALTERNATIVE ASSESSMENT

The project grew out of our dissatisfaction and frustration with mandated standardized modes of assessment. Standardized tests do not reflect how we teach, the effects of our teaching on children, or how we adapt instruction to individual learners. Wolf and colleagues write that "the design and implementation of alternative modes of assessment will entail nothing less than a wholesale transition from what we call a testing culture to an assessment culture." They continue:

> The observable differences in the form, the data, and the conduct of standardized testing and its alternatives are in no way superficial matters or mere surface features. They derive from radical differences in

From *Educational Leadership,* vol. 49, no. 8, May 1992, 58–61. © 1992 by the Association for Supervision and Curriculum Development. Reprinted with permission.

underlying conceptions of mind and of the evaluation process itself. Until we understand these differences and their network of consequences, we cannot develop new tools that will allow us to ensure that a wide range of students use their minds well. (1991, p. 33)

Obviously, we had our work cut out for us. What did we do to reaffirm our commitment to a concept of learning incompatible with standardized testing? First, we did a good deal of reading; engaged in lengthy discussions about values, community building, and conferencing; and consulted with experts. We also became more deliberate about making time to visit one another's classrooms and to share and refine our observations of children. Next we began defining the questions to which we were seeking answers. Our first questions were global:

- How do we define learning?
- Where does learning take place?
- How do we recognize learning?
- How do we report instances of learning?

As we answered these larger questions, our concerns became more specific. How can we communicate about children's learning experiences with parents in ways that:

- authentically describe the child,
- speak to issues of accountability and maintain the integrity of our beliefs about children and how they learn,
- reflect the different ways that teachers organize instruction, and
- provide concrete information compatible with parents' expectations?

## A COMPATIBLE THEORY

Some background information about our school provides a context for our project and how we went about answering these questions. Crow Island is a public JK–5 school in Winnetka, Illinois, an affluent suburb of Chicago's north shore. The Winnetka Public Schools include three elementary schools and one middle school for grades 6–8. Our lower schools have enrollments of 360–390. Although a public school system, we have a strong tradition in the progressive philosophy of education that is distinguished by:

- a commitment to a developmental orientation to instruction,
- the priority placed on consideration of the "whole child" and his or her individual mode of learning,
- the absence of letter grades until 7th grade,
- high regard for teachers as professionals.

In acknowledging the uniqueness of a child's mode of learning, the district has placed a high priority on conferencing with parents. For many years, pupil progress has been reported to parents in a conference format three times per year. Teachers had prepared narrative descriptions of children using the following organizers: language arts, math, social studies, science, growth of the child as a group member.

> Gardner's theory provided a good scaffold for our thinking.

One expert who influenced our thinking about alternative assessment was Howard Gardner, whose "Theory of Multiple Intelligences" (musical, linguistic, logical-mathematical, spatial, bodily-kinesthetic, interpersonal, and intrapersonal) challenges the more traditional concepts of intelligence. The main thrust of Gardner's theory as applied to schools is that children may demonstrate the different kinds of intelligences in ways not necessarily associated with traditional school subjects and certainly not associated with traditional modes of assessment. Gardner's theory resonated with the themes of progressive education to which we at Crow Island are devoted.

## A VISUAL FORMAT

Gardner's theory provided a good scaffold for our thinking. The next step was to put our thoughts into a visual format. Our first rough attempt began to capture the idea of multiple dimensions of a child's learning. This primitive model consisted of a stick figure surrounded by floating boxes. As you may expect, there was much discussion about the number, size, and positioning of the boxes, but we finally agreed on a format. We call it our Learning Experiences Form (see Fig. 1 for a composite example of the form, shortened for space).

Our next concern was to identify our organizers on the Learning Experiences Form. Being committed to the multiple intelligences perspective, we readily included music, art, and physical education. We wanted to recognize these teachers' long-term relationships with

## Figure 1
## Learning Experiences Form

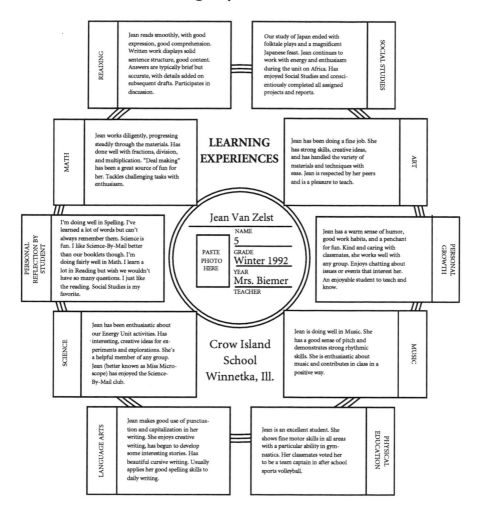

**READING**
Jean reads smoothly, with good expression, good comprehension. Written work displays solid sentence structure, good content. Answers are typically brief but accurate, with details added on subsequent drafts. Participates in discussion.

**SOCIAL STUDIES**
Our study of Japan ended with folktale plays and a magnificent Japanese feast. Jean continues to work with energy and enthusiasm during the unit on Africa. Has enjoyed Social Studies and conscientiously completed all assigned projects and reports.

**MATH**
Jean works diligently, progressing steadily through the materials. Has done well with fractions, division, and multiplication. "Deal making" has been a great source of fun for her. Tackles challenging tasks with enthusiasm.

**LEARNING EXPERIENCES**

**ART**
Jean has been doing a fine job. She has strong skills, creative ideas, and has handled the variety of materials and techniques with ease. Jean is respected by her peers and is a pleasure to teach.

**PERSONAL REFLECTION BY STUDENT**
I'm doing well in Spelling. I've learned a lot of words but can't always remember them. Science is fun. I like Science-By-Mail better than our booklets though. I'm doing fairly well in Math. I learn a lot in Reading but wish we wouldn't have so many questions. I just like the reading. Social Studies is my favorite.

Jean Van Zelst
NAME
5
GRADE
PASTE PHOTO HERE
Winter 1992
YEAR
Mrs. Biemer
TEACHER

**PERSONAL GROWTH**
Jean has a warm sense of humor, good work habits, and a penchant for fun. Kind and caring with classmates, she works well with any group. Enjoys chatting about issues or events that interest her. An enjoyable student to teach and know.

**SCIENCE**
Jean has been enthusiastic about our Energy Unit activities. Has interesting, creative ideas for experiments and explorations. She's a helpful member of any group. Jean (better known as Miss Microscope) has enjoyed the Science-By-Mail club.

Crow Island School
Winnetka, Ill.

**MUSIC**
Jean is doing well in Music. She has a good sense of pitch and demonstrates strong rhythmic skills. She is enthusiastic about music and contributes in class in a positive way.

**LANGUAGE ARTS**
Jean makes good use of punctuation and capitalization in her writing. She enjoys creative writing, has begun to develop some interesting stories. Has beautiful cursive writing. Usually applies her good spelling skills to daily writing.

**PHYSICAL EDUCATION**
Jean is an excellent student. She shows fine motor skills in all areas with a particular ability in gymnastics. Her classmates voted her to be a team captain in after school sports volleyball.

students, the value of their programs, and their insights about children's learning. But what about the other Learning Experience organizers? The dialogue went something like this:

Q: How should I specify my organizers?
A: That depends on how you organize instruction.
Q: But what if mine are different from someone else's?

A: That's OK. You organize instruction differently. We already know that about one another. Now we're just writing about it.

Q: But we organize instruction differently for different students.

A: Your Learning Experiences Form will then reflect the flexibility of your teaching.

This was a crucial stage in our thinking because discussing the form brought to the surface what I term the "bilingualism" of teachers. *Inside language*—what we do in our classrooms—reflects our beliefs and values, years of teaching experience, observations of children and of other good teachers, and confidence in knowing what we know. *Outside language*—what we say we do in our classrooms—is influenced by community values, comfort level within the school environment, political pressures, district and administrative policies, test scores, and curriculum.

> **Teachers must construct their own knowledge of children, how they learn, and how to evaluate that learning.**

The nature of our project necessitated our speaking "inside language," a more difficult discourse because it requires feelings of safety and security. Gradually, though, we were able to experience the sharing of values that leads to the creation of a secure, thoughtful environment for children, teachers, and parents.

## A CLOSE LOOK AT OURSELVES

In order to change how we evaluated children's learning, we realized we needed to take a close look at ourselves. We soon found ourselves undergoing an intensive assessment of our teaching, our beliefs about children, and our views of the school and its relationship to our community.

At this point, the project quite naturally proceeded from an emphasis on student assessment to a more powerful staff development focus. In order for this to occur in any school, administrators must commit to providing the kind of school environment where such a climate can flourish. Administrators also have to acknowledge that all teachers do not arrive at the same point in their growth together. As we emphasize with the children, teachers must construct their own knowledge of children, how they learn, and how to evaluate that learning. We have to be patient and sufficiently open to allow for dif-

ferent stages of understanding, yet focused enough to provide clarity
and vision to the effort.

## IMPROVEMENT TO THE PROCESS

We began using the Learning Experiences Form in a variety of ways.
Some teachers were more conservative, using traditional school subject labels on their forms. Others coined new organizers that reflected their teaching styles. As they struggled with the new format,
teachers became more thoughtful; and parents, sensing the positive
energy and concern of teachers, responded enthusiastically. After the
first conference using the new form, the response from both parents
and teachers was overwhelmingly positive.

Over four years, we've refined the form to meet the suggestions
of teachers at kindergarten, primary, and intermediate levels. In response to our concern about how to separate out curriculum specif-
ics and descriptions of a child's learning, one of our teachers
designed a Curriculum Overview, to be printed on the back of the
form, that consists of mini-statements of curriculum objectives for
that portion of the year. This addition freed up the front of the form
for more focused descriptions of children's learning.

Noting the absence of the child's input to the form, we designated a space for a "child's reflection" about his or her learning. The
older students write their own thoughts; teachers take dictation for
the 1st graders. We've also begun to include parents' thoughts about
their child's learning experience in our assessment form.

## STUDENTS TELL THEIR STORIES

The next step was to have our students create portfolios. Portfolios
are compatible with Crow Island's agenda for effective teaching, authentic assessment, and faculty growth. One of the best definitions in
the current literature comes from Paulson and Paulson (1991):
"Portfolios tell a story . . . put in anything that helps tell the story."
With these authors, we also agree about the importance of the child's
participation in selecting the contents of the portfolio and with a focus more on process than on content (1991, p. 1).

At present, each of our students has a portfolio that represents
work across all domains. Students maintain their portfolios all year
and frequently have conferences with the teacher about works in

progress, additions, and deletions. At the end of the year, their portfolios are combined with past years' work and stored in our Student Archives. The archives are alphabetically arranged in open shelving in our Resource Center along with historical documents, publications, and photographs of our school and students.

## PORTFOLIO EVENINGS

Three years ago we added a new element to our assessment project. Encouraged by the kinds of thinking that children have expressed in their Student Reflections, we realized that they were capable of much more. Getting them more involved in the process of assessment seemed to make good sense.

In preparation for "Portfolio Evenings," children review their portfolio/archive as teachers guide them with questions like:

> At present, each of our students has a portfolio that represents work across all domains.

- How has your writing changed since last year (or since September)?
- What do you know about numbers now that you didn't know in September?
- Let's compare a page from a book you were reading last year and a book you are reading now and include copies of each in your portfolio (an idea from Denise Levine, Fordham University, New York).
- What is unique about your portfolio?
- What would you like Mom and Dad to understand about your portfolio? Can you organize it so it will show that?

The idea is to ask guiding questions that help children reflect on their learning. Students are encouraged to write about their learning and to include these thoughts as part of their portfolios. Developing the metacognitive process in students, even at a young age, heightens their awareness and commitment to a critical assessment of their learning.

In preparation for Portfolio Evenings, the teacher divides the class into small groups of six or seven at the primary level (and larger groups at grades 4 and 5) and assigns a night for each group of students and their parents. Primary-level Portfolio Evenings are held in February. We hold intermediate-level Portfolio Evenings in May, because older students prepare more extensive projects.

On Portfolio Evenings, which last for about an hour and a half, the children sit with their parents and present their portfolios. The teacher and I circulate, visiting each student and highlighting particular milestones each youngster may have attained. We are available for questions but try not to intrude, because this is really the children's evening, and they need to "run the show" as much as possible. Parents and teachers have been impressed with the leadership and independence that even our youngest students have demonstrated in this setting.

## A POWERFUL LEARNING EXPERIENCE

We are continuing to refine our assessment project. Some issues we're addressing are practical in nature, for example, storage containers for the portfolios/archives. Others are more fundamental, like how to use portfolios to link children's early, strong expressions of interest in a particular topic to more sophisticated elaborations later in their school careers. We are also contemplating how to gain the community's support for these alternative modes of assessment as part of a viable system of accountability. And, finally, as a faculty we are trying to preserve the cohesive and bold spirit that nurtured this project along its way.

The entire process has been a powerful learning experience for our faculty as well as for the children and their parents. It has expressed the fundamental values of our school district and represents our joint exploration of the complex issues of children and their learning. We are encouraged to go forward by the positive effects this project has had on the self-esteem and professionalism of the individual teachers and the inevitable strengthening of the professional atmosphere of the entire school. We have improved our ability to assess student learning. Equally important, we have become, together, a more empowered, effective faculty.

*Author's note:* For further reading on student archives, consult the writings of Pat Carini and teachers from the Prospect School in Bennington, Vermont, The Prospect Archive and Center for Education and Research, Bennington, VT 05257.

## REFERENCES

Gardner, H. (1983). *Frames of Mind: The Theory of Multiple Intelligences.* New York: Basic Books.

Paulson, F. L., and P. R. Paulson. (Copyright, February 1991). "Portfolios: Stories of Knowing." Prepublication draft.

Paulson, F. L., P. R. Paulson, and C. Meyer. (1991). "What Makes a Portfolio a Portfolio?" *Educational Leadership* 48, 5: 60–63.

Wolf, D., J. Bixby, J. Glen, and H. Gardner. (1991). "To Use Their Minds Well: Investigating New Forms of Student Assessment." In *Review of Research in Education* 17, edited by G. Grant, p. 33. Washington, D.C.: American Educational Research Association.

# The Power in Portfolios: "A Way for Sitting Beside" Each Learner

by Evangeline Harris Stefanakis

Imagine a classroom where grading is based on the evidence of learning over time visible in student work—selected samples of writing, math, science, and social studies, project work, art, journals, quizzes, tests, or other classroom activities. Imagine a classroom where teachers and students regularly *sit beside* one another *to assess* these collections of student work and to define the next steps in their teaching and learning process. Imagine classrooms where teachers regularly look at student's work and look at *how* students *do their work* to better understand the multiple intelligences (Gardner 1983) of these individuals. This ongoing practice of examining daily class work allows teachers and students to be "co-learners"; to discover, to use, and to build on an individual child's abilities.

Teachers and students in these classrooms use *portfolios* or collections of student work, to guide their interactions related to teaching, learning, and assessment. Portfolios are a tool that can help teachers in their efforts to reach and to teach every child. To understand the power in using portfolios as an assessment tool and in using multiple intelligences as a tool to identify a student's strengths, I suggest we look to expert teachers and listen to what they have to say.

Manuel, a skilled second grade teacher in an urban school, "keeps track" of his students' individual progress by collecting their work in portfolios. Portfolios are more than a place to keep "student work"; for Manuel these collections are evidence of what his students *care about* and are *excited to learn*. These portfolios, he suggests, are collections of work that document student growth. In his words:

> I keep a portfolio of the children's writing and other things they make. What they want to save is important so I ask them to help me select the work we keep. This to me is the data on a child— my memory is not enough—looking into their work and how it is made helps me see *how they each are smart.* I observe when the child is making a piece, then I listen to what the child says about their work. I try to make a note of what they are telling me about the work and themselves— what excites them as they learn. This data—the work and how it is created—becomes my mental file on each child. Student work is what I use to think about what I should be teaching next to help these individuals grow.

An individual student's work and how it is created—is, according to Manuel, the data on a child. It can reveal for the teacher "how an individual is smart." Using the portfolio as a guide, Manuel actually creates what he calls "mental files" or profiles of each individual in his class. Using the theory of multiple intelligences as an analytic tool, Manuel looks at student work over time to gather information about an individual child's strengths, whether they be mathematical, visual/spatial, linguistic, bodily/kinesthetic, musical, interpersonal, or intrapersonal. A single piece of an illustrated project can tell a teacher, like Manuel, something about a child's visual/spatial abilities, shown in art or diagrams; linguistic and logical/mathematical abilities, in the writing and problem solving activities; or even intrapersonal abilities in a written reflection about doing projects. Students' work, for teachers like Manuel, becomes a window into the multiple intelligences of children—it provides evidence of a collection of skills whether they be in the arts, in sports, in languages, in mathematics, or in self-understanding. (For further details, see Gardner 1993.)

Teachers like Manuel are able to personalize the educational process for their students—finding ways to tap into an individual's abilities in activities which may include the arts, problem-solving, model building, or group work. Creating curricula that offer students multiple ways for showing what they know (be it oral presentation, in writing, or through performances) is one way that multiple intelligences theory can be applied in classroom practice.

The major question is, "How does a skilled teacher create a profile on each student and do this for a whole class of second graders?" As Manuel explains:

> I make time to *sit beside* each of my students to watch and note what
> they do. Then I sit beside them again, as often as I can, to look at their
> portfolio of work. I ask them questions about what some pieces mean
> to them. I feel like these two practices, looking at them and looking at
> their work, help me really know each of them as an individual and
> find ways to use their abilities in activities we do.

When a teacher like Manuel *sits beside* a student, periodically looking
at her work and listening to her reflections, he understands more
about how that individual child thinks and learns. Simply stated, sitting beside an individual student to look carefully at class work helps
a teacher gather information about her multiple intelligences—
understanding the rich combinations of abilities in that child—
creating a "mental file" or profile of that learner. According to
Manuel, his "mental file" on a student helps him think, plan, and
create a collection of classroom activities to address children's interests and abilities.

It is my belief that this position—*sitting beside* a child—is the
best way to actively understand that individual and create a profile
using the tool of multiple intelligences theory. I chose these phrases
carefully because each one has a significant image to convey. Where
teacher and student are sitting when they look into portfolios is the
first subtle but significant shift.

When teachers sit *next to, instead of in front of* students and ask
them about their classroom creations, they begin to show that they
care to know "how that individual child has made meaning" out of
an assignment or a project. The ongoing conversations between students and teachers about the work they create together in the classroom offers them both a chance to better understand their
interactive learning process.

But it is not only the teacher that benefits from looking at student work in a portfolio. The fact that a teacher regularly cares
enough to examine an individual student's work and talk to her
about it means a great deal to that learner. This makes curriculum
building a shared experience for teacher and for student—a co-
designed process—guided by what teacher and student want to
know and want to learn.

After years as a researcher, "sitting beside" teachers who were
judged to be skilled at using portfolios, I discovered that the majority
of their curriculum and daily assessment was based on systematically

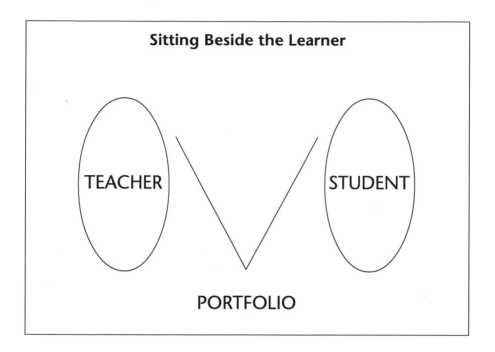

looking at student work. Looking together at student work, whether it be in journals, in stories, or in math problem sets, showed them what the students actually thought about during this mysterious interaction called teaching and learning (Harris Stefanakis 1995). Simply stated, looking at student work allows both individuals—teacher and student—to see *what the student learned from what the teacher taught* in a given lesson sequence.

Hannah, a Grade 1/2 teacher, states that portfolios help her see what students need to learn and what she needs to teach:

> I share with my children that we have a folder and we keep our work in it. In this folder I usually find some of their self-portraits, stories with pictures, projects, journal entries, math story problems, whatever we are doing. They help choose the work that goes into the folder. When you combine a portfolio of student work with your own journal writing on the child, it gives you a richer understanding of that child and what you can do for that child.

Hannah, like Manuel, suggests that using portfolios for classroom assessment helps the teacher create a mental file of each child's multiple intelligences and then use this information to personalize the teaching process.

Maria, a bilingual teacher, suggests that *looking at student work* and *looking at the student at work* tell her how to develop language and literacy skills for children in her multilingual classroom.

> I keep folders with my students . . . I keep samples of their handwriting . . . their drawing . . . their artwork . . . we date it. Look at the work in October . . . Look at the journals through the year . . . this is what I use to develop our lessons. Here is Jon's book he made in December . . . in the beginning he was doing simple drawings . . . now . . . in May . . . look at the drawings . . . they are more elaborate and now he is writing an elaborate story to go with them. Now I know it's time to work on punctuation. These are the samples of work I see in my children's portfolios . . . they really tell me a lot—each day I see more about how they are really smart!!!

Finally, I believe that adopting portfolios as an assessment tool asks teachers to "sit beside" learners on a regular basis, to actively reflect on the work that is generated in their classroom.

Second, using the portfolios as a story of learning allows teachers and learners to engage in regular conversations, which allows them to continually assess and set new standards for the assignments and products they create. When teachers look at student work and use the ideas that come from students' interests to teach, they notice that everyone's motivation to learn increases. This frequent interaction in looking at work allows teachers and students to be "co-learners," to discover what is motivating and to use individuals' strengths as a bridge to address weaknesses. This is one way, I believe, to improve the quality of teaching and learning and to serve the diverse individuals in everyday classrooms. Portfolios are a tool that can help teachers in their efforts to reach every child.

Teachers I have talked to confess that a key part of this sitting beside students to examine portfolios is the realigning of power relations that happens between the individuals in the classroom. Realigning this power relationship actually gives *each* of the individuals (teacher and student) *more* power. Teachers learn to feel better about their teaching because they see how students' questions and curiosity become the catalyst for new learning in their classrooms.

Students feel a different sense of power in "asking questions and voicing their interests" since these may become the springboards for what the class studies. Students learn that they can have choices in what and how they learn. As Manuel so clearly describes:

Mostly, I collect samples of the child's work. I look at the samples and when they happen. And then I sit down with the child. I listen to what they say about their work . . . It's feedback for me and for them. . . I know what they are telling me is important. From the student portfolios I am collecting ongoing ideas about what this child is thinking and enjoying in my class. Now I know what to teach to excite them and interest them.

For Manuel, instead of report cards, the portfolio is the long- and short-term evidence of his students' work and ongoing learning. This authentic classroom work is what he values and prefers to share with parents and other teachers at conferences as evidence of how individuals learn in relation to their multiple intelligences.

As portfolio assessment enters public school classrooms, I ask professional educators to pay attention to teachers using portfolios to create profiles of individual students. They are learning how to personalize the educational process for the diverse learners in their classes. These are the individuals, I believe, whose judgments count when it comes to evaluating the power of portfolios as a tool to improve teaching and learning. As Marshall (1992) reminds us:

> Assessment is not an end in itself. It is a process that facilitates appropriate instructional decisions by providing information on two fundamental questions; How are we (teacher and learner) doing, and how can **we** (teacher and learner) do better? (p. 3)

---

## REFERENCES

Gardner, H. 1983/1993. *Frames of mind.* New York: Basic Books.

Gardner, H. 1993. *Multiple intelligences: The theory in practice.* New York: Basic Books.

Harris Stefanakis, E. 1995. Whose judgment counts: Case studies of teachers' classroom assessment of linguistic minority children. Ph.D. diss., Harvard Graduate School of Education.

Marshall, S. 1992. Managing the culture: The key to effective change. *School Organization*, 13 (3), 255–68.

# Domain Projects as Assessment Vehicles in a Computer-Rich Environment

by Joseph Walters and Howard Gardner

## INTRODUCTION

This paper reviews recent research that has been conducted at Project Zero at the Harvard Graduate School of Education on the topic of assessment. In the paper we argue that an assessment built around an interesting and challenging project that explores a particular domain (such as music, writing, drawing, mathematics, science, or programming) offers an important alternative to traditional standardized tests. As students work through such projects, they reveal most vividly the skills and aptitudes that we want to assess. We refer to these assessment instruments as *domain projects*.

The theory of multiple intelligences provides much of the conceptual underpinning of our view of assessment, and the paper begins with a brief synopsis of this theory. Next, we review examples of domain projects under development in two different research initiatives at Project Zero–Arts PROPEL and Catalyst. Drawing from these examples, we list the salient characteristics of this project-based assessment and outline the design of one such project that uses computer technology.

The paper concludes by indicating directions for future research and development.

## ASSESSMENT AT PROJECT ZERO

For the past twenty years, Project Zero has taken as its research agenda the systematic study of children and their symbol-using skills

From *Center for Technology in Education,* Technical Report No. 5, August 1990. Copyright © 1990 by Officers and Fellows of Harvard University and Howard Gardner. Reprinted with permission.

by exploring such diverse areas as drawing, metaphoric language, musical ability, storytelling, written language, mathematics, and computer programming. The diversity of this research is responsible for the development of the view of human cognition that we call the theory of "multiple intelligences" (Gardner 1983).

With respect to assessment, we draw two conclusions from this particular view of human cognition. First, an evaluation of achievement or aptitude must be specified within a domain of human activity. Second, the assessment must be drawn based on a true performance in that domain. In this section, we will build the argument by reviewing the central ideas of multiple intelligences and then outlining the implications of the theory for assessment.

## Multiple Intelligences

The theory of multiple intelligences claims that human beings have evolved at least seven different forms of knowing or processing information. These different forms, called "intelligences," include the skills for manipulating language, logic and mathematics, musical ability, spatial information, bodily-kinesthetic information, knowledge of other persons (interpersonal), and knowledge of oneself (intrapersonal). All normal human beings possess some capacity in each of these intellectual spheres, but the interaction of genetic and environmental factors produce marked differences in the profiles of the various intelligences in individuals.

This theory was designed to serve two goals: (1) to synthesize a large set of findings about human cognition, including neurobiological evidence, cross-cultural analysis, and developmental milestones; and (2) to provide an alternative to the widespread belief in a single faculty—intelligence—that can be adequately assessed by paper-and-pencil "intelligence tests."

In the theory of multiple intelligences, the specific skills of human cognition—the intelligences—are mobilized for solving problems within particular domains of activity. Each *intelligence* is an evolved biopsychological potential that is manifested as a particular cognitive skill. In contrast, the *domain* of that potential is defined by the culture as an arena in which the various cognitive skills are mobilized. In the theory of multiple intelligences, analysis of problem solving requires consideration of both the cognitive functioning of the intelligences (and their combination) and the context of a domain specific within a particular culture.

The theory of multiple intelligences stipulates that the various intelligences are independent. For instance, when an individual displays a high degree of competence with one intelligence, this ability does not imply similar competencies in other areas. Similarly, disability in one intelligence does not imply disabilities in the others.

Although the intelligences are independently structured in this way, they do not function independently. Any reasonably complex adult task requires the simultaneous functioning of several of the intelligences. For example, the task of writing a research paper makes primary use of the linguistic intelligence, but it also taps the logical-mathematical intelligence at the same time. Playing the violin for an audience—first and foremost a musical task—also makes demands on bodily-kinesthetic and interpersonal faculties. How an individual combines these separate intelligences is part of that individual's personal endowment, just as are the intelligences themselves.

> The theory of multiple intelligences has important implications for the problem of assessment.

These two outcomes of the theory of multiple intelligences—that the intelligences are independent and that they operate in concert—has important implications for the problem of assessment. First, an assessment must pose problems in which individuals work with the actual materials of the domain being examined. Second, a complete assessment must pose a number of problems that yield to a variety of solutions in order to reveal an accurate picture of the talents and skills of a given individual.

To illustrate the first point, consider the task of assessing an individual's musical competence. If the assessment consists of a number of questions in a multiple-choice format, the assessment is less a measure of the musical intelligence and more a measure of linguistic facility or test-taking skill. As an alternative, the assessment might ask the student to compose an ending to a simple melody. To take this problem, the student must manipulate musical notation, select musical sounds, and use musical terminology. In this task, the student makes demands directly on the musical intelligence—the problem is not filtered through a linguistic or logical-mathematical assessment instrument, as it is in the multiple-choice example. This is what we mean when we say that to elevate an underlying intelligence, an assessment must pose problems that require the individual to manipulate the actual materials of the domain of that intelligence. We must examine true performance and not just a verbalization of a problem solution.

Second, the fact that cognition is composed of several independent intelligences operating in concert implies that an assessment must pose a variety of problems that yield to different types of solutions if it is to establish a complete picture of the profile of intelligences for an individual. For instance, by asking a student to solve our music composition task, we do not learn much about that student's ability to write short stories. Similarly, we cannot infer that individuals who do not write well are equally disinclined to perform well on tasks that require interpersonal skills, spatial abilities, or musical prowess. Any simple task, even when it requires genuine performance with the materials of a domain, does not reveal the complete profile of an individual's talents. Therefore, a complete assessment of an individual must make demands on all the intelligences, not just a select few.

Finally, the theory of multiple intelligences underscores the importance of the "personal" skills in daily life. Working cooperatively in a group is recognized as an important feature of many dynamics. Also, understanding one's self, the intrapersonal skill, is highlighted in the theory. For instance, a strength in the musical realm may be underutilized by an individual who does not fully understand that strength, whereas an individual with a strong intrapersonal intelligence may be better equipped to combine modest strengths or to compensate for weaknesses efficiently. A complete assessment should take both of the personal skills into account, and the assessments we describe below consistently feature both small group collaboration and reflection on learning.

**Assessment through Projects**

To summarize, assessments of ability and learning must engage students in performances in which they handle the actual materials of a given domain and mobilize a number of different intelligences. We believe that problems that meet both criteria can often be formatted as *projects*.

At Project Zero, we have been devising a number of exemplar projects in a variety of domains. These projects are at once open-ended, structured, and oriented towards products. In order to pose rich, complex, and engaging problems, the projects are open ended—they offer opportunities to find alternative solutions and unexpected outcomes using different strategies and different combinations of intelligences. At the same time, the projects are structured—the results can be analyzed in terms of what students are learning. Finally, as students work through projects, they are called on to create original products—songs, essays, drawings—and this gives them a stake in the outcome of the project.

> Projects are open ended—they offer opportunities to find alternative solutions and unexpected outcomes using different strategies and different combinations of intelligences.

The products that students create in working on a project are evaluated by the teacher and the student together. We follow the work of Collins and Frederiksen (1989) in designing these evaluations. First, the evaluations consider only the performances that reveal directly the skills and competencies that we are interested in; again, we ask students to exhibit skills, and not simply to describe those skills. Second, the scope of each project is designed such that every skill that we are interested in is exhibited; we do not design evaluations that test only a sample of the desired skills. Finally, all of these criteria are articulated at the outset of the project, making them transparent to the students. In the final section of the paper, we will return to these principles of problem design and evaluation.

Currently, two research initiatives at Project Zero are developing specific examples of assessment projects. Arts PROPEL is designing instruments in the arts; and Project Catalyst has created a series of computer-based projects. We will outline these projects in the next two sections. Following this, we will describe a project that we are developing for the Center for Technology in Education that embodies these several design principles.

## DOMAIN PROJECTS IN ARTS PROPEL

Arts PROPEL is a five-year research effort sponsored by the Rockefeller Foundation. Its primary goal is to create and test new techniques for fostering and assessing artistic development in secondary school students. The project brings together researchers from Project Zero and the Educational Testing Service and teachers of music, visual arts, and imaginative writing in the Pittsburgh public schools.

Arts PROPEL has designed two assessment techniques for arts classrooms: portfolios and domain projects. A portfolio is a collection of materials that the student assembles during the process of creating a finished piece and includes sketches, early drafts, and notes as well as the final piece itself. These selections may be supplemented with a written journal in which the student reflects on the process of creating the piece.

It is the second technique, the domain project, that is directly relevant to the present discussion. Each domain project in Arts PROPEL is composed of a clearly defined set of classroom tasks that focus students on a central issue in the art form. We will illustrate Arts PROPEL domain projects with examples drawn from the domains of music and imaginative writing, but projects are also developed in the visual arts. These descriptions begin with a summary of the project along with a description of the products that the students create. This is followed by a discussion of the various assessment techniques which include reflection exercises and teacher judgments.

### Sample Projects

*Musical Performance: Ensemble Critique*
In musical performance, rehearsal is the main avenue for developing instrumental skill. In a typical rehearsal session, the teacher leads a number of student instrumentalists, guiding their development by pointing out errors, highlighting certain areas for additional private practice, adjusting the ensemble sound, and suggesting stylistic interpretation.

In the Ensemble Critique project, students begin to make judgments about their performances of the sort that were previously made by the teacher. At the beginning of the project, the teacher leads a discussion of critique and gives the students special scoring sheets that they will use to critique a performance. The class then examines the score of the piece they will perform, considering the style, the key, and other important features.

Next, the students perform the piece as an ensemble and tape record their performance. They evaluate their performance from memory; then they listen to the tape and compare what they hear with what they remember. Finally, they fill out their score sheets as a formal critique of the performance, focusing on both the performance of their part as well as the entire ensemble.

This performance and critique process is repeated two more times during the semester. In later performances, students can compare their performances with earlier recordings. As the student musicians become increasingly proficient at the process of critique, they begin to take over other tasks of the rehearsal, including conducting the ensemble in rehearsal, determining which portions of the piece require additional attention, and even making stylistic changes in the performance.

> With practice, students become more precise in their ability to evalute the performance, and this in turn makes them more proficient in their ability to rehearse.

Assessment of the Ensemble Critique project consists of the reflection activities that students carry out at each of the three checkpoints. As they fill out the critique score sheets, they assess the performances of individuals as well as the ensemble as a whole. The teacher also evaluates these performances and students can compare their self-assessments with those of the teacher. With practice, students become more precise in their ability to evaluate the performance, and this precise evaluation in turn makes them more proficient in their ability to rehearse themselves.

This project is not designed as an assessment of performance. Instead, it is an assessment of the students' ability to critique a performance and to adjust their rehersal accordingly. In this project the students begin to share responsibility for decisions that are usually made by the director alone.

*Imaginative Writing: Writing Dialog*

All students read plays in English class but very few write them. In the typical class, for example, the plays of Shakespeare are treated as literature that can be studied and analyzed, not as scripts to be performed and interpreted. The PROPEL project called Writing Dialog provides students with a set of structured activities that develop their skill at creating original dramatic dialogue. Brief passages from contemporary drama are examined and judged using the same criteria that are used to critique the students' work.

The Writing Dialog project is conducted over seven class sessions. Throughout these sessions, students are learning to articulate the criteria by which dialogues can be critiqued. In each session, written work is read out loud and discussed.

First, the teacher introduces the project by circulating several clipboards around the class. Each clipboard has written at the top a single line of dialogue and each student adds an additional line. When the sheet is filled, the class reads the resulting dialogues out loud and discusses the results. Next, working in pairs, students imagine a setting and write a simple scene with two characters that takes place in that setting. The students in each pair write alternate lines in the dialogue. Again, the class reads the scenes out loud and discusses the results. This process of writing and rewriting continues for several class sessions.

All writing done for the project is saved in a folder, and in this class session the students select a piece from that folder to work from, adding approximately ten lines of dialogue to the scene. At the conclusion of the project, students review their collection of dialogues. They record their observations of the changes they have seen in their own writing over the course of the project.

In this project, students begin writing dialogues with no instruction. They can then use these first efforts to begin to explore those features that make for a "good" dialogue—sense of character, scene, motivation, and so on. As their dialogue writing continues, they elaborate these criteria and practice using them to evaluate their own dialogues as well as dialogues from published plays. By looking back over their earlier work, students can see a general improvement through the project; they can also see that they have a deeper understanding of what makes a dialogue work. In this way, the project helps the students to use their own productions to construct the criteria they need later to reflect on their own work.

Assessment in this project focuses on the collection of written material that the students create in the seven working sessions. At the end of the project, students evaluate their entire collection, looking for evidence of their developing skill at writing dialogue. This self-examination is then compared with the teacher's review of the same material.

These sample projects, Ensemble Critique and Writing Dialog, illustrate the breadth of projects that have been created in Arts PROPEL. These domain projects, as well as a number of others, have been extensively tested in the Pittsburgh Public Schools. They became available for broader dissemination in 1990.

### Analysis

To summarize, PROPEL projects are sets of activities that are presented over the course of the school year. Each project poses problems that students solve by creating original work. In producing original work, the students use the work of others or reproductions of master works for points of contrast. Throughout this process students critique their own work.

> In producing original work, the students use the work of others or reproductions of master works [to] critique their own work.

Teachers can use the PROPEL projects to assess students by evaluating the final products, by documenting the change in skills displayed over the course of the project or between two projects, and by measuring their students' growing abilities to recognize positive and negative elements in their own work. The PROPEL project assessments are not designed to measure static competencies nor to determine precisely what has been "learned" in a specific curriculum unit. Instead, they demonstrate learning over a period of time.

These projects are designed to incorporate the features of assessment drawn from the theory of multiple intelligences. The PROPEL domain projects require students to deploy a variety of intelligences as they engage specific problems. Students produce a product in each project, such as a musical piece or a dramatic dialogue. They also work in groups throughout the project, featuring the interpersonal skills of collaboration and group discussion. Finally, the PROPEL tasks tap intrapersonal skill by asking students to reflect on their unique approach to the problems posed in that project. In the PROPEL model, assessment is the continuing process of taking stock of one's current position and comparing that state to the desired state. As students become more sensitive to their current state and how it compares with the desired state, they begin to take on more responsibility for their own learning.

Second, the PROPEL projects provide students with multiple opportunities for problem solving. In this program assessment does not rest on the results of a single PROPEL project but is drawn from students' performances over a series of projects given throughout the year.

## CATALYST PROJECTS

Catalyst is a five-year investigation funded by the John and Mary R. Markle Foundation to explore how children and adults learn with microcomputers. We focused this investigation on the experiences of individuals as they approached some area of endeavor for the first time, examining novices' performance in music and visual art, and more recently in mathematics, writing, and computer programming. Since the difficulties that novices experience in various areas are well documented, we wondered if the computer could alleviate some of those problems. We felt that this research question would shed some interesting light on the general issue of computer-aided learning.

This initial research effort demonstrated that even when assisted by powerful, straightforward, and inexpensive software tools, novices did not make a sustained entry into a domain when they worked on their own. Although these novices did not have difficulty with the software itself, their lack of experience with the domain prevented them from using the software effectively. At the same time, however, this early research determined that novices could use such software most productively when they were presented with an inviting task and considerable help.

Here is an example. We asked novice adults to use a music composition computer program to solve a number of simple harmony tasks. We (and the subjects themselves) were surprised to find that even with little musical training these beginners could solve the problems quite proficiently. However, when we then posed a more open-ended problem, like composing an original melody, we discovered that our novices were much less successful. Even with the computer as an aid, they could not tackle the more unstructured problem effectively on their own.

We took this research finding as a starting point for the design of computer-enhanced projects that would enable novices to work effectively in a new domain. Three prototype Catalyst projects have been developed in the past year to test this idea. What follows is a description of these projects along with the principles we used in designing them. Our current research initiative, also funded by the Markle Foundation, is to evaluate the efficacy of these projects.

### Design of the Catalyst Projects

Each Catalyst project consists of three essential components:

1. *A powerful software tool.* Each project is built around a powerful computer program. We select software that is inexpensive, readily available, and powerful enough for professionals in the domain. Examples include music composition tools, computer program editors, and word processing software.

   The software tool reduces the barrier posed by the prerequisite skills that make up the craft of the domain, which an expert would hone through years of practice. In music, for example, the computer produces the performance of the composition and can even flag several kinds of syntactic errors.

2. *An on-disk library.* Each project contains detailed information in the form of computer files. In the projects described below, this library can contain songs, programming procedures, or historical information.

   The library of examples in the project gives the novice ready access to a repertoire of experiences, examples, or illustrations relevant to the problem at hand. The expert has internalized this repertoire through experience.

3. *Strategies and instructions.* The project also provides strategies in the form of step-by-step instructions along with expert advice and sample solutions. The user follows these instructions to complete the project.

   The strategies and instructions of the project guide the novice through the solution of the problems inherent in each step of the task. The ability to find effective solutions to common problems quickly is the hallmark of expert problem solving.

## Three Illustrations of Catalyst Projects

Three projects that meet these criteria have been created and are currently being tested at Project Zero: *SongSmith* (Walters, Meyaard, and Scripp 1989); *Just Enough Pascal* (Walters and Morrison 1988); and *Immigrant 1850* (Project Zero 1990).

*Catalyst Project in Music:* SongSmith

   *The Project:* To write a short poem (a limerick) and set it to music by composing an original melody, duet part, bass line, and chords. Working alone, an individual with moderate musical experience can expect to spend ten to fifteen hours completing the project.

   *The Computer Tool: Deluxe Music Construction Set* (Electronic Arts), an inexpensive but powerful music editing program that can perform the composition in up to four voices using a variety of synthesized timbres, and can print the composition as sheet music.

*The Library:* Examples of good solutions illustrate each step in the process of writing a song. Illustrations from experienced composers link the task to music history. Using nontechnical language, the project also makes connections with concepts in music theory.

*The Instructions:* The project guides the user through a step-by-step process of writing a song. It begins with the task of creating the lyric and setting it to an original melody. The project concludes with the creation of harmony with a bass line.

The *SongSmith* project poses the central problems of music composition—text setting, voicing, contour, and harmony. It offers a chance for the beginner to explore various solutions to these problems and structures the experience in such a way as to guarantee a product (an original song) as an outcome.

*Catalyst Project in Programming:* Just Enough Pascal

*The Project:* To assemble the Pascal program *GridWalker*—a game in which small creatures intelligently find their way through mazes—from a set of Pascal procedures supplied with the project. An individual with no Pascal programming experience can complete the project in about twenty-five hours.

*The Computer Tool: THINK Pascal* (Symantec), an integrated system for writing, editing, and debugging compiled Pascal programs. The debugging features of this development system pinpoint many of the novice programmer's errors. Special windows give the programmer valuable information about the current state of the program and display the values assigned to variables at any given point.

*The Library:* The kit includes all the necessary Pascal pieces to assemble the complete program *GridWalker*. These program pieces are also fully explained in the accompanying manual.

*The Instructions:* The *Just Enough Pascal* kit provides concise instructions on how to assemble the pieces of Pascal code in the editor. The kit also includes instructions for "tinkering" with the program, making those changes to the program that reveal important underlying concepts such as loops, variables, conditionals, and events. It also exemplifies modular program design and issues of user interface.

*Just Enough Pascal* gives the novice an insider's look at programming through the process of building an elaborate program one step at a time.

*Catalyst Project in Social Studies:* Immigrant 1850

*The Project:* To explore the experiences of the Irish immigrants to Boston in 1850 by making the same decisions these immigrants made when they arrived in the United States. After a brief introduction to the computer software, an individual can complete the project in five hours.

*The Computer Tool:* Either Microsoft Works (Microsoft) or AppleWorks (Apple). These integrated programs include modules for word processing, database, and spreadsheet calculations.

*The Library: Immigrant 1850* provides a complete list of the actual passengers of four ships that arrived in Boston from Ireland in 1850. It also provides information about available jobs (location, wages, necessary experience), housing (location and rent), and transportation costs of the time. A spreadsheet document displays a market basket of food and clothing prices in 1850.

*The Instructions:* The project poses the problem of adopting one family from the passenger list, and making several important decisions for that family—finding them a place to live, jobs, transportation, food. The users record these decisions in the family diary (a word-processing document) and they summarize the family budget on a spreadsheet.

The *Immigrant* project takes on many aspects of a simulation in a game-like format. In working through the project, the user makes decisions and reviews the results. The full impact of each decision can be assessed by playing the game a second time and making particular decisions differently. *Immigrant* also demonstrates how structured information accessed through a powerful tool can be used to gather insights about an historical era.

The *Immigrant* project provides the individual with "raw" or unstructured information about a period in history, and the individual must organize that information to make decisions and to generate insights about the period and the social group that is being studied.

These three Catalyst projects were designed to give novices first-hand experiences with the materials and problems in three domains. At the end of each project the novice has created a finished piece—a song, a computer program, or a diary. This product provides a "stake" for the student, the motivation and context for following the instructions of the task. For example, in *SongSmith* the discussions of musical notation, terms, and concepts are presented in the context of an individual's own emerging song. In *Just Enough Pascal,* the student creates a computer program, and in *Immigrant 1850* a personal diary of experiences.

> At the end of each project the novice has created a finished piece—a song, a computer program, or a diary.

These three examples are different from the PROPEL projects in some important ways: They are not designed to facilitate assessment; they are not designed to fit seamlessly into the school curriculum; and they make explicit use of computer technology. Nevertheless, the Catalyst projects offer important features for our assessment projects by illustrating how projects—sustained activity on a single problem to produce an outcome—can tap into specific intelligences and reveal how individuals approach the same task differently.

## DESIGNING PROJECTS THAT COMBINE TECHNOLOGY AND ASSESSMENT

As a partner in the Center for Technology in Education at Bank Street College, Project Zero researchers are developing assessment instruments that make the best possible use of technology. In our approach, technology functions in two distinct ways. First, technology is used directly in solving the problem at hand. For example, the music composition software actually performs the composition as it is being written, allowing the composer to judge by ear the quality of the work. Writers can use outlining software to study and manipulate the structure of an essay and use word processing programs to simplify the task of rewriting and editing a manuscript.

Technology operates in a second way in the assessment of student progress. The computer "opens up" the process of problem solving, making it more visible to both the problem solver and to the evaluator. For instance, students can easily revise and save drafts as they complete them for later review. When students work in small groups at the computer, their decisions, made visible on the computer screen, can be easily observed by both the members of the group and the teacher. In these ways, using the computer to compose allows the student and the evaluator to study the process of composition as well as the final product.

To develop assessment instruments that use technology as a facilitating instrument and that build on the design principles drawn from the theory of multiple intelligences, we are creating domain projects that embody features taken from the projects in both PROPEL and Catalyst:

- Assessment is drawn from student performance as they complete projects that focus on central issues in the curriculum.
- To complete a project, the student creates one or more original products.
- Assessment includes both interim and final evaluations of student products.
- Students evaluate their own work throughout the project and compare these self-evaluations with the teacher's judgments.
- The computer is an indispensable tool which students learn to use effectively during the project.

Domain projects designed to these specifications allow students to work directly with the materials of the domain. These projects pose problems that can be solved in a variety of different ways. They provide an opportunity for students to develop a stake in the outcome of that problem solving. Finally, projects designed in this way incorporate technology as a tool that facilitates problem solving in the domain. The use of technology opens up the process of completing the project to assessment.

### A Prototype Project

The domain project *Immigrant 1850* provides a starting point for developing one such domain project. Like the other Catalyst projects, *Immigrant 1850* uses a powerful computer tool (AppleWorks) to analyze information. The design of the assessment component is drawn from the domain projects constructed for Arts PROPEL. Because we are presenting this project as a prototype, we would like to describe it in a little more detail.

In the *Immigrant 1850* project, students work in small groups. First, they examine the passenger list of a ship that arrived in Boston in 1850. This list includes the name, age, occupation, and country of origin of the passengers, all of whom list Ireland as their country of origin. Students sort the list to divide the names into groups that might make up individual families. For example, they find that the list contains several adults with the same last name, but by using the age and occupation information, they make decisions about which individuals might plausibly be considered a family. Each working group "adopts" one family and begins to make a number of decisions from the point of view of this adopted family. Students begin a first-person-account diary for the family which describes their voyage, their arrival in Boston, and the family's plans for the future.

Next, the students peruse other database documents. One document lists jobs that were available in Boston during that period, including the location of each job, the wage it pays, and the skills required. A second database records typical housing, its location, cost per week, and a brief description of the property. A third database covers the costs of commuting from one location in the city to another. Using these three sources of information, the students make the decisions that their adopted family had to make. The students locate their selected jobs and housing on a map of the Boston area and they calculate how much it would cost and how long it would take to commute from home to work. Using a spreadsheet document, students "purchase" food and dry goods supplies for their adopted family. As they select items from the list, the spreadsheet calculates the total cost.

With all of this information in hand—family members and their ages, jobs and salaries, the location and rent of housing, the cost of food and clothing, the distance and charges for transportation—students begin to calculate a yearly budget for their family. They enter all of the information they have gathered into the budget spreadsheet, which then computes the results of these expenditures over the course of one year. Students examine the result, and if the family is losing money, they return to the other documents to reconsider their decisions.

For example, the students may decide that the children in the family should be sent to work in factories instead of going to school. Or they might send older children to work as servants, because these jobs pay room and board in addition to a small wage. The parents in the family can decide to work six days a week instead of five. The family may select less expensive housing. In this way, the students adjust their decisions for the family so that income and expenses balance.

Throughout this process of getting their family settled, students enter the decisions they make into their family diary. They also compare the decisions they make for their family with the decisions of other working groups. For instance, the class can plot where individual families decided to live on a single map of Boston. This summary displays the distribution of this particular group of Irish immigrants across the city, which can be compared with published demographic maps of Boston of the period. Students also compare the experiences and decisions of different families. For instance, some families will have many children to support, others may have a single parent (many immigrants died at sea), and some families will consist only of young adults. The decisions and experiences of these different families will themselves be very different.

This core activity—using the various tools in AppleWorks to make decisions for an adopted family—is supplemented with several other activities. In one, students review newspapers written for the Irish immigrants during this period and use these as models for writing their own newspapers. In another activity, students produce a skit depicting some aspect of the Irish experience. In a third activity, students compare the cost of feeding a family of four in 1850 with the cost of making the same purchases in 1990.

## Student Products

*Immigrant 1850* supports the production of a range of products in a variety of formats. To illustrate, we will consider three written products that students create. First, they keep track of their decisions by writing a diary from the point of view of one member of their adopted family. To complete this diary, students supplement the factual information they are given in the various databases with historically realistic but fictional details. In writing this diary, students exercise their "historical imagination."

Students write a second essay as an historian or sociologist of the period. The questions that guide this piece may require additional research. For example, as historians, students would be asked to explain why so many Irish immigrants came to Boston at this particular time, and how their arrival changed the city. As sociologists, students could be asked to explain why the immigrants lived where they did, and to speculate on what impact adding a trolley system to the city might have, or how prejudice toward the immigrants was manifested.

> **Students reflect on how they made decisions, how effectively their group functioned, and what they would do differently if they were to work through the project a second time.**

In a third writing assignment, students consider questions about the unit itself. For example, they reflect on how they made decisions, how effectively their group functioned, and what they would do differently if they were to work through the project a second time. They consider what information is missing from the simulation and how the project would change if that information was added. Or, they discuss how an immigrant's experience today compares with that of the Irish immigrants 140 years ago.

### Techniques for Assessment

Three different techniques are brought to bear in assessing this student work: (1) evaluation of the three written pieces; (2) assessment of group work using a checklist; and (3) review of students' self-assessment activities.

### Written Work

As teachers read the written work, they offer several specific points for improvement. Students redraft the assignment taking these points into account, and the new draft is graded. Checklists of writing performance used in Arts PROPEL tasks will be adapted to this portion of the assessment. As in Arts PROPEL writing assignments, students create a portfolio of drafts that lead to the completion of the finished piece, which they use when reflecting on changes in their writing.

### Checklist on Group Activities

In a second assessment technique, the teacher evaluates how the various teams of students function as a group to accomplish the assigned tasks. To facilitate this, the teacher uses a detailed checklist to record pertinent incidents and interactions. The aspects of group work that are listed on this checklist include interpersonal dynamics, group efficiency and creativity in problem solving, flexibility of roles, and responsiveness to suggestions.

This checklist is important for several reasons. First, it attempts to capture the interpersonal dynamics of the project, which may otherwise remain undetected because students rarely comment spontaneously on such features of their work in their own writing. Second, the checklist gives the teacher the opportunity to step back from the class and observe classroom interactions in a structured and purposeful manner. The checklist also provides the teacher a chance to observe the work of students who may not write well or speak up in class frequently.

Finally, the checklists offer yet another dimension to the grading process—here the teacher can take stock of the classroom atmosphere, how people are working as groups rather than individuals, and the differences in working style among these groups. Since group work is a large part of the project, it is important that assessment procedures take it into account. The results of the checklist will be shared with students as groups and individually when appropriate.

> Students evaluate their own work and comment on the project itself—its function, limitations, and assumptions.

### Student Reflection

Students' reflections on the project take two forms. They evaluate their own work (both process and product), and they comment on the project itself—its function, limitations, and assumptions. In both instances, reflection is linked directly to what students produce over the course of the project.

To structure the process of self-assessment, students create a portfolio of their drafts of the essays they write as they work through the project, along with their teacher's comments and suggestions. At the end of the project, they review all of the materials collected in the portfolio. They compare what they accomplished on this project with those of previous projects; or they contrast their observations and reflections with those of other students.

At the conclusion of the project, students critique the materials of the project itself, including the relationship of specific activities of the project to general questions in the subject area. Students can consider the nature of the simulation, its limitations and implications, and its relationship to history.

The goal of this reflective component is to get students to play a significant part in their own education by casting a critical eye toward their accomplishments and toward the project itself. To do that, they must think about what they are doing, why they are doing it, and how good the results are when compared with their capabilities and expectations. As these reflections become more precise, they can be used to guide students' work in later stages of the project.

### Analysis of the Assessment Techniques

As a tool for assessment, the *Immigrant 1850* project is designed with the theory of multiple intelligences in mind. In the project, students work with the materials of social studies—the historical records and documents of the period being studied. Furthermore, students can approach the project from a number of different perspectives and engage the variety of intelligences in different combinations. They can mobilize the logical-mathematical intelligence to analyze quantitative data or to select from among competing sources of evidence. They can use the linguistic intelligence to fashion poignant written documents, the interpersonal intelligence to collaborate with their peers, and the spatial intelligence in locating neighborhoods on a map.

> Because skills of interest are evaluated directly, the domain project approach stands in sharp contrast to the traditional test situation.

Although the theory of multiple intelligences informs the design of this assessment project, it does not speak to the issue of the actual assessment itself. How do we distinguish between an "adequate" solution of the Immigrant problem from an "inadequate" one? To consider this question, we will follow Frederiksen and Collins' analysis of assessment: *directness, scope,* and *transparency.*

First, as an assessment instrument, the domain project blends learning and evaluation and it targets *directly* the skills and concepts that the teacher wants the students to learn. For example, in a special studies class, students are evaluated on their ability to gather and collate information, to analyze and interpret the results, to get help when necessary, and to write a description of what they have uncovered. These are precisely the tasks they must perform to complete the project.

Because the skills of interest are evaluated directly, the domain project approach to assessment stands in sharp contrast to the traditional test situation. With direct assessment, both teacher and student focus on the skills themselves; in contrast, with tests the teacher must infer the presence of desired skills from students' performance on tests that measure those skills only indirectly. When a student answers a multiple-choice question correctly, the teacher must infer from that response that the student has some understanding of the concepts that provide a basis for the correct answer. Furthermore, as Frederiksen and Collins point out, indirect tests of skills often lead students to concentrate on the skills that are directly related to taking the test rather than on the skills that can only be inferred from the tests.

Second, the domain project assessment is more complete in *scope* than the traditional test in that it attempts to capture most of what is required to complete the desired activity. Interpersonal skills are manifested in the group interactions, mathematical and spatial abilities appear in the tasks of manipulating data and working with maps, and performance styles can be observed throughout the project.

Of course, different students will display very different profiles of performance along the dimensions represented by these different skills. The challenge to the assessment procedure is to document the breadth of these skills in useful detail. For example, the checklist of group activities directs the teacher to many skills that might easily be overlooked in the written components of the project. Similar instruments are yet to be devised for observing and recording other skills that are represented in the project.

In contrast, a traditional test must select a representative sample of skills for evaluation. From this sample, the teacher then infers the degree to which the untested skills have been mastered. Furthermore, certain important skills—such as planning, negotiating, collaborating, revising, reflecting, or persevering—are rarely represented at all on multiple-choice tests.

Finally, the terms of assessment must be defined explicitly for both the teacher and the students. This makes the assessment *transparent*. In the Immigrant domain project, for example, all criteria of the assessment are shared with the students when the project begins. As the students complete portions of the project, they use these criteria to gauge their own work. They can even use the group process report card to evaluate the performance of their group.

### Practice with Assessment

Because the domain project is direct in method and broad in scope, it allows students to "study for the test" or to practice with the features of assessment that permeate the project from beginning to end. Furthermore, if several domain projects are given throughout the year, an individual's accomplishments in one project can serve as signposts that direct learning on later projects. We hope that as they complete a series of these projects, students will gain confidence and experience with the demands of assessment. And because these assessments tap the very skills that the teacher is interested in, this practice with assessment becomes part of the educational process itself. Ultimately, the goal of domain projects is to teach students to assess their own work efficiently and to use this self-assessment to improve their performance on similar tasks in the future.

> Students will develop sophisticated skills of self-assessment only through repeated practice with feedback.

Although adults might find reflection in a domain project to be straightforward, high school students probably will not. Therefore, the teacher must model the process by posing typical questions and then offering answers. As the students attempt to assess their own work, the teacher can review these first attempts and make suggestions where appropriate. Again, students will develop sophisticated skills of self-assessment only through repeated practice with feedback.

## CONCLUDING REMARKS

Our goal in developing domain projects for assessment is to create a realistic model of an alternative to the traditional test-based approach to measuring competency or achievement. We will be examining this model in the classroom next year. We will attempt to determine if the assessment is practical and reliable and if it yields information about students efficiently with a reasonable amount of teacher effort. We will also consider the subjective nature of teacher judgments. We must determine which assessments capture insights and aspects of student performance that may have been overlooked otherwise and to what degree teachers agree with one another in these judgments.

The domain projects we are developing are not designed as large-scale replacements for what currently transpires in the classroom. Instead, they serve as models of how one might develop strategies for assessment that meet the criteria we have identified and can coordinate with existing curricula.

We hope that these domain projects will move the discussion of assessment away from tests, measurement, and large-group comparisons toward a consideration of careful documentation of student learning, self-assessment, and growth.

## REFERENCES

Collins, A., and Frederiksen, J. 1989. A systems approach to educational testing. *Educational Researcher, 18,* 27–32.

Gardner, H. 1983. *Frames of mind.* New York: Basic Books.

Project Zero. 1990. *Immigrant 1850.* Cambridge, MA: Harvard Graduate School of Education.

Walters, J. 1988. *Just enough Pascal.* Bedford, MA: Symantec.

Walters, J., Meyaard, J., and Scripp, L. 1989. *SongSmith: Songwriting on the Macintosh.* Cambridge, MA: Walters Associates.

# Alternative Assessments and Educational Practices

The final section is devoted to the issues inherent in putting alternative assessments to use in making educational decisions. One such decision involves identifying gifted students—a task often assigned to standardized tests. Two chapters by Maker and colleagues look at giftedness identification from an MI standpoint. Giftedness, the authors assert, is too narrowly defined according to the traditional model. They identify a set of "problem types" which can be crossed with the intelligences to yield a matrix showing many areas in which giftedness can be revealed.

Gardner's chapter ties together many of the themes that emerge in this book, including problems with standardized tests, the need for intelligence-fair assessment, and the desirability of assessment in context. Encouraging educators to rethink our society's use of testing as the exclusive mode of assessment, Gardner calls for an "assessing society" that is concerned less with standardization and more with individual differences and student growth. Such a move, Gardner argues, is not a regression toward a subjective form of evaluation but a forward step toward individual-centered educational practices.

# Giftedness, Diversity, and Problem Solving

by C. June Maker, Aleene B. Nielson, and Judith A. Rogers

## MULTIPLE INTELLIGENCES AND DIVERSITY IN EDUCATIONAL SETTINGS

*My autumn eyes behold*
*Spooky costumes skipping in*
*Halloween night*
*White ghost dancing by my house.*
*Orange pumpkin nestled on my window*
*Black witches gliding across the*
*full moon*
*Red golden leaves falling softly*
*from the tree.*

by Melissa Begay

Melissa's test scores did not identify her as gifted; her writing did. Her poem shows an unusual sensitivity to the rhythm of language, a delicate imagery, sophisticated choices of descriptive words, and ideas that are unusually advanced for a 9-year-old child. Melissa likes to write, read, and listen to other children read. She and other children like her often are excluded from special programs that would benefit them greatly, because their scores on standardized intelligence and achievement tests are not high enough.

From *TEACHING Exceptional Children*, Fall 1994, 4–19. © 1994 by The Council for Exceptional Children. Reprinted with permission.

## A Need for Change

The cultural and linguistic character of the U.S. population has changed significantly since the early 1900s. These changes have accelerated dramatically in the past ten years (National Association for Bilingual Education 1993; Waggoner 1993) from a predominance of persons of European ancestry to a multicultural mix of immigrants from Latin America and Asia. According to the 1990 Census, the total number of persons born outside the United States increased by 40% between 1980 and 1990. A related fact is that 14% of the current school population does not speak English at home (Waggoner 1993).

Perceptions of giftedness and beliefs about what abilities should be recognized and developed in U.S. schools also have changed dramatically over the years (Feldman 1991; Gardner 1983; Renzulli 1979; Sternberg 1981; Treffinger 1991). In spite of these significant changes, many educators continue to rely on identification instruments and procedures that were designed to measure giftedness as it was perceived early in this century (Bernal 1990; Klausmeier, Mishra, and Maker 1987; Renzulli 1979; Richert, Alvino, and McDonnel 1982). Most tests of intelligence have been based on or judged against the classic Stanford Binet test developed by Lewis M. Terman in the early 1900s (Nielson 1993). These tests, although criticized widely, continue to be used as the sole or major criterion to determine whether or not a particular student is considered gifted (Maker 1994).

The widespread use of intelligence tests as they are presently normed and constructed does not result in equitable representation of the culturally and linguistically diverse populations of the United States in programs for gifted students. A survey conducted by the U.S. Office of Civil Rights revealed a significant underrepresentation of Hispanic students in programs for the gifted. Similar discrepancies exist for American Indians, Asian/Pacific Islanders, and African Americans. The cultural and linguistic diversity of this country needs to be honored, valued, and represented in our special programs for gifted students, but unless significant changes occur, this will not be possible. Many recommendations have been made, and many solutions proposed, but they either are not implemented on a wide-scale basis or, if implemented, are not working. The situation is getting worse rather than better. As stated by Callahan and McIntire (1994) "the challenge for public schools is to recognize alternative culturally relevant indicators of outstanding talent that will be translated into effective assessment strategies and programming models for children not from the dominant culture " (p. 7).

## The Theory of Multiple Intelligences

Many solutions to the problems outlined have been limited in scope, often involving only minor changes in identification practices. However, Gardner's (1983) Theory of Multiple Intelligences has offered educators a comprehensive framework within which fundamentally different solutions can be devised and implemented. According to Gardner,

> The problem lies less in the technology of testing than in the ways in which we customarily think about the intellect and in our ingrained views of intelligence. Only if we expand and formulate our view of what counts as human intellect will we be able to devise more appropriate ways of assessing it and more effective ways of educating it. (p. 4)

To Gardner (1983), intelligence involves the use of problem-solving skills that enable people to resolve unique problems, create effective products, and find or create new problems. Both the problems and the products must be relevant in a particular cultural context. Gardner has identified seven different intelligences possessed by most people: linguistic, logical-mathematical, spatial, musical, bodily-kinesthetic, interpersonal, and intrapersonal. Most of us, however, are not gifted or highly competent in all seven. Gardner believes that development of high-level competence requires innate capacity, motivation, and opportunity. Environment, cultural context, and language may influence all of these important factors.

Gardner (1983) has implied, and we believe strongly, that culture, language, and environment do not determine whether or not an individual will be gifted; instead, they influence the specific ways in which giftedness is expressed. For example, oral storytelling may be a common form of linguistic giftedness in some cultures, while writing novels may be more common in others. The form of a particular language also may influence the expression of giftedness. Navajo has many rich, descriptive words and few nouns, while English has many nouns and categories. In Spanish, nouns precede adjectives, while in English, adjectives precede nouns. Such differences may influence the expression of both linguistic and logical-mathematical giftedness. For example, using languages in which nouns come first may contribute to a holistic style of thinking, while using languages in which adjectives come first may contribute to a more linear, analytic style of thinking (Maker 1994). Environment, family values, and a host of other factors can influence opportunities and motivation for developing any form of giftedness. Thus, children who grow up in isolated rural areas may have fewer opportunities to develop certain interpersonal skills but more chances for self-reflection and introspection than those who grow up in cities. Children whose parents are musicians have many more opportunities to develop musical ability than children whose parents have little interest in music.

**Theory into Practice**

Gardner's ideas constitute a useful theoretical framework; however, specific applications must be designed if the framework is to be practical in an educational setting. We have added two important components to enhance the usefulness of the theory. The first is a definition of giftedness that guides both assessment and curriculum, and the second is a definition of problem types (see Table 1) that, when combined with varied intelligences, forms a problem-solving matrix for designing assessment procedures and developing curriculum. A gifted person is a problem solver—one who enjoys the challenge of complexity and persists until the problem is solved in a satisfying way. Certainly, gifted people are capable of solving simple problems, and they may do so quickly and effectively (Maker 1994). Often they redefine simple problems into complex ones or complex problems into simple ones. This problem-solving ability may be demonstrated within each of the intelligences, and it is demonstrated by some children across all intelligences.

> A gifted person is a problem solver—one who enjoys the challenge of complexity and persists until the problem is solved in a satisfying way.

*Problem Types and the Problem-Solving Matrix*

Based on the work of researchers in creativity and problem solving, Maker (1992) and Schiever (1991) developed a continuum of problem types that affords many, varied ways for learners to interact with content and demonstrate competence.

Problem Types I and II require convergent thinking and are most similar to the types of questions found on standardized intelli-

## Table 1
## Matrix of Problem Types for Gardner's Seven Intelligences

| | Type I<br>Clearly defined.<br>Use method.<br>Solve correctly. | Type II<br>Clearly defined.<br>Select method.<br>Solve correctly. | Type III<br>Clearly defined.<br>Choose from<br>range of methods.<br>Range of answers. | Type IV<br>Clearly defined.<br>Discover method.<br>Create solution. | Type V<br>Lacks definition.<br>Define problem.<br>Discover method.<br>Create solution. |
|---|---|---|---|---|---|
| Linguistic | | | | | |
| Logical-Mathematical | | | | | |
| Spatial | | | | | |
| Musical | | | | | |
| Bodily-Kinesthetic | | | | | |
| Interpersonal | | | | | |
| Intrapersonal | | | | | |

gence and achievement tests. Type I problems are highly structured. The solver knows the solution method and must recall or derive the correct answer. Type II problems also are highly structured, but the solver must decide on the correct method to use to produce a correct solution. By definition, no Type I or Type II problems can be posed for intrapersonal intelligence. The problem presenter cannot "know" a right answer about an individual that the individual does not know.

Type III problems are clearly structured, but a range of methods can be used to solve them and they have a range of acceptable answers. Solutions require a combination of divergent and convergent thinking. Problem Types IV and V are more open ended, less structured, and require much more divergent thinking. In Type IV, the problem is clearly stated, but the learner must select a method and set evaluation criteria for the solution. Type IV problems are commonly found in tests of creativity. Type V problems are extremely ill structured. The solver must explore the possibilities, identify the questions to be answered, and determine the criteria by which an effective solution will be recognized. "Real world problems" (Renzulli and Reis 1985) are a good example of Type V as they are represented in this matrix.

> To move from simply accommodating differences to honoring, valuing, and developing them, we must change both practices and beliefs.

### Diversity and Giftedness

The concept of diversity includes not only cultural and linguistic factors but also a diversity of gifts and talents, interests, and means of self-expression. Within and across all cultures, many individual differences exist. Differing opportunities, values, and motivation result in varied patterns of abilities. To move from simply accommodating differences to honoring, valuing, and developing them, we must change both practices and beliefs. Gardner's theory, when combined with a different definition of giftedness and a matrix of problem types, can be used successfully to design ways to identify and serve students with diverse gifts, interests, skills, languages, cultures, and values.

The following sections provide specific applications of these ideas, including a description of an assessment process and examples of curriculum planning and teaching strategies. Questions about the topic were posed to individuals who represent the diversity of cultures, languages, and environments found in the United States, and their answers are interspersed throughout.

## ASSESSMENT OF PROBLEM-SOLVING ABILITIES IN MULTIPLE INTELLIGENCES

Using the problem continuum presented in Table 1, we have designed a process called DISCOVER for assessing problem solving in multiple intelligences. Results from approximately three years of use with multicultural populations (African American, Anglo American, Navajo, Tohono O' Odham, Mexican American) are exciting. The characteristics of students identified using this process closely resemble the characteristics of the communities from which they come (Nielson 1993), and the process is equally effective with boys and girls. Students identified through this process make gains equal to or greater than students identified by traditional standardized tests when placed in specific enrichment programs (Maker 1992). Use of this process also results in identification of equitable percentages of students from various ethnic, cultural, linguistic, and economic groups (Nielson, 1993). Studies are in progress to evaluate the long-term validity of the process when used in a variety of settings.

The essence of the DISCOVER assessment process is that children engage in problem-solving activities in their regular classroom setting. For three of the activities, they use materials that are novel, fun, and versatile, and they interact with their peers while a trained observer records their problem-solving behaviors and describes their products. Two of the exercises do not require observers: a creative writing task and a math worksheet. In Table 2 are listed the activities, problem types, and intelligences for grades K through 2.

Because the children work together in small groups and interact with an observer, they can demonstrate their interpersonal abilities. The students solve interpersonal problems as they occur, and the observers record what happens. Since the open-ended writing activity includes personal experiences as a possible subject, we also get infor-

## Table 2
## DISCOVER Process Problem Types, Activities, and Intelligences, Grades K–2

| Activities and Intelligences | Problem Type | | | | |
|---|---|---|---|---|---|
| | Type I | Type II | Type III | Type IV | Type V |
| Spatial | Find a piece shaped like a ☐. (Teacher shows a shape.) | Find pieces that look like a rainbow. (Observer shows pictures.) | Find pieces and make mountains. (Observer shows pictures.) | Make any animal with as many pieces as you need. Tell about your animal if you want. (Observer provides connectors.) | Make anything you want to make. Tell about it if you wish. |
| Mathematical-Spatial | Complete simple tangram puzzles with a one-to-one correspondence between the tangram pieces and the puzzles. | Complete simple tangram puzzles with more than one solution that works. | Complete complex tangram puzzles with multiple solutions. | Make a square with as many tangram pieces as you can. | Make a design or a pattern with pieces. |
| Mathematical | Complete one- and two-digit addition and subtraction problems. | Complete magic squares using addition and subtraction. | Write correct number sentences using numbers given (in any order). | Write as many correct number problems as you can with an answer of 10. | None |
| Linguistic | Provide a label for toys given. | Make groups of toys and tell how items in the group are alike. (Some are obvious.) | Make different groups of toys and tell how items in each group are alike. (Encourage going beyond the obvious.) | Tell a story that includes all your toys. | Write a story about a personal experience, something you made up, or anything you wish. |

mation about intrapersonal abilities from children who choose to write about themselves.

### Spatial Intelligence Problem Solving (Pablo)
During the first activity, children are directed to build certain constructions (e.g., a rainbow, mountains, an animal) and then to make anything they want to make. The difficulty of the tasks varies with the age of the student: Younger children may make an animal while older children make a machine.

### Logical-Mathematical and Spatial Problem Solving (Tangrams)
For the next activity, the children begin by making a geometric figure such as a square, a triangle, or a parallelogram using as many of the tangram pieces as possible from a 21-piece set. Next, the children solve a set of six increasingly complex puzzles. Observers record the time needed to complete puzzles, the number completed, and the problem-solving strategies used.

### Linguistic Problem Solving (Storytelling)
Finally, the children are given a bag of toys. After a short period of play, they talk about some of these toys and tell a story involving any or all of them. An adult transcribes the story verbatim and encourages each child to tell the story in his or her native or dominant language. Older students may tape record their stories, write them, or tell them to an adult.

### Logical-Mathematical and Linguistic Problem Solving
After the observers leave the classroom, the teachers conduct two more activities: a math worksheet, which includes both computation and open-ended problem solving, and a writing task in which students write about anything they choose.

After observing the students, scoring their math papers, and analyzing their responses to the open-ended writing exercise, we enter all information on checklists of observable behaviors. We then study the information and develop a profile of the students' strengths across five intelligences: spatial, logical-mathematical, linguistic, interpersonal, and intrapersonal. In the future, the assessment also will include musical and bodily-kinesthetic problem solving.

## Figure 1
## Logical-Mathematical Problem Solving by Krystal and Another Student with the Same Standardized Math Test Score

Use these numbers to write true addition or subtraction problems:

11.  2  5  3  $2+8=5$  $3+2=5$  $5-3=2$  $5-2=3$ ✓

12.  9  1  8  $1+8=9$  $8+1=9$  $9-8=1$  $9-1=8$ ✓

13.  4  3  7  $4+3=7$  $3+4=7$  $7-4=3$  $7-3=4$ ✓

14.  12  2  10  $10+2=12$  $2+10=$  $12-10=2$  $12-2=10$ ✓

Write as many problems as possible that have 10 as the answer. You may use the back of this paper.

$1+9=10$ ✓
$2+8=10$ ✓
$3+7=10$ ✓
$4+6=10$ ✓
$5+5=10$ ✓
$6+4=10$ ✓
$7+3=10$ ✓
$8+2=10$ ✓

$9+1=10$ ✓
$10+0=10$ ✓
$11-1=10$ ✓
$12-2=10$ ✓
$13-3=10$ ✓
$14-4=10$ ✓
$15-5=10$ ✓
$16-6=10$ ✓

$17-7=10$ ✓
$18-8=10$ ✓
$19-9=10$ ✓
$20-10=10$ ✓
$21-11=10$ ✓
$22-12=10$ ✓
$23-13=10$ ✓
$24-14=10$ ✓

$100-90=10$ ✓

Use these numbers to write true addition or subtraction problems:

11.  2  5  3  $= 2-5=3$

12.  9  1  8  $= 9-1=8$ ✓

13.  4  3  7  $= 4+3=7$ ✓

14.  12  2  10  $12-2=10$ ✓

Write as many problems as possible that have 10 as the answer. You may use the back of this paper.

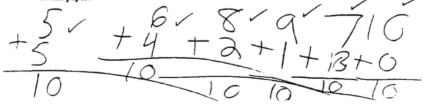

## Case Studies

Using the DISCOVER process, many children have been identified as gifted who would not have been recognized if traditional paper-and-pencil tests were used. The three children introduced here have been involved in enrichment programs for three years, and their giftedness is evident in their responses to these programs.

### Krystal

Krystal showed her giftedness in response to open-ended math questions, as shown in Figure 1. A response from another eight-year-old girl with exactly the same quantitative reasoning score on the Developing Cognitive Abilities Test (DCAT) (9th percentile) illustrates why we consider Krystal gifted in logical-mathematical problem solving. Rather than giving only one answer to each of questions 11 through 14, as the other child did, Krystal chose to provide all the possible combinations of numbers and demonstrated an early understanding of reversibility of operations. For the last question, Krystal not only wrote a variety of problems, but also demonstrated another important aspect of mathematical reasoning: logical thought. She used a clear, logical strategy for generating alternatives $(1 + 9, 2 + 8, 3 + 7, 4 + 6, \ldots 1\text{-}1, 12\text{-}2, 13\text{-}3 \ldots)$. When solving tangram puzzles, she took them apart without prompting and solved them before anyone else in her group, all without specific clues. Krystal has demonstrated these strengths consistently when using numbers or manipulatives. A section from the problem-solving behavior checklist (see Figure 2) shows the observers' final decisions about Krystal's strengths in logical-mathematical problem solving.

### Marquis

Marquis is an artist who enjoys making detailed drawings of living things. Marquis demonstrates his spatial abilities when drawing, painting, writing, and solving puzzles. During the Pablo activity, Marquis continually elaborated on his constructions, attended to the designs on the pieces, made detailed constructions, and developed delicate color and line balance. Like Krystal, he consistently has solved difficult tangram puzzles, and his scores on *The Raven Progressive Matrices* reflect increasing skills and confidence in test taking (75th, 67th, and 92nd percentiles, respectively, in grades 1, 2, and 3). A section from the problem-solving checklist (see Figure 3) shows the observers' decisions about Marquis's strengths in spatial ability.

# Figure 2
# Problem-Solving Behavior Checklist for Krystal

Student Name _____Krystal_____

4. Logical/Mathematical:  Strength?

___ unknown ___ maybe ___ probably ✓definitely

### 4.1 Problem-Solving

| | Pablo | Tang. | Math | Story | Writ |
|---|---|---|---|---|---|
| 3.1.1 takes apart puzzles when necessary without prompting | | ✓ | | | |
| 3.1.2 makes puzzles in more than one way | | | | | |
| 3.1.3 answers to open-ended math questions show use of a strategy (e.g. 1 +9 = 10, 2 + 8 = 10, 3 + 7 = 10) | | | ✓ | | |
| 3.1.4 checks size of pieces by putting one on top of the other | | | | | |
| 3.1.5 makes square, triangle, or parallelogram in a "logical" way. (e.g. starts with a shape and adds pieces) | | | | | |
| 3.1.6 solves complex problems quickly | | ✓ | | | |
| 3.1.7 solves all problems without specific clues | | ✓ | | | |
| 3.1.8 uses a logical strategy for adding or substituting pieces | | | | | |
| 3.1.9 uses negative numbers | | | | | |
| 3.1.10 other _____ | | | | | |
| 3.1.11 other _____ | | | | | |

### 3.2 Product (s)

| | Pablo | Tang. | Math | Story | Writ |
|---|---|---|---|---|---|
| 3.2.1 groupings are made by additions of attributes. (e.g., they are red or green) | | | | | |
| 3.2.2 groupings are made by multiplication of attributes (e.g., they have 4 legs and are mammals) | | | | | |
| 3.2.3 problems are correct | | | ✓ | | |
| 3.2.4 answers to magic squares have been checked vertically and horizontally | | | ✓ | | |
| 3.2.5 many math problems are written for open-ended questions | | | ✓ | | |
| 3.2.6 problems written for open-ended math questions are correct | | | ✓ | | |
| 3.2.7 answers show understanding of associative, commutative, and distributive properties | | | ✓ | | |
| 3.28 a variety of problem types are written for open-ended questions, (e.g., addition, subtraction, multiplication, division, fractions) | | | ✓ | | |
| 3.2.9 in math problems 13–16 more than one operation is used for each | | | ✓ | | |
| 3.2.10 includes algebraic equations | | | | | |
| 2.2.11 other _generates all possible alternatives for 13–16_ | | | ✓ | | |
| 2.2.12 other _____ | | | | | |

# Figure 3
## Problem-Solving Behavior Checklist for Marquis

Student Name _____ *Marquis* _____

2. Spatial: Strength? __ unknown __ maybe __ probably ✓ definitely

| 2.1 | **Problem-Solving** | Pablo | Tang. | Math | Story | Writ |
|---|---|---|---|---|---|---|
| 2.1.1 | adds pieces to a construction to make it into something different | ✓ | ✓ | | | |
| 2.1.2 | sees which pieces will complete a puzzle without physically manipulating them (e.g., chooses shapes without turning) | | ✓ | | | |
| 2.1.3 | takes pieces off | | ✓ | | | |
| 2.1.4 | sees shapes as objects, animals, or something in environment | ✓ | ✓ | | | |
| 2.1.5 | makes square, triangle, or parallelogram in an unusual way. (e.g. stacks several pieces to make a 3-D square) | | ✓ | | | |
| 2.1.6 | makes square, triangle, or parallelogram in a visual way, (e.g., makes outline and fills in with pieces) | | ✓ | | | |
| 2.1.7 | completes puzzles 3, 5, or 6 before any other group member | | ✓ | | | |
| 2.1.8 | sees how to substitute pieces for others to make the same shape or puzzle | | ✓ | | | |
| 2.1.9 | makes more than one square, triangle or parallelogram | | ✓ | | | |
| 2.1.10 | directs the spatial component of a group effort | | | | | |
| 2.1.11 | other *attends to delicate balance of color* | | ✓ | | | |
| 2.1.12 | other _____ | | | | | |

| 2.2 | **Product (s)** | Pablo | Tang. | Math | Story | Writ |
|---|---|---|---|---|---|---|
| 2.2.1 | constructions are asymmetrical with attention to interest and design | ✓ | ✓ | | | |
| 2.2.2 | constructions are symmetrical | ✓ | ✓ | | | |
| 2.2.3 | constructions show attention to design(s) on pieces | ✓ | | | | |
| 2.2.4 | constructions are detailed | ✓ | ✓ | | | |
| 2.2.5 | Makes a variety of types of constructions | ✓ | ✓ | | | |
| 2.2.6 | makes many constructions/designs | ✓ | ✓ | | | |
| 2.2.7 | uses many pieces to make a large square, triangle, or parallelogram | | ✓ | | | |
| 2.28 | constructions are 3-dimensional | ✓ | | | | |
| 2.2.9 | constructions are complex, (e.g., many pieces are used, several pieces in one end of a connector, connectors used in interesting ways) | ✓ | ✓ | | | |
| 2.2.10 | constructions are humorous | ✓ | | | | |
| 2.2.11 | constructions show movement | ✓ | | | | |
| 2.2.12 | constructions show clear resemblance to what student says they are | | | | | |
| 2.2.13 | other _____ | | | | | |
| 2.2.14 | other _____ | | | | | |

*Carey*

Carey is quietly creative and well behaved. Even though her test scores (69th percentile on the Raven) did not identify her as gifted, she was considered a superior problem solver in all areas in which she was assessed. Her writing is clear and expressive: She tells interesting stories with a clear plot and many details. She used a logical strategy for generating alternative answers to the math problems presented; solved difficult tangram puzzles; and made detailed, complex constructions. She won second place in an art show for drawing with an unusual framing and sensitive detail. Carey is an artist and a high achiever in academic subjects. She is a leader in both small- and large-group settings. Every suggestion she makes is followed joyfully by those in her group, and other students look to her for guidance. She has won many awards in art shows and recently won the fourth-grade spelling bee at her school.

The final page on the checklist of problem-solving behaviors is one in which behaviors and characteristics of products that can be observed across all intelligences are listed (see Figure 4). When students demonstrate these behaviors during all activities, we consider them to be gifted in general problem-solving—a type not included in Gardner's theory. Children whose strengths are demonstrated in one area are found more frequently than those whose abilities are superior in two or more. Students like Carey are much less common.

Krystal, Marquis, and Carey are all gifted. They have diverse profiles of abilities, diverse interests, and diverse needs. Can this diversity be accommodated in one classroom by one teacher? We believe the answer is "Yes," and invite you to explore several approaches outlined by the teachers who were asked to respond to questions about their classrooms and to examine the problem-solving matrix as it is used in curriculum planning and described next.

## CURRICULUM PLANNING WITH THE PROBLEM-SOLVING MATRIX

To build on the diversity afforded by new identification procedures, educators also must have new tools for planning learning activities. A matrix based on multiple intelligences (Gardner 1983) and the continuum of problem types (Maker 1992) is used in the curriculum planning process.

# Figure 4
# Problem-Solving Behavior Checklist for Carey

Student Name _____ *Carey* _____

7. General: Strength? __ unknown __ maybe __ probably ✓definitely

| 7.1 Problem-Solving | Pablo | Tang. | Math | Story | Writ |
|---|---|---|---|---|---|
| 7.1.1 makes more than one grouping of a set of items | | | ■ | ✓ | ■ |
| 7.1.2 invents new, different, or original ways to solve problems, (e.g., checks different set of tangrams, checks new pieces before removing others) | ✓ | ✓ | ■ | | ■ |
| 7.1.3 makes own product(s) rather than copying product(s) of others | ✓ | ✓ | | ✓ | |
| 7.1.4 attends to own work | ✓ | ✓ | | ✓ | |
| 7.1.5 shows "hitchhiking" on ideas or constructions of others without duplicating or copying | ✓ | | | ✓ | |
| 7.1.6 asks questions about task requirements | ✓ | ✓ | | | |
| 7.1.7 does not want to quit even when others are finished | ✓ | ✓ | | | |
| 7.1.8 increases in motivation or enjoyment as problems increase in open-endedness | ✓ | ✓ | ■ | ✓ | ■ |
| 7.1.9 follows through to completion | ✓ | ✓ | ✓ | ✓ | |
| 7.1.10 continuously working (e.g., on construction, stories, puzzles) | ✓ | ✓ | | ✓ | |
| 7.1.11 persists on tasks that are difficult for him/her | | ✓ | ■ | | ■ |
| 7.1.12 solves problems quickly | ✓ | ✓ | ■ | ✓ | ■ |
| 7.1.13 incorporates clues and new information into problem-solving strategy | | ✓ | | | |
| 7.1.14 shows nonverbal enjoyment of task (smiling, laughing, playing) | ✓ | ✓ | | ✓ | |
| 7.1.15 shows involvement in task (e.g., focuses on own work rather than others, not easily distracted) | ✓ | ✓ | | ✓ | |
| 7.1.16 organizes materials | | ✓ | | | |
| 7.1.17 verbalizes enjoyment of task | ✓ | ✓ | | ✓ | ■ |
| 7.1.18 stretches boundaries of task | | | | | |
| 7.1.19 exhibits "problem-finding" abilities | ✓ | | | | |
| 7.1.20 other _____ | | | | | |
| 7.1.21 other _____ | | | | | |

| 7.2 Product (s) | Pablo | Tang. | Math | Story | Writ |
|---|---|---|---|---|---|
| 7.2.1 shows humor when interacting with others, (e.g., students, observer(s), teacher(s) | ✓ | | ■ | ✓ | ■ |
| 7.2.2 products or solutions are new, original, or different | ✓ | ✓ | ✓ | ✓ | ✓ |
| 7.2.3 products are constructed of unique perspective | ✓ | | ■ | ✓ | ✓ |
| 7.2.4 products reflect an environment removed from that in which student lives | ✓ | | | | |
| 7.2.5 other _____ | | | | | |
| 7.2.6 other _____ | | | | | |

The problem-solving matrix incorporates most of the curriculum modifications recommended for gifted students (Maker 1982). Content can be abstract, complex, varied, and organized in such a way that several disciplines can be integrated into a coherent whole. The process modifications of higher-level thinking, open endedness, discovery, freedom of choice, group interaction, pacing, and variety are inherent in the matrix design. Evidence of reasoning can be incorporated into many of the problems. The learning environment also must be changed to allow independence, promote autonomy, and center on learners. Because students are doing related but different activities, competition is deemphasized and the environment becomes psychologically safer, more open, and more accepting. A variety of grouping options is available, and students are free to move about the classroom and school (and perhaps the community) to obtain the information and resources necessary to solve their problems effectively.

Perhaps the greatest modifications are in student products. Students seldom have the same solutions to the problems, and they often use different intelligences to perform their work. Solutions to real problems and presentations to real audiences are emphasized. Few problems allow a student to excel through simple recall; most products require synthesis of information and transformation into new forms. The student-selected format of solutions to Type IV and Type V problems provides variety and requires a new approach to evaluation. All learners, in conference with teachers or mentors, should specify evaluation criteria and evaluate their own work. The products also may be evaluated by experts in a domain and/or by peers.

The problem-solving matrix has been used to design and implement varied activities for spelling; an integrated unit on westward expansion in the United States; and integrated theme studies of change, patterns, relationships, and environment. The teachers and coordinators of programs for gifted students in the Charlotte-Mecklenburg School District used this matrix to structure their curriculum on Native Americans and North Carolina history.

When students have had some experience solving problems designed by educators and have learned about multiple intelligences and the continuum of problem types, most of them will be able to use the matrix to design independent study projects or group investigations. More complex projects that require high competence in

# Table 3
# Using the Problem Continuum to Develop Thematic Curricula in Multiple Intelligences

| Intelligences | Problem Type | | | | |
| --- | --- | --- | --- | --- | --- |
| | Type I | Type II | Type III | Type IV | Type V |
| Verbal/ Linguistic | Read a road map of North Carolina. List the Native American place names on the map. | Study Native American symbols. Write a message using some of these symbols. | After listening to several Native American legends, use that format to write a legend to explain life in the 1990s. | Use Native American symbols to create a pictograph. Write a story about the event(s) symbolized in the pictograph. | Create your own symbolic alphabet or icons that reflect current cultural values. |
| Logical/ Mathematical | Compute the number of miles Cherokees walked per day during the Trail of Tears. | Research the Native American calendar. Compare it to calendars in use now. | Graph the Native American population at selected times in the past and in the present. Predict and graph future population trends for Native Americans in North Carolina. | Create a calendar that might have been used by a Native American tribe or that might be used by a future tribe. | Create a code. Send a message in the code. Evaluate the effectiveness of your code. |
| Visual/ Spatial | Trace the route of the Trail of Tears on a modern-day map. | Choose a Native American house form that works effectively with the environment. Illustrate your choice. | Study Native American legends about dreams. Make a dreamcatcher that would reflect your personality. | Research costumes and decorations used by various tribes. Design costumes for a Native American opera/drama. | Create an original work of art inspired by your Native American studies. |
| Bodily/ Kinesthetic | Demonstrate a Native American game that teaches the skills of hunting. | Teach a Native American game to others. | Using rhythms you studied, create a dance to celebrate a Native American ritual. | Create a dance that tells a Native American legend. | Use your body to create a nonverbal interpretation of an event from Native American history. |
| Musical/ Rhythmic | Find a recording of Native American music and share it with your classmates. | Select, prepare, and present Native American songs that convey tribal customs and emotions. | Make models of musical instruments invented by Native Americans from North Carolina. | Write an opera dramatizing one of the Native American stories. | Create an original work of music inspired by your Native American studies. |
| Interpersonal | Identify the problems specific Native American groups have had with settlers in North Carolina. Which was the most severe? Why? | Choose a charismatic leader of a Native American tribe. Identify the ways that leader recruited and persuaded followers. | Trace the relationships of a present-day Native American family to a tribal ancestor. Create an artifact or event to honor the ancestor. | With your team, select a Native American ritual or custom and role play the preparation for the event. | Create an original way to communicate with others that is inspired by your studies of Native Americans. |
| Intrapersonal | | | Choose your favorite event(s) from Knots on a Counting Rope. Show in some way the role you would play in the event(s). | Create a totem pole, mask, shield, or medicine pouch inspired by your study of Native Americans that represents your own personal beliefs. | Visualize yourself as a Native American personality. Create a legend you would want to pass down to descendants. |

several intelligences can be designed as components to be completed by student specialists in the particular intelligences and then assembled into a coordinated whole. In the curriculum matrix presented in this article, for example, musically and linguistically talented students might collaborate to write a Native American opera; spatially talented students might design and construct the sets and the costumes; kinesthetically talented students might create the dances; students who are highly competent in logical-mathematical tasks might plan and monitor the integration of the components; and students highly competent in interpersonal relationships might coordinate the production and keep everyone working together.

## COMMON ELEMENTS IN PROGRAMS

Children with diverse gifts—like Melissa, Krystal, Marquis, and Carey—and those who are from varied cultural and linguistic backgrounds will have many opportunities to develop and appreciate their gifts in programs like the ones described in this article. These programs have the following characteristics.

- Providing opportunities for problem solving in both realistic and fantasy situations.
- Giving opportunities to design products using strengths and interests as a guide.
- Providing opportunities for students to acquire skills and information using multiple intelligences and multiple symbol systems.
- Involving students in solving problems ranging from well structured to ill structured (Sternberg 1985a, 1985b).
- Planning learning experiences around abstract themes.
- Bringing the students' own culture and experiences into the curriculum while expanding from this base into other related areas.
- Modeling.
- Emphasizing strengths but encouraging acknowledgment and effort to develop in areas of weakness.
- Learning and thinking actively.
- Connecting with and learning from the community.
- Interacting with parents and extended families.
- Learning in independent, small-group, and large-group settings.

One of the most important goals of these programs is to increase the individual learner's control of the learning process and opportunities for decision making in situations involving both learn-

**Figure 5**
**Letter from Mary Vuke's EXCEL Class**

Dear Dr. Maker,
    We would be happy to let you use our 4th and 5th grade Excel quotes for your article on multiple Intelligence. Thank you for asking. We are very happy about seeing our qoutes in your article

       Sincerly,
        Megan Mamds
        writing for
        4th and 5th
        grade Excel
        class

ing and other aspects of living. To us, this is true empowerment—an essential but often neglected part of education. An incident involving Mary Vuke's class provides an excellent example of this principle in action.

Mary Vuke and her (EXCEL) students attended the Southern Arizona conference of the Arizona Educators of the Gifted and Talented. They are planning a conference and want to learn how real professionals have conferences. At this conference, they presented their unit and some of their self-perceptions. June Maker was in the audience. After the session, she told them about this article and asked if we could publish some of their ideas. They said they would have a meeting and decide. A week later, June received this note (see Figure 5).

We invite each of you to try the activities we have presented with learners of all ages regardless of whether you believe they may be gifted, average, or have disabilities. We believe you will be pleasantly surprised at the gifts and ability you may observe.

## REFERENCES

Bernal, E. M. 1990. The identification blues and how to cure them. *CAG Communi-cator, 20* (3), 1, 27.

Callahan, C. M., and McIntire, J. A. 1994. *Identifying outstanding talent in American Indian and Alaska Native students.* Washington, DC: U.S. Department of Education, Office of Educational Research and Improvement.

Feldman, D. H. 1991. Has there been a paradigm shift in gifted education? In N. Colangelo, S. G. Assouline, and D. L. Ambroson (Eds.), *Talent development: Proceedings from the 1991 Henry B. and Jocelyn Wallace National Research Symposium on Talent Development* (pp. 89–94). Boston: Trillium Press.

Gardner, H. 1983. *Frames of mind: The theory of multiple intelligences.* New York: Basic Books.

Klausmeier, K., Mishra, S. P., and Maker, C. J. 1987. Identification of gifted learn-ers: A national survey of assessment practices and training needs of school psychologists. *The Gifted Child Quarterly, 31* (3), 135–37.

Maker, C. J. 1994. *Identification of gifted minority students: A national problem and an emerging paradigm.* Manuscript submitted for publication.

———. 1994. National Association for Bilingual Education. (1993). Census reports sharp increase in number of non-English language speaking Americans. *NABE News, 16* (6), 1, 25.

———. 1992. Intelligence and creativity in multiple intelligences: Identification and development. *Educating Able Learners, 17* (4), 12–19.

———. 1982. *Curriculum development for the gifted.* Austin, TX: Pro-Ed.

Nielson, A. B. 1993. *Demographic characteristics of families of children placed in pro-grams for the gifted in a large multicultural school district.* Ph.D. dissertation, University of Arizona.

Renzulli, J. S. 1979. *What makes giftedness: A reexamination of the definition of the gifted and talented* (N/S - LTI - G/T Brief #6). Ventura, CA: Ventura County Superintendent of Schools.

Renzulli, J. S., and Reis, S. M. 1985. *The schoolwide Enrichment Model: A compre-hensive plan for educational excellence.* Mansfield Center, CT: Creative Learning.

Richert, E. S., Alvino, J. J., and McDonnel, R. C. 1982. *National report on identifica-tion: Assessment and recommendations for comprehensive identification of gifted and talented youth.* Sewell, NJ: Educational Information and Resource Center.

Schiever, S. W. 1991. *A comprehensive approach to teaching thinking.* Boston: Allyn and Bacon.

Sternberg, R. J. 1981. A componential theory of intellectual giftedness. *Gifted Child Quarterly, 25* (2), 86–93.

—————. 1985a. Teaching critical thinking, Part 1: Are we making critical mistakes? *Phi Delta Kappan, 67* (3), 104–8.

—————. 1985b. Teaching critical thinking, Part 2: Possible solutions. *Phi Delta Kappan, 67* (4), 277–80.

Treffinger, D. 1991. Future goals and directions. In N. Colangelo and G. Davis (Eds.), *Handbook of gifted education* (pp. 439–49). Boston: Allyn and Bacon.

Treffinger, D. J., and Isaksen, S. G. 1992. *Creative problem solving: An introduction.* Sarasota, FL: Center for Creative Learning.

Waggoner, D. 1993. 1990 Census shows dramatic change in the foreign-born population in the U.S. *NABE News, 16* (7), 1, 18–19.

# Authentic Assessment of Problem Solving and Giftedness in Secondary School Students

by C. June Maker

S everal words in the title of this article need to be defined to provide a framework for the methods described. First, "problem" is defined as "a question or situation that presents doubt, perplexity, or difficulty; a question offered for consideration, discussion, or solution" (Webster's II: New Riverside University Dictionary, 937). Thus, much of what people think about can be considered "problems," and a "problem" is not necessarily negative, but contains a challenge of some sort. "Solving " a problem involves a variety of behaviors and processes, including "work out, figure out, resolve, find the answer, disentangle, unravel, penetrate, explain, make clear, unriddle" (Rodale 1978, 1, 134).

In current work that forms the basis of ideas presented in this article, we (Maker, Rogers, and Nielson 1994) have used a problem continuum to define a range of problem types helpful in research and practice related to problem solving (Schiever and Maker 1991). The degree of structure inherent in the problem, the range of possible methods, and the degree of latitude possible in the solutions determine the problem types.

Problem Types I and II require convergent thinking and are most similar to the types of questions found on standardized intelligence and achievement tests. Type I problems are highly structured. The solver knows the method for solution, and must recall or derive the correct answer. Type II problems also are highly structured, but the solver must decide on the correct method to use and produce a correct solution.

From *The Journal of Secondary Gifted Education*, Fall 1994, 19–29. Copyright © 1994 by C. June Maker. Reprinted with permission.

Type III problems are clearly structured, but have a range of methods that can be used to solve them and a range of acceptable answers. Solutions require a combination of divergent and convergent thinking. Problem Types IV and V are open-ended, less structured, and require much more divergent thinking. In Type IV, the problem is stated clearly, but the learner must select a method and set evaluation criteria for the problem solution. Type IV problems commonly are found in tests of creativity. Type V problems are extremely ill-structured. The solver must explore the possibilities, identify the questions to be answered, and determine the criteria by which an effective solution will be recognized. "Real world problems" (Renzulli and Reis 1985) are a good example of Type V as they are represented in this continuum.

> For maximum benefits to both the individual and the surrounding community, assessment must be as genuine and true-to-life as possible.

The next word needing definition is "authentic," which has become a word with many confusing meanings especially when combined with "assessment." Assessment, to me, is the process of gathering information about the skills, abilities, interests, and knowledge of an individual for the purpose of assisting that individual and the surrounding community. "Authentic" simply means genuine, real, and true-to-life, and provides an important goal for assessment. For maximum benefits to both the individual and the surrounding community, the assessment must be as genuine and true-to-life as possible. Authentic assessment of problem solving in which a well-defined, structured problem (Type I) is involved is different from authentic assessment of problem solving when a "fuzzy" situation or real-life problem (Type V) is involved.

Finally, the word "gifted" or "giftedness" needs to be defined. In some circles, gifted has come to mean "high IQ," "creative, motivated, and able," or a whole range of other traits. The definition employed here is based on a series of cross-cultural studies of people considered gifted in a variety of intelligences: "the key element in giftedness or high competence is the ability to solve the most complex problems in the most efficient, effective, or economical ways. In addition, gifted or highly competent individuals are capable of solving simple problems in the most efficient, effective, or economical ways" (Maker 1993, 71). Simply put, an assessment of problem solving is an assessment of giftedness; and assessment of the ability to solve complex problems gives more information about giftedness than does assessment of ability to solve simple problems. Using the problem continuum again as a framework, assessment of problem solving in the context of all five problem types is essential to understanding giftedness, but assessment in the context of a Type V problem will provide the most information about giftedness.

The purpose of this article is to describe how to develop authentic assessment of problem solving abilities in secondary school students. To achieve this purpose, I will present criteria for use in constructing and evaluating such assessments, and after each criterion, provide examples of assessments that meet the criterion. Finally, some implicit assumptions are listed to help in development and evaluation of such assessments.

## CRITERIA FOR ASSESSMENT

Howard Gardner (1992) uses the term "assessment in context" rather than authentic assessment. However, the criteria he presents are useful and comprehensive for the purpose of this article: emphasis on assessment rather than testing; assessment as simple, natural, and occurring on a reliable schedule; ecological validity; "intelligence-fair" instruments; multiple measures; sensitivity to individual differences, developmental levels, and forms of expertise; use of intrinsically interesting and motivating materials; and application of assessment for the student's benefit.

### Emphasis on Assessment Rather than Testing

The two words "assessment" and "testing," although sometimes used in a similar way, have different meanings. "Test" often is viewed as "a means employed to examine, try, or prove" (Webster's II: The New Riverside University Dictionary, 1, 196), while "assess" is "to appraise or evaluate" (Webster's II, 131). A test generally is considered to be "objective" and standardized, and is used to find out whether or not an individual meets certain criteria. Assessment generally seems to imply an evaluation of strengths and weaknesses, and has as its purpose the use of this information to inform rather than to judge.

Often, testing involves administering formal instruments in neutral, decontextualized settings. While this procedure may be appropriate for our Type I problems, which are defined clearly and have methods and solutions pre-determined by the presenter of the problem, it is much less appropriate for Type V problems, which are by nature, imbedded in a context, and must permit the problem solver to design and implement his or her own methods and solutions rather than being restricted to "finding out" the solution determined by the one who designed the problem. Perhaps testing does have its place in educational settings. However, we must recognize that "most American schoolchildren spend hundreds of hours engaged in a single exercise—the formal test—when few if any of them will even encounter a similar instrument once they have left school" (Gardner 1992, 91).

Earlier in this article, I defined the purpose for assessment as one of assisting an individual and the surrounding community. If the individual and the surrounding community are concerned about predicting performance on other similar tests, then testing provides needed information. If, however, the individual and the surrounding community wish to find out about skills, abilities, and interests that may enable an individual to achieve success in careers or in high-level, non-academic settings, tests provide very little useful information (Baird and Richards 1968; Howieson 1981; Neisser 1976; Resnick 1976; Richard, Holland, and Lutz 1967; Sternberg and Salter 1982; Wallach 1976; Wing and Wallach 1971).

> We find that if teachers have told students they will be tested, they are visibly more tense, hesitant, and fearful.

Assessment has a much broader meaning than test and can have important implications for everyone involved. Even the use of the word "test" or "testing" may need to be avoided to enable students to view the process as it is intended. We find, for example, that if teachers have told students they will be tested, they are visibly more tense, hesitant, and fearful than when teachers tell them they are going to "do some problem solving activities and observe how they solve the problems." In the assessments described in this article, a student's performance is not a "mystery" to the student or the teacher. Observers often sit at tables with students, writing what they say and do, drawing sketches of their products, tape recording them, and taking photographs. Observer notes are open and available to everyone, and students often examine the drawings to determine their accuracy and quality.

Another important component of assessment that distinguishes it from testing is involvement of the students in the process and the interpretation of results. One high school teacher with whom I have worked closely for many years (Maker 1982) audiotapes all problem solving discussions, using a weekly rotation system so that every small group is recorded at least once weekly. Students listen to these tapes individually and record their behaviors on a simple form. They then reflect on this information, either completing a Likert-type rating scale or writing an open-ended statement of strengths, weaknesses, and goals for the future. Using her own rotation system, the teacher reviews these tapes periodically, focusing on each student at least twice during each semester. If students request her perceptions of their problem solving skills, she reviews tapes more frequently. Videotapes also can be used to pick up nonverbal behaviors, but she uses these less frequently because of the intrusiveness of the video camera.

Eventually, such external aids may become less important, and a more natural process can occur. Students may first need to apply criteria for assessment that have been developed by the teacher. However, as they reflect upon their own processes, certain needs may emerge that are different from the teacher's focus. A gradual change from teacher-designed criteria to cooperatively designed and applied criteria, and finally to student-generated and student-applied criteria parallels the process by which novices become experts in most fields of endeavor. As a writer, for example, I now rely less on external reviews of my writing and more on my own internal standards. If I feel a need for another opinion I seek out certain individuals for specific purposes. Students at all levels must be encouraged and allowed to move in these same directions.

### Ecological Validity

As Gardner (1992) notes, and much research confirms, when assessment occurs under "actual working conditions" predictions about future performance are much better. Applying this idea to the assessment of problem solving in secondary school students results in an interesting situation. Educators often are concerned with predicting two very different sets of problem solving behaviors: future performance in school and future performance in solving real-life problems. What is the appropriate context? Is it the classroom? Is it an on-the-job experience or performance? My answer would not be neither, but both. In fact, an educator's task is complicated by the fact that dual goals are operating and both must be met.

Achieving ecological validity in the assessment process would necessitate involving students in solving problems of all five types as well as engaging them in problem solving activities in a wide variety of settings, ranging from individual solving of personal problems to group solving of simulated problems and group solving of real-life problems. Sternberg (1985a, 1985b) concludes that in school, we tend to teach critical thinking and problem solving in a context in which the problem is defined clearly, the method is known at least to the teacher, and the solution is known to the teacher (problem Types I and II), while in most real-life situations problems are not formulated clearly, have no pre-determined methods, and no known or agree-upon solutions (Types IV and V).

> Much problem solving occurs in contexts in which people can interact with others, use the appropriate "tools," and revise or rework their products.

Research on the performance of experts shows that experts often fail or perform poorly on formal measures of problem solving, but exhibit these skills at a high level when engaged in ordinary tasks on a daily basis (Kay 1991; Lave 1980; Rogoff 1982; Scribner 1986). Thus, to achieve greater ecological validity in the assessment of problem solving, one must assess individuals in the many contexts in which problem solving occurs and must describe the context as a part of the description of performance. Most important, however, educators must realize that much problem solving occurs in contexts in which people can interact with others, use the appropriate "tools," and revise or rework their products. In our assessment of linguistic problem solving in secondary students, for instance, students are provided with dictionaries, synonym finders, and thesauruses, and are taught how to use them. After several warm-up exercises in small groups, they produce written or oral linguistic products of their choice, and are encouraged to discuss their ideas, use all available tools, and ask for suggestions for improvement from everyone in the room. Most writers I know (myself included) seldom engage in serious writing tasks without their favorite "tools," which may be a word processor, a favorite pen, a dictionary, a thesaurus, a synonym finder, and various "style" manuals. Without such conditions, the authenticity of assessments of linguistic problem solving is jeopardized.

### "Intelligence-Fair" Instruments

Testing instruments and assessment procedures frequently are heavily loaded with two types of abilities—linguistic and logical/mathematical. Yet, many human occupations and many daily activities involve a variety of other abilities (e.g., spatial, bodily/kinesthetic, interpersonal, intrapersonal, and musical [Gardner 1983]). I will never forget the best mechanic I have ever had. My "vintage" car had no problem he could not fix. Yet, he failed every test of mechanical ability given in school because he could not read the manuals and answer the multiple-choice questions correctly.

> Incomplete observations often lead to inaccurate conclusions and are not useful assessments of problem solving.

A practice frequently employed in assessment is self-reflection, which often is narrowed further to written learning logs, journals, or checklists. Learning logs and journals rely on linguistic abilities (particularly written language) while self-assessment checklists draw upon logical/mathematical abilities. Expanded assessment procedures that enable a more "intelligence-fair" assessment would include oral reflection; interactive discussions with peers or teachers (interpersonal); diagrams, models, photographs, collages, drawings, and paintings (spatial); performances, and exhibitions (bodily/kinesthetic or musical). A teacher could suggest, for example, that a student's learning log consist of a series of drawings or photographs selected carefully to document his or her learning process.

Increasing the "intelligence-fairness" of assessment also necessitates the addition of a technique common to real-life assessment: direct and continuous observation. Many times, decisions and conclusions are reached as a result of an observer (teacher or group leader) moving around a room, going from small group to small group or surveying the room from the vantage point of a desk or favorite corner. Unfortunately, such incomplete observations often lead to inaccurate conclusions and are not useful assessments of problem solving skills. Three types of observations could occur. At times, the teacher or leader could stay with a group throughout the entire process, recording as much information as possible about each participant and the group as a whole. At other times, a time-sampling process could be used in which the teacher or leader stays in a group for a pre-determined length of time (e.g., 10 minutes), and then moves to the next group and spends the same amount of time. For maximum usefulness, each group should be observed for an extended period of time (10–15 minutes), and all groups should be observed an equal number of times. With assistance from other teachers, students from other classes, counselors, and others (such as retired teachers), a third option is available: observation by trained individuals who are not familiar with the students and who can be impartial and free of preconceptions about individual students. In addition, a rotating tape recorder could capture verbal interactions, or a rotating video camera could record both verbal and non-verbal interactions to supplement personal observations.

> In a normal classroom setting, all problem types need to be included to enable development of a complete picture of problem-solving abilities.

Without such direct and continuous observations of a variety of behaviors and processes, teachers often overestimate the problem solving abilities of students whose strengths are in the linguistic or interpersonal areas and underestimate the problem solving abilities of students whose strengths are in nonverbal areas (e.g., spatial, bodily/kinesthetic, logical/mathematical). These students with nonverbal strengths may be able to do a rotation or construct a model, but be unable to explain it to others or convince the group to adopt their methods.

To increase the "intelligence-fairness" of assessment of problem solving at the secondary level, we have constructed tasks or situations in which the contribution of other intelligences is minimized, both in the directions and the development of products (see Table 1). Please note that varied problem types are represented, but that not all problem types are included in each area. When we attempted to include all types in an observational assessment, the length of time necessary to complete the process made it impractical. In a normal classroom setting, however, all problem types need to be included to enable development of a complete picture of problem solving abilities.

In the spatial problem solving tasks, few words are used. Students watch while techniques are demonstrated, and then implement them with assistance as needed. All products are visual, and minimal instructions are needed. The same is true of logical/mathematical problem solving using tangrams. These materials are visual, and students need minimal verbal ability to understand the directions. The

## Table 1
## Assessment of Problem Solving in Multiple Intelligences

| Problem Type | Intelligence | | | | |
|---|---|---|---|---|---|
| | Spatial | Logical/ Mathematical | Linguistic | Interpersonal | Intrapersonal |
| I | Demonstrate correct use of pastels, watercolor, clay, and mechanical techniques after being shown. | | Demonstrate appropriate and correct use of writing tools. | | (By definition no Type I or Type II problems can be posed for intrapersonal intelligence. The problem presenter cannot "know" a right answer about an individual that is unknown to the individual.) |
| II | | Solve tangram puzzles that have one correct solution. | Make a chart showing words with the same meaning as "big" arranged from common to uncommon. | In a group, make a square using as many tangram pieces as possible. Each group member has a 21-piece set. | |
| III | Choose one of five photographs and make what is in it using any of the materials available. | Solve tangram puzzles that have several correct solutions. | Choose words written about a photograph and develop a "word chart" showing synonyms arranged from common to uncommon in more than one language. | | |
| IV | | Make a rhombus using as many pieces as possible from a 21-piece set. | While watching slides write any thoughts, ideas, or impressions that come to mind. | | Write or otherwise indicate which of the activities were preferred and in which performance was best. |
| V | Make anything using any of the materials or tools available. | | Choose a photograph, imagine yourself in it, and create something using words to describe your experience or perceptions. | Solve problems as they occur during the task of making a square or during other group activities. | Explain or otherwise indicate reason for conclusions about preferences and strengths. |

interpersonal problem is a visual one, and students can employ both verbal and non-verbal strategies depending on their strengths. I once observed a group of Navajo boys who accomplished the task very quickly, and who spoke only five words during the entire activity. In contrast, I also have watched groups in which all members talk constantly—both to themselves and to the other members of the group.

### Multiple Measures

A comprehensive, authentic assessment process must include multiple instruments, multiple contexts, and multiple observers. One interpretation we have made of this criterion is to recommend at least three general types of assessment: individual, classroom-based development of portfolios with items chosen by both students and teachers; individual, classroom-based development of portfolios with certain required elements (e.g., all portfolios must include at least two pieces that demonstrate growth in all seven of the intelligences identified by Gardner [1983]; all portfolios must include pieces resulting from solving all five problem types); and standard assessment tasks implemented in the classroom setting, directed by the teacher, but with observations made by a team well-trained in making behavioral observations and without preconceived notions about the abilities of the students. The first two types of assessment are on-going and should occur throughout the year. The third can be conducted as needed, and is useful to do on at least a yearly basis to benefit both students and teachers. If observers are teachers from other schools, and exchanges are made regularly, the assessment also can be of great benefit to the observers, who will continually refine their skills in watching students.

Another application of the concept of multiple measures is to place learners in real and simulated problem solving situations, both in and out of the classroom setting, and to record as much of the process as possible (e.g., combining audiotaping, observer notes, videotaping, photography, and collection of products). All this documentation is collected and reviewed by individuals from varied backgrounds and different perspectives. For example, during a recent assessment of problem solving, a team of observers watched students as they participated in several problem solving activities, including the spatial intelligence problem solving tasks presented in Table 1. Observers sat with groups of four to six students, watching their processes and interactions, and documenting the evolution of their products using sketches and/or photographs. One group was selected randomly as the one to be videotaped.

Information obtained during this process was analyzed in several ways by different individuals.

- The observers noted which students in the groups seemed to be superior problem solvers.
- The team of observers shared their perceptions of individual students and described the behaviors of the students they considered superior problem solvers.
- One individual reviewed all observer records and documents noting any inconsistencies and listing problem solving behaviors that seemed consistent across students considered superior and across observers.
- Experts from the various domains were asked to review selected videotapes, photographs, and products and to indicate which students they would consider outstanding in their areas of expertise, and to identify the behaviors or characteristics of products that led them to that conclusion. A visual artist might be asked to review a videotape and products of a student the observers considered superior in the visual arts, while an engineer might be asked to review a tape of a group in which a student constructed a mechanical toy using Capsela. Photographs of this construction could be used to supplement information on the videotape.
- All these reviews resulted in a list of problem solving processes and characteristics of products considered useful or valuable in this drawing and constructing task.

Using this list of behaviors and product characteristics as a guide, a description of the performance of each student was provided.

A similar version of this type of process often is followed at the professional level in student teaching or internships. Student teachers are placed in real-life teaching situations and are observed on a continuing basis by their "cooperating" teachers. Occasionally, however, the supervising teacher (often the university professor responsible for assigning a grade) visits the classroom or analyzes audio and videotapes to provide another perspective on the performance of the student teacher. Sometimes, the children or adolescents are asked to provide their perspectives, resulting in a more complete picture of the abilities of the teacher-in-training. A similar process can be followed when high school students are placed in internships, mentorships, and other real-life situations.

### Sensitivity to Individual Differences, Developmental Levels, and Forms of Expertise

One of the greatest challenges in designing authentic assessment at the high school level is to present a set of problems that will challenge the capabilities of the most able students within a particular domain, but will not be so difficult that those less able within that domain will not even attempt them. Students at the high school level have had more time to "specialize" and develop skills in areas of interest and strength than have younger students. Thus, a wider variety of developmental levels can be found, especially in certain content areas. An example of this difficulty, using the problem sets presented in Table 1, is the development of tangram puzzles. In some of the earlier versions of our puzzle booklets, the most able students could complete the entire set of six puzzles in five to ten minutes while less able students could not solve even the first puzzle. In a situation like this, little useful information is gained about the problem solving abilities of either the most or least logical/mathematically able students. Puzzle booklets have been redesigned so that they include a wider variety of difficulty levels than necessary at the other grade levels we assess.

> Students at the high school level have had more time to "specialize" than have younger students.

When designing a set of spatial problem solving tasks, sensitivity to varied forms of expertise is particularly important. Spatial abilities are necessary and can be assessed in a wide variety of often unrelated content areas and occupations: visual arts (both two-dimensional such as drawing, painting, weaving, and three-dimension such as sculpture, ceramics, basketry), engineering, mechanics, cartography, set construction, and building. After trying a number of tasks considered "generic," and feeling that we missed the most gifted in the domain, we settled upon a varied set of materials, a varied set of "subjects" for construction, a student choice of both subject and material. Another aspect of this concept is the necessity of having available the appropriate "tools" for problem solvers at various levels. Recently, for example, an observer noted that at least one set of real horsehair brushes needed to be available for students who were accustomed to their quality, and who would be unable to create a painting that met their personal standards using the inexpensive brushes that had been included. On-going assessment of problem solving abilities must be sensitive to forms of expertise, and must parallel closely both the context, content, and tools of the practitioner, yet be sensitive to the developmental differences between adolescent students and adult experts.

### Use of Intrinsically Interesting and Motivating Materials

Paper-and-pencil tasks, administered under strict testing procedures, often using machine-scorable answer sheets, may be intrinsically interesting and motivating to some students. However, I suspect that boxes of brightly-colored materials, sets of tangrams and puzzles, slides, photographs, markers, chart paper, and various tools will be more interesting and motivating to most, if not all, students.

> **Projects and tasks that "genuinely engage" students will likely bring out their best and provide the most useful assessment information.**

Perhaps more important, thought, is that these materials are available for the students to use in the context of solving problems, working on projects, and developing products of interest to them. Projects and tasks that "genuinely engage" students will be much more likely to bring out their best and provide the most useful assessment information. During one of our most recent assessments of high school students, we discovered that several students had skipped their regular classes and "sneaked" into the classrooms in which problem solving assessments were occurring. These students had enjoyed the activities so much that they wanted to do them again and again. Many students also requested that they be allowed to come back on their own time (during a free period or after school) to make something else, write about another photograph, or work more tangram puzzles. These were the acid tests of intrinsic interest for the materials.

### Application of Assessment for the Student's Benefit

My view of this criterion is that all assessment must be used to describe and inform rather than to rank order students from best to worst or most able to least able on a particular task or skill. To me, a single score is not descriptive. Nor is it "objective" as some would like to believe. Someone somewhere assigned a value to a particular response or behavior and a different value must be made known to all who participate in or use assessment or interpret scores. Many of these values have become a mystery to both teachers and students in attempts to avoid teaching the test.

Most important, however, is the usefulness of the information obtained from assessments. If a student is concerned about his or her possibilities of receiving an academic scholarship or being admitted to an academically oriented college, then rankings and percentiles will provide needed information. If, on the other hand, students and parents are concerned about what skills students have and which skills they need to develop to succeed in certain careers or activities, descriptions of their behaviors and products will be more useful.

One of the most important aspects of the assessments we have designed is a behavior checklist that includes both problem solving processes and characteristics of products that we have observed in students of various ages. These checklists consist of observable behaviors and characteristics of products rather than inferences or value judgments. For example, in the logical/mathematical category we would record "takes apart puzzles when necessary without prompting" or "makes puzzles in more than one way" rather than "flexible in thinking." All behaviors and characteristics are positive, and the activities in which they are observed are clearly indicated on the checklist.

Figure 1 is an excerpt from this checklist that shows some of the interpersonal problem solving behaviors and characteristics of products we have found in superior problem solvers.

A note about the development of this and other checklists is important here. Construction of many checklists begins with searches of the literature to determine traits of, for example, gifted people. In the past, since the operational definition of a gifted student was one with a high IQ, characteristics included on checklists were those found in high IQ students, but not in their low IQ peers. Due to an intense interest in cultural, ethnic, and linguistic diversity, and a paucity of research on problem solving in which open-ended, real-life problems (Type V) are included (Rogers 1993) our approach has been different. In an earlier section of this article, under the heading of "Multiple Measures," a five-step process used in the development of a behavior checklist for the drawing and constructing task was described. This same process has been followed in the development of all checklists. First, tasks are constructed and field tested in a variety

## Figure 1
## Excerpts from Problem Solving Behavior Checklist for High School Students

Student Name _____

4. Interpersonal Strength?    __ unknown  __ maybe  __ probably  __definitely

| | Dr/Cst | 1 Tan | G Tan | Word | Writ |
|---|---|---|---|---|---|
| **4.1 Problem-Solving** | | | | | |
| 4.1.1 shows humor when interacting | | | | | |
| 4.1.2 others listen and respond to him/her | | | | | |
| 4.1.3 others follow his/her suggestions | | | | | |
| 4.1.4 evaluates others by making positive comments or giving constructive criticisms (rather than destructive) | | | | | |
| 4.1.5 shows interest in what observers are writing about | | | | | |
| 4.1.6 shows interest in observer as a person | | | | | |
| 4.1.7 shows pleasure when others solve a a problem or complete a construction (e.g. gives a compliment) | | | | | |
| 4.1.8 competes with others | | | | | |
| 4.1.9 encourages others to attempt difficult tasks | | | | | |
| 4.1.10 verbalizes confidence in others | | | | | |
| 4.1.11 gives help to others (e.g. gives away own pieces, gives hints, supplies a needed word) | | | | | |
| 4.1.12 organizes group activity | | | | | |
| 4.1.13 assumes responsibility for writing, recording, or facilitating the activity | | | | | |
| 4.1.14 assists observer in accomplishing his/her purposes | | | | | |
| 4.1.15 attempts to involve all group members in activity | | | | | |
| 4.1.16 keeps mood of group light and cheerful | | | | | |
| 4.1.17 makes suggestions to group without dominating | | | | | |
| 4.1.18 changes behavior if it seems to affect group in a negative way | | | | | |
| 4.1.19 demonstrates interpersonal behaviors valued by own and/or dominant culture | | · | | | |
| **4.2 Product** | | | | | |
| 4.2.1 characters created have recognizable personalities | | | | | |
| 4.2.2 products demonstrate knowledge/ understanding of emotions and motivation of others | | | | | |
| 4.2.3 language demonstrates knowledge/ understanding of social relationships | | | | | |

of settings, and revised as needed. Then, tasks are implemented with diverse populations, in different settings, and by many observers.

Each time, lists of behaviors and characteristics of products are generated. At some point, we have found that no new behaviors or characteristics seem to emerge, and a checklist is developed. The checklist currently in use at grades K–8, for instance, was not considered complete until we had observed more than 5,000 children from the following groups: multicultural urban and suburban settings in the southwest, midwest, southeast, and northeast; varied linguistic groups (e.g., Spanish, Navajo, English, Tohono O'Odham, Yaqui, Arabic); varied economic groups; students with disabilities; students with varied ethnic and cultural backgrounds (e.g., Anglo-American, Asian-American, Australian, Baharaini, Hualapai, Mexican-American, Navajo, Tohono O'Odham); and students living in rural, isolated areas such as the Navajo and Tohono O'Odham Indian reservations.

> Educators must remain open to the possibility that behaviors other than those they expect may constitute effective, efficient, and economical problem solving.

Although extensive observations such as these may not be possible or practical, the important point to remember is that a variety of behaviors may be desirable, and educators must remain open to the possibility that behaviors other than those they expect or are looking for may constitute effective, efficient, and economical problem solving. Educators also must realize that answers or solutions they may think are "wrong" or "inappropriate" because they fall outside the boundaries of traditional views of appropriate products may be richer sources of information about students than the products we expect. During an observation of a problem solving activity, our observers are taught to record everything they see, take photographs of all products, and accept all responses and products with their initial reactions or beliefs about the quality of the products.

During the Type I spatial problem solving task (Table 1), one student began to weave the watercolor techniques demonstration into an abstract construction. The observer's initial reaction was to remind the student that she would have time to make a painting later. However, common sense (or perhaps good preparation) took over, and he simply watched the student and took pictures of the painting, growing more and more fascinated with the student's artistic abilities. In another case, a student wrote a visual, metaphorical short story about the killing of ram. The inclination of some teachers and observers was to dismiss the student as a "Satanist" and to ignore the excellent linguistic qualities of his writing. Equal appreciation must be expressed and all products must be valued.

The main point of this discussion is that the purpose of the assessment must be kept in mind at all times, and assessment that is not shared with the individual being assessed, or is unusable to that individual because it cannot be understood, interpreted, or applied, is not beneficial to the student. Similarly, such assessment must be beneficial to teachers, parents, guardians, counselors, administrators, and others involved in helping students to grow and develop their problem solving abilities.

## CONCLUSION

In conclusion, I would like to review some implicit assumptions underlying the ideas and methods presented. First, authentic assessment of problem solving must involve many types of problems and many domains of knowledge or expertise. Second, it must involve documentation of processes as well as descriptions of products, including description of products throughout their development, not just at the end. Third, students must be involved in all phases of assessment, including decisions about the appropriateness of the tasks, evaluations of their own performance, and interpretations of results. Fourth, observation is essential, and needs to include "being there" as well as videotaping and photographing for later analysis—both by the observer and by others with different perspectives or forms of expertise. Finally, those responsible for designing, implementing, and evaluating assessments always must be aware of their own biases, values, perspectives, and experiences; and understand the powerful effects these personal traits can have on their decision-making. Such awareness can and must lead to inclusion of other people and other belief systems, and ultimately to more fair, true-to-life, genuine descriptions of the problem solving abilities of secondary school students.

## REFERENCES

Baird, L. L. & Richards, J. M. Jr. (1968). *The effects of selecting college students by various kinds of high school achievements.* (ACT Research Report No. 23). Iowa City, IA: American College Testing Program.

Gardner, H. (1983). *Frames of mind: The theory of multiple intelligences.* New York: Basic Books.

———. (1992). Assessment in context: The alternative to standardized testing. In B. R. Gifford & M. C. O'Connor (Eds.), *Alternative views of aptitude, achievement, and instruction.* Boston: Lummer.

Howieson, N. (1981). Longitudinal study of creativity—1965–1975. *Journal of Creative Behavior, 15* (2), 117–134.

Kay, S. (1991). The figural problem solving and problem finding of professional and semi-professional artists and nonartists. *Creativity Research Journal, 4*(3), 233–252.

Lave, J. (1980). What's special about experiments as contexts for thinking? *Quarterly Newsletter of the Laboratory of Comparative Human Cognition, 2,* 86–91.

Maker, C. J. (1982). *Curriculum development for the gifted.* Austin, TX: PRO-ED, Inc.

———. (1993). Creativity, intelligences, and problem solving: A definition and design for cross-cultural research and measurement related to giftedness. *Gifted Education International, 9,* 68–77.

Maker, C. J., Rogers, J. A. & Nielson, A. B. (1994). *Giftedness, diversity, and problem solving.* Teaching Exceptional Children.

Neisser, U. (1976). General, academic, and artifical intelligence. In L. Resnick, (Ed.), *The nature of intelligence* (pp. 135–144). New York: John Wiley & Sons.

Renzulli, J. S. & Reis, S. M. (1985). *The schoolwide enrichment model: A comprehensive plan for educational excellence.* Mansfield Center, CT: Creative Learning Press.

Resnick, L. B. (1976). Changing conceptions of intelligence. In L. Resnick (Ed.). *The nature of intelligence* (pp. 1–10). New York: John Wiley & Sons.

Richards, J. M., Jr., Holland, J. L. & Lutz, S. W. (1967). Prediction of student accomplishment in college. *Journal of Educational Psychology, 58,* 343–355.

Rodale, J. I. (1978). *The synonym finder.* Rodale Press, Emmaus, PA.

Rogers, J. A. (1993). *Understanding spatial intelligence through problem solving in art: An analysis of behaviors, processes, and products.* Unpublished dissertation, The University of Arizona, Tucson.

Rogoff, B. (1982). Integrating content and cognitive development. In M. Lamb & A. Brown (Eds.), *Advances in developmental psychology (Vol. 2)*. Hillsdale, NY: Lawrence Erlbaum.

Schiever, S. & Maker, C. J. (1991). Enrichment and acceleration: An overview and new directions. In N. Colangelo and G. Davis (Eds.), *Handbook no. 5 of gifted education* (pp. 99–110). Boston: Allyn and Bacon.

Scribner, S. (1986). Thinking in action: Some characteristics of practical thought. In R. Sternberg & R. K. Wagner (Eds.), *Practical intelligence*. New York: Cambridge University Press.

Sternberg, R. J. (1985a). Teaching critical thinking, Part 1: Are we making critical mistakes? *Phi Delta Kappan, 67*(3), 104–108.

————. (1985b). Teaching critical thinking, Part 2: Possible solutions. *Phi Delta Kappan, 67*(4), 277–280.

Sternberg, R. J. & Salter, W. (1982). Conceptions of intelligence. In R. J. Sternberg (Ed.), *Handbook of human intelligence* (pp. 3–24). Cambridge: Cambridge University Press.

Wallach, M. A. (1976). Tests tell us little about talent. *American Scientist, 64,* 57–63.

Webster's II: *New Riverside University Dictionary*. (1984). Boston: Houghton Mifflin Co.

Wing, C. W. & Wallach, M. A. (1971). *College admissions and the psychology of talent*. New York: Holt, Rinehart, & Winston.

# Assessment in Context: The Alternative to Standardized Testing

by Howard Gardner

## CONTRASTING MODELS OF ASSESSMENT

A familiar scene almost anywhere in the United States today: Several hundred students file into a large examination hall. They sit nervously, waiting for sealed packets to be handed out. At the appointed hour, booklets are distributed, brief instructions are issued, and formal testing begins. The hall is still as students at each desk bear down on number two pencils and fill in the bubbles which punctuate the answer sheets. A few hours later, the testing ends and the booklets are collected; several weeks later, a sheet bearing a set of scores arrives at each student's home and at the colleges to which the students have directed their scores. The results of a morning's testing become a powerful factor in decisions about the future of each student.

An equally familiar scene in most pre-industrial societies over the centuries: A youth of ten or eleven moves into the home of a man who has mastered a trade. Initially, the lad is asked to carry out menial tasks as he helps the master to prepare for his work or to clean up the shop at the end of the day. During this initial phase, the lad has the opportunity to watch the master at work, while the master monitors the youth to discover his special talents or serious flaws. Over the months the apprentice slowly enters into the practice of the trade. After initially aiding in the more peripheral aspects of the trade, he eventually gains familiarity with the full gamut of skilled work. Directed by the tradition, but also guided by the youth's par-

From *Multiple Intelligences: The Theory in Practice,* edited by Howard Gardner, published by Basic Books, New York. Copyright © 1993 by Howard Gardner. Reprinted with permission.

ticular skills and motivation, the master guides his charge through the various steps from novice to journeyman. Finally, after several years of supervised training, the youth is ready to practice the craft on his own.

**Aspects of the apprenticeship model are consistent with current knowledge about how individuals learn and how their performance might best be assessed.**

While both of these scenes are idealized, they should be readily recognizable to anyone concerned with the assessment and training of young people. Indeed, they may be said to represent two extremes. The first "formal testing" model is conceived of as an objective, decontextualized form of assessment which can be adopted and implemented widely, with some assurance that similar results will be obtained. The second "apprenticeship" model is implemented almost entirely with a naturally occurring context in which the particularities of a craft are embedded. The assessment is based upon a prior analysis of the skills involved in a particular craft, but it may also be influenced by subjective factors including the master's personal views about his apprentice, his relationship with other masters, or his need for other kinds of services.

It should be evident that these two forms of assessment were designed to meet different needs. Apprenticeships made sense when the practice of various crafts was the major form of employment for non-rural youths. Formal testing is a contemporary means of comparing the performance of thousands of students who are being educated in schools. Yet these forms of assessment are not limited to the two prototypical contexts described above. Despite the overwhelmingly agrarian nature of Chinese society, formal tests have been used there for over two thousand years in selecting government officials. And, by the same token, in many art forms, athletic practices, and areas of scientific research (Polanyi 1958), apprenticeships and the concomitant ongoing, context-determined forms of assessment continue to be used in our highly industrialized society.

Thus, the choice of "formal testing" as opposed to "apprenticeship" is not dictated solely by the historical era or the primary means of production in the society. It would be possible in our society to utilize the apprenticeship method to a much greater extent than we do. Most observers today (myself included) do not lament the passage of the obligatory apprenticeship system, with its frequent excesses and blatant sexism; from several points of view, contemporary formal testing represents a fairer and more easily justifiable form of assessment. And yet, aspects of the apprenticeship model are consistent with current knowledge about how individuals learn and how their performance might best be assessed.

Our society has embraced the formal testing mode to an excessive degree; I contend that aspects of the apprentice model of learning and assessment—which I term "contextualized learning"—could be profitably reintroduced into our educational system (see Collins, Brown, and Newman 1989). Following an account of the origins of standardized testing and the one-dimensional view of mentation often implied by such testing methods, I review several lines of evidence from the cognitive, neural, and developmental sciences which point to a far more capacious view of the human mind and of human learning than that which informed earlier conceptions.

Our task here is to envision forms of education and modes of assessment which have a firm rooting in current scientific understanding and which contribute to enlightened educational goals. In the latter half of the chapter I describe in general terms the characteristics of these novel forms of assessment. I then introduce educational experiments in which my colleagues and I have become engaged, at levels from preschool to college admissions. These educational experiments demonstrate alternative ways in which information relevant to guidance and selection could be obtained. I conclude with a description and endorsement of a possible "individual-centered" school-of-the-future, in which the lines between assessment and curriculum, students and disciplines, school and community are newly drawn. Such a school can be fashioned within a society that spurns standardized testing-in-isolation and favors assessment-in-context.

## BINET, THE TESTING SOCIETY, AND THE "UNIFORM" VIEW OF SCHOOLING

The widespread use of formal testing can be traced to the work on intelligence testing carried out in Paris at the turn of the century by Alfred Binet and his colleagues. Binet was asked by city educational leaders to assist in determining which students would succeed, and which would likely fail, in elementary school (Binet and Simon 1905; Block and Dworkin 1976). He hit upon the inspired idea of administering a large set of items to young school children and identifying which of the items proved most discriminating in light of his particular goal. The work carried out by the Binet team ultimately led to the first intelligence tests, and the construct of intelligence quotient, or IQ.

So great was the appeal of the Binet method that it soon became a dominant feature of the American educational and assessment landscape. To be sure, some standardized tests—ranging from the California Achievement Tests to the Scholastic Aptitude Test—are not direct outgrowths of the various intelligence tests. And yet it is difficult to envision the proliferation of these instruments over just a few decades without the widely esteemed examples of the Stanford-Binet, the Army Alpha, and the various Wechsler intelligence instruments (Brown and Herrnstein 1975).

In the United States especially, with its focus on quantitative markers and its cult of educational efficiency, there has been a virtual mania for producing tests for every possible social purpose (Gould 1981; Hoffman 1962). In addition to standardized tests for students, we have such tests for teachers, supervisors, soldiers, and police officers; we use adaptations of these instruments to assess capacities not only in standard areas of the curriculum but also in civics and the arts; and we can draw on short-answer measures for assessing personality, degrees of authoritarianism, and compatibility for dating. The United States is well on the way to becoming a "complete testing society." We could encapsulate this attitude thus: If something is important, it is worth testing in this way; if it cannot be so tested, then it probably ought not be valued. Few observers have stopped to consider the domains in which such an approach might *not* be relevant or optimal, and most have forgotten the insights which might be gained from modes of assessment favored in an earlier era.

> In the United States especially, there has been a virtual mania for producing tests for every possible social purpose.

It is risky to attempt to generalize across the thousands of "formal instruments" which are described in books like the Buros's (1978) *Mental Measurements Yearbook*. Yet, at the cost of doing some violence to certain instruments, it is worth indicating the features which are typically associated with such instruments.

There is within the testing profession considerable belief in "raw," possibly genetically based potential (Eysenck 1967; Jensen 1980). The most highly valued tests, such as IQ tests and the SAT, are thought to measure ability or potential performance. There is no necessary reason why a test cannot assess skills which have been learned, and many "achievement" tests purport to do this. Yet, for tests that purport to measure raw ability or potential, it is important that performance cannot be readily improved by instruction; otherwise, the test would not be a valid indicator of ability. Most authorities on testing believe that performance on ability and achievement tests reflects inherent capacities.

Adherents of testing also tend to embrace a view of human development which assumes that a young organism contains less knowledge and exhibits less skill than a more nature organism, but that no qualitative changes occur over time in human mind or behavior (Bijou and Baer 1965). Making such assumptions enables the testmaker to use the same kinds of instruments for individuals of all ages; and he or she can legitimately claim that descriptions of data at a certain point in development can be extended to later ages, because one is dealing with the same kind of scale and the same property of mind or behavior. Thus the makers of a test called the QT (Quick Test) claim in a regularly run advertisement that their instrument "handles two-year-olds and superior adults within the same short series of items and the same format."

> Most testmakers and buyers place a premium on instruments which are efficient, brief, and can be readily administered.

Reflecting general American technological pressures, as well as the desire for elegance and economy, most testmakers and buyers place a premium on instruments which are efficient, brief, and can be readily administered. In the early days of testing, assessment sometimes took hours and was individually administered; now, group-administered instruments are desired. Virtually every widely used test has spawned a "brief" version. Indeed, some of the standardized supporters of formal intelligence tests hope to strip them down even further: Arthur Jensen (1987) has embraced "reaction time" measures, Michael Anderson (1987) looks to sensory discrimination, and Hans Eysenck (1979) has called for the examination of patterns of brain waves.

Accompanying a fealty to formal testing is a view of education which I have termed the "uniform view of schooling." This view does not necessarily entail the wearing of uniforms, but it does call for homogenized education in other aspects. According to the uniform view, as much as possible students should study the same subject matter. (This may include a strong dosage of the values of the dominant culture or subculture—see Bloom 1987; Hirsch 1987; Ravitch and Finn 1987). Moreover, as much as possible that subject matter ought to be conveyed in the same way to all students.

In the uniform view, progress in school ought to be assessed by frequent formal tests. These tests should be administered under uniform conditions, and students, teachers, and parents should receive quantitative scores which detail the students' progress or lack thereof. These tests should be nationally normed instruments, so that the maximum comparability is possible. The most important subject matters are those which lend themselves readily to such assessment, such as mathematics and science. In other subjects, value is assigned to the aspects which can be efficiently assessed (grammar rather than "voice" in writing; facts rather than interpretation in history). Those disciplines which prove most refractory to formal testing, such as the arts, are least valued in the uniform school.

In putting forth this picture of Binet, the testing society, and the uniform view of schooling, I am aware that I am overemphasizing certain tendencies and lumping together views and attitudes in a way which is not entirely fair to those who are closely associated with formal testing. Some individuals intimately involved with testing have voiced the same concerns (Cronbach 1984; Messick 1988). Indeed, had I put this picture forth fifteen or twenty years ago it might have seemed an outrageous caricature. However, the trends within American education since the early 1980s bear a strong resemblance to the views I have just sketched. At the very least, these views serve as a necessary "contrast case" to the picture of contextualized and individualized assessment and schooling which I present later in the chapter; they should be taken in that contrastive spirit.

## SOURCES FOR AN ALTERNATIVE APPROACH TO ASSESSMENT

While the testing society has responded more to pragmatic needs than to scientific dictates, it does reflect a certain view of human nature. The scientific ideas on which the testing society has been based derive from an earlier era in which behaviorist, learning theoretical, and associationist views of cognition and development were regnant (see Gardner 1985 for a summary). According to these views, it made sense to believe in "inborn" human abilities, in a smooth, probably linear curve of learning from infancy to old age, in a hierarchy of disciplines, and in the desirability of assessing potential and achievement under carefully controlled and maximally decontextualized conditions.

Over the past few decades, however, the various assumptions on which this testing edifice was based have been gradually undermined by work in developmental, cognitive, and educational studies, and a quite different view has emerged. It is not possible in this chapter to review all of the evidence on which this shifting psychological conception has been based. But because my alternative picture of assessment builds on the newly emerging picture of human development, it is important to highlight the principal features of this perspective and to indicate where it may clash with standard views of testing.

### The Necessity for a Developmental Perspective

Owing to the pioneering work of Jean Piaget (1983), it is widely recognized that children are not simply miniature versions of adults. The infant or the toddler conceives of the world in a way which is internally consistent but which deviates in important particulars from a more mature conception. Here are some of the most familiar instances from the Piagetian canon: the infant does not appreciate that an object continues to exist when it has been removed from view; the toddler does not understand that material remains constant in quantity, even when its physical configuration has been altered (for example, squashing a ball of clay); the young school child is unable to reason solely from the implications of one proposition to another but instead proceeds on the basis of knowledge of concrete instances and perceived empirical regularities.

According to Piaget's view, children pass through a number of qualitatively different stages called sensori-motor, pre-operational, concrete operational, and formal operational. A child at one stage in one area of knowledge will necessarily be at the same stage in other domains of experience. Few investigators hold any longer to a literal version of this "structured-stage" perspective; there have been too many findings which do not support it (Brainerd 1978; Gelman

1978). But most developmental psychologists continue to subscribe to the point of view that the world of the infant or toddler has its own peculiar structures; many developmentalists believe that there are stage sequences within particular domains of experience (for example, language, moral judgment, understanding of physical causality); and nearly all emphasize the need to take into account the child's perspective and level of understanding (Case 1987; Feldman 1980; Fischer 1980).

Another feature of this approach is its assumption that development is neither smooth, nor unilinear, nor free of perturbations. While details differ among theorists, most researchers believe that there may be critical or sensitive periods during which it is especially easy—or especially difficult—to master certain kinds of materials. Similarly, while youngsters tend to improve in most areas with age, there will be periods of more rapid growth and periods of stasis. And a minority of researchers believes that in some domains there may actually be regressions or "U-shapes" with younger children performing in a more sophisticated or integrated fashion than students in middle childhood (Strauss 1982).

It is possible to construct measurement instruments which reflect the developmental knowledge recently accrued. In fact, some batteries have been devised which build specifically on Piagetian or allied notions (Uzgiris and Hunt 1966). For the most part, however, American tests have been insensitive to developmental considerations.

### The Emergence of a Symbol-System Perspective

At the height of the behaviorist era there was no need to posit any kind of mental entity, such as an idea, a thought, a belief, or a symbol. One simply identified behaviors or actions of significance and observed these as scrupulously as possible; so-called thoughts were simply "silent" movements or musculature.

Over the past few decades, however, there has been increasing recognition of the importance in human cognition of the capacity to use various kinds of symbols and symbol systems (Gardner, Howard, and Perkins 1974; Goodman 1976; Langer 1942). Humans are deemed the creatures par excellence of communication, who garner meanings through words, pictures, gestures, numbers, musical patterns, and a whole host of other symbolic forms. The manifestations of the these symbols are public: all can observe written language, number systems, drawings, charts, gestural languages, and the like.

However, the mental processes needed to manipulate such symbols must be inferred from the performances of individuals on various kinds of tasks. Unexpectedly potent support for the belief in internal symbol-manipulation has come from invention and widespread use of computers; if these human-made machines engage in operations of symbol use and transformation, it seems ludicrous to withhold the same kinds of capacities from the humans who invented them (Newell and Simon 1972).

> **Nearly all formal tests presuppose that their users will be literate in the second-level symbol systems of the culture.**

Considerable effort has been expended in the relevant sciences to investigate the development of the human capacity for symbol use. It is widely (though not universally) agreed that infants do not use symbols or exhibit internal symbolic manipulation and that the emergence of symbol use during the second year of life is a major hallmark of human cognition. Thereafter, human beings rapidly acquire skill in the use of those symbols and symbol systems which are featured in their culture. By the age of five or six most children have acquired a "first draft" knowledge of how to create and understand stories, works of music, drawings, and simple scientific explanations (Gardner 1982).

In literate cultures, however, there is a second level of symbol use. Children must learn to utilize the *invented symbol* (or *notational*) systems of their culture, such as writing and numbers. With few exceptions, this assignment is restricted to school settings, which are relatively decontextualized. Mastering notational systems can be difficult for many students in our society, including students whose mastery of "practical knowledge" and "first-order symbol systems" has been unproblematic. Even those students who prove facile at acquiring notational systems face a non-trivial challenge: they must mesh their newly acquired "second-order" symbolic knowledge with the earlier forms of "practical" and "first-order" symbolic knowledge they brought with them to school (Bamberger 1982; Gardner 1986; Resnick 1987).

Nearly all formal tests presuppose that their users will be literate in the second-level symbol systems of the culture. These tests thus pose special difficulties for individuals who, for whatever reason, have had difficulty in attaining second-level symbol knowledge or cannot map that knowledge onto earlier forms of mental representation. Moreover, it is my belief that individuals with well-developed second-level symbolic skills can often "psych out" such tests, scoring well even when their knowledge of the subject matter which is ostensibly being assessed is modest (Gardner 1983). At any rate, what the exact relations are which exist among "practical," "first-order," and "second-order" symbolic knowledge and the best way to assess these remain difficult issues to resolve.

**Evidence for the Existence of Multiple Faculties or "Intelligences"**
When intelligence tests were first assembled, there was little attention paid to the underlying theory of intelligence. But soon the idea gained currency that the different abilities being tapped all fed into or reflected a single "general intelligence." This perspective has remained the view-of-choice among most students of intelligence, though a minority has been open to the idea of different "vectors of mind" or different "products, content, and operations" of intellect (Guilford 1967; Thurstone 1938). This minority has based its conclusions on the results of factor analyses of test results; however, it has been shown that one can arrive at either unitary or pluralistic views of intellect, depending upon which assumptions guide factor analytic procedures (Gould 1981).

In recent years, there has been a resurgence of interest in the idea of a multiplicity of intelligences. Mental phenomena have been discovered that some researchers construe as evidence for mental *modules*—fast-operating, reflex-like, information-processing devices which seem impervious to the influence of other modules. The discovery of these modules has given rise to the view that there may be separate analytic devices involved in tasks like syntactic parsing, tonal recognition, or facial perception (Fodor 1983).

A second source of evidence for a multiplicity of intelligences has been the fine-grained analysis of the mental operations involved in the solution of items used in intelligence tests (Sternberg 1977, 1985). These analyses have suggested the existence of different components which contribute to success on any standard intellectual assessment. Individuals may differ from one another in the facility with which the different components operate, and different tasks may call upon a differential use of the various components, meta-components, and sub-components.

My proposal for a set of "multiple intelligences" (Gardner 1983, 1987a) has been prompted by a different set of considerations. Initially I was impressed in my research by two lines of findings: (1) normal children can distinguish themselves in one or two areas of performance with no predictive value about how they will perform in other areas and (2) brain-damaged individuals may lose capacities in one or two areas but otherwise appear to be as competent as before (Gardner 1975).

I subsequently surveyed research on the development of different capacities in normal children; the breakdown of these capacities under different varieties of brain damage; the existence in special populations of highly jagged cognitive profiles (prodigies, idiot savants, autistic children, individuals with learning disabilities); the sets of abilities found in individuals from different cultures; the evolution of cognition over the millennia in humans and in infrahuman species; and two kinds of psychological evidence—correlations among psychometric tests and the results of studies of transfer and generalization of skills.

Pulling together the results of this massive survey, I isolated the existence of seven different mental facilities or intelligences. As outlined in *Frames of Mind: The Theory of Multiple Intelligences* (Gardner 1983), humans have evolved as a species to carry out at least seven kinds of computations or analyses: those involving language (linguistic intelligence, as exemplified by a poet); logical-mathematical analysis (in a scientist, mathematician, or logician); spatial representation (for instance, the painter, sculptor, architect, sailor, geometer, or engineer); musical analysis; bodily-kinesthetic thinking (for example, the dancer, athlete, mime, actor, surgeon, craftsman); and two forms of personal understanding—interpersonal knowledge (of other persons, as in a salesman, teacher, therapist, leader) and intrapersonal knowledge (the ability to know one's own desires, fears, and competences and to act productively on the basis of that knowledge).

According to my analysis, most formal testing—whatever the area that is allegedly being tested—engages primarily the linguistic and logical-mathematical faculties. If one has high linguistic and logical-mathematical intelligences, one is likely to do well in school and in formal testing. Poor endowment or learning in one or both of these intelligences is likely to result in poor standardized scores.

If life consisted solely of schooling, most formal tests would serve their purpose well—though last year's grades would fulfill the same predictive purposes equally well. Schooling, however, is supposed to be a preparation for life, and there is ample evidence that formal testing alone is an indifferent predictor for success once a student has left school (Jencks 1972).

> There is ample evidence that formal testing alone is an indifferent predictor for success once a student has left school.

I therefore call for assessment which is "intelligence-fair"—which looks *directly* at an individual's skills in areas such as music, spatial knowledge, or interpersonal understanding, rather than looking through the "window" of linguistic and/or logical-mathematical prowess. It is the desire for modes of assessment that can detect capacities in the other intelligences, even in the face of indifferent linguistic or logical-mathematical capacities, which animates much of the applied research program described below.

While my research documents that individuals differ from one another in the profile of intelligences which they exhibit, it is not clear how particular intelligences are distributed in the population. Indeed, in the absence of adequate measures of nonscholastic intelligences, quantitative questions about strength and distribution of intelligences cannot be answered at the present time. It cannot, therefore, be maintained *a priori* that each individual stands out in one or more intelligences or that every person has clear deficiencies as well as strengths. There may be individuals with potency in every intelligence, as well as others who have only "relative strengths" or "relative weaknesses." Still there is reason to think that, given a broader gamut of indexes, more individuals will emerge as competent on at least some measure and that such competence in turn can have beneficent effects on self-concept and on productivity.

### Recognition of Vast Individual Differences

A consequence of the "multiple intelligences" perspective is the recognition that instead of a single dimension called intellect, on which individuals can be rank-ordered, there are vast differences among individuals in their intellectual strengths and weaknesses and also in their styles of attack in cognitive pursuits (Kagan and Kogan 1970).

Our own evidence suggests that these differences may be evident even before the years of formal schooling.

The literature on different individual strengths, as well as the findings on diverse cognitive styles, has crucial educational implications. To begin with, it is important to identify strengths and weaknesses at an early point so that they can become part of educational planning. Striking differences among individuals also call into question whether individuals ought to all be taking the same curriculum and whether, to the extent that there is a uniform curriculum, it needs to be presented in the same fashion to all individuals.

> **Striking differences among individuals also call into question whether individuals ought to be taking the same curriculum.**

Formal tests can be an ally to the recognition of different cognitive features, but only if the tests are designed to elicit—rather than mask—these differences (Cronbach and Snow 1977). It is particularly important that instruments used in "gatekeeping" niches (like college admissions) be designed to allow students to show their strengths and to perform optimally. Until now, little effort has been made in this regard and tests are more frequently used to point up weaknesses than to designate strengths.

### A Search for Human Creative Capacities

During most of the first century of formal testing interest fell heavily on assessment of individual intelligence, and there was relatively little concern with other cognitive capacities. In the post-Sputnik era, when scientific ingenuity was suddenly at a premium, American educators became convinced of the importance of imaginativeness, inventiveness, and creativity. They called for the devising of instruments which would assess creativity or creative potential (Guilford 1950). Regrettably (from my perspective), in their search for creativity measures they repeated most of the mistakes that had been made throughout the history of intelligence testing. That is, they tried to devise short-answer, timed measures of the abilities they thought central to creativity—the capacity to come up with a variety of answers to a question (divergent thinking) or to issue as many unusual associations as possible to a stimulus (ideational fluency).

While the field of intelligence testing is currently filled with controversy, there is consensus that creativity tests have not fulfilled their potential (Wallach 1971, 1985). These instruments are reliable, and they do measure something other than psychometric intelligence, but they cannot predict which individuals will be judged as creative on the basis of their productions within a domain. Rather than attempting to devise more and better "creativity tests," researchers have instead begun to examine more closely what actually happens when individuals are engaged in problem-solving or problem-finding activities (Gruber 1981; Sternberg 1988).

These recent studies have yielded two major findings. On the one hand, creative individuals do not seem to have at their disposal mental operations which are theirs alone; creative individuals make use of the same cognitive processes as do other persons, but they use them in a more efficient and flexible way and in the service of goals which are ambitious and often quite risky (Perkins 1981). On the other hand, highly creative individuals do seem to lead their lives in a way different from most others. They are fully engaged in and passionate about their work; they exhibit a need to do something new and have a strong sense of their purpose and ultimate goals; they are extremely reflective about their activities, their use of time, and the quality of their products (Gruber 1985).

Except rhetorically, the quest for creativity has not been a major goal of the American educational system. However, to the extent that the fostering of creative individuals is a desirable goal for an educational institution, it is important that this goal be pursued in a manner consistent with current analyses of creativity (Gardner 1988a). In some of the programs described in this chapter, an attempt is made to foster the kinds of personal habits which appear to be associated with creative individuals—rather than to engender the kinds of fluency which have typically been monitored in so-called creativity tests.

### The Desirability of Assessing Learning in Context

When standardized tests and paradigmatic experimental designs were first introduced into non-Western cultural contexts, they led to a single result; preliterate individuals and others from non-Western societies appeared to be much less skilled and much less intelligent than Western control groups. An interesting phenomenon was then discovered. Simple alterations of materials, test setting, or instructions frequently elicited dramatic improvements in performance. The "performance gap" between the subjects from another culture

and the subjects from our own culture narrowed or even disap-
peared when familiar materials were used, when knowledgeable and
linguistically fluent examiners were employed, when revised instructions were given, or when the "same" cognitive capacities were
tapped in a form which made more sense within the non-Western
context (Laboratory of Comparative Human Cognition 1982).

Now a huge body of experimental evidence exists to indicate
that assessment materials designed for one target audience cannot be
transported directly to another cultural setting; there are no purely
culture-fair or culture-blind materials. Every instrument reflects its
origins. Formal tests that make some sense in a Western context do
so because students are accustomed to learn about materials at a site
removed from the habitual application of such materials; however,
in unschooled or lightly schooled environments, most instruction
takes place in situ, and so it only makes sense to administer assessments which are similarly in context.

Building upon this cross-cultural research, there is also an accu-
mulation of findings about the cognitive abilities of various kinds of
experts. It has been shown that experts often fail on "formal" measures of their calculating or reasoning capacities but can be shown to
exhibit precisely those same skills in the course of their ordinary
work—such as tailoring clothes, shopping in a supermarket, loading
dairy cases onto a truck, or defending one's rights in a dispute (Lave
1980; Rogoff 1982; Scribner 1986). In such cases, it is not the person
who has failed but rather the measurement instrument which purported to document the person's level of competence.

### Locating Competence and Skill Outside the Head of the Individual

The research just reviewed has yielded another novel conceptualization. In many cases it is erroneous to conclude that the knowledge
required to execute a task resides completely in the mind of a single
individual. This knowledge can be "distributed": that is, successful
performance of a task may depend upon a team of individuals, no
single one of whom possesses all of the necessary expertise but all of
whom, working together, are able to accomplish the task in a reliable
way (Scribner 1986). Relatedly, it is too simple to say that an individual either "has" or "does not have" the requisite knowledge; that
knowledge may show up reliably in the presence of the appropriate
human and physical "triggers" but might be otherwise invisible to
probing (Squire 1986).

It makes sense to think of human cognitive competence as an emerging capacity, one likely to be manifest at the intersection of three different constituents: the "individual," with his or her skills, knowledge, and aims; the structure of a "domain of knowledge," within which these skills can be aroused; and a set of institutions and roles—a surrounding "field"—which judges when a particular performance is acceptable and when it fails to meet specifications (Csikszentmihalyi 1988; Csikszentmihalyi and Robinson 1986; Gardner and Wolf 1988). The acquisition and transmission of knowledge depends upon a dynamic which sustains itself among these three components. Particularly beyond the years of early childhood, human accomplishment presupposes an awareness of the different domains of knowledge in one's culture and the various "field forces" which affect opportunity, progress, and recognition. By focusing on the knowledge that resides within a single mind at a single moment, formal testing may distort, magnify, or grossly underestimate the contributions which an individual can make within a larger social setting.

The foregoing research findings point to a differentiated and nuanced view of assessment, one which, in at least certain ways, might more closely resemble traditional apprenticeship measures than formal testing. An assessment initiative being planned today, in light of these findings, should be sensitive to developmental stages and trajectories. Such an initiative should investigate human symbolic capacities in an appropriate fashion in the years following infancy and investigate the relationship between practical knowledge and first- and second-level symbolic skills. It should recognize the existence of different intelligences and of diverse cognitive and stylistic profiles, and it should incorporate an awareness of these variations into assessments; it should possess an understanding of those features which characterize creative individuals in different domains. Finally, a new assessment initiative should acknowledge the effects of context on performance and provide the most appropriate contexts in which to assess competences, including ones which extend outside the skin of the individual being assessed.

It is a tall order to meet all of these needs and desiderata. Indeed, an attraction of formal testing is that one can bracket or minimize most of the features which I have just outlined. However, if we seek an assessment which is both true to the individual and reflective of our best understanding of the nature of human cognition, then we cannot afford to ignore the lines of thinking which I have just outlined.

## GENERAL FEATURES OF A NEW APPROACH TO ASSESSMENT

If one were to return to the drawing board today and lay out a fresh approach to assessment, one might attempt to incorporate the following principal features:

### Emphasis on Assessment Rather than Testing

The penchant for testing in America has gone too far. While some tests are useful for some purposes, the testing industry has taken off in a way which makes little sense from the point of view of a reflective society. Many who seek to understand the underlying theoretical or conceptual basis of findings of validity are disappointed. It seems that many tests have been designed to create, rather than to fulfill, a need.

While I have ambivalent feelings about testing, I have little ambivalence about assessment. To my mind, it is the proper mission of educated individuals, as well as those who are under their charge, to engage in regular and appropriate reflection on their goals, the various means to achieve them, their success (or lack thereof) in achieving these goals, and the implications of the assessment for re-thinking goals or procedures.

I define assessment as the obtaining of information about the skills and potentials of individuals, with the dual goals of providing useful feedback to the individuals and useful data to the surrounding community. What distinguishes assessment from testing is the former's favoring of techniques which elicit information in the course of ordinary performance and its general uneasiness with the use of formal instruments administered in a neutral, decontextualized setting.

In my view, those in the psychological and educational communities charged with the task of evaluation ought to facilitate such assessment (see Cross and Angelo 1988). We ought to be devising methods and measures which aid in regular, systematic, and useful assessment. In some cases we would end up producing "formal tests." But not in most cases, I expect.

### Assessment as Simple, Natural, and Occurring on a Reliable Schedule

Rather than being imposed "externally" at odd times during the year, assessment ought to become part of the natural learning environment. As much as possible it should occur "on the fly," as part of an individual's natural engagement in a learning situation. Initially, the assessment would probably have to be introduced explicitly; but after a while, much assessment would occur naturally on the part of student and teacher, with little need for explicit recognition or labeling on anyone's part.

The model of the assessment of the cognitive abilities of the expert is relevant here. On the one hand, it is rarely necessary for the expert to be assessed by others unless engaged in competition. It is assumed that experts will go about their business with little external monitoring. However, it is also true that the expert is constantly in the process of assessing; such assessment occurs naturally, almost without conscious reflection, in the course of working. When I first began to write, I was highly dependent upon the detailed criticism of teachers and editors; now most of the needed assessment occurs at a preconscious level as I sit at my desk scribbling, or typing a first draft, or editing an earlier version of the material.

As assessment gradually becomes part of the landscape, it no longer needs to be set off from the rest of classroom activity. As in a good apprenticeship, the teachers and the students are always assessing. There is also no need to "teach for the assessment" because the assessment is ubiquitous; indeed, the need for formal tests might atrophy altogether.

### Ecological Validity

A problem for most formal tests is their validity, that is, their correlation with some criterion (Messick 1988). As noted, creativity tests are no longer used much because their validity has never been adequately established. The predictive validity of intelligence tests and scholastic aptitude tests is often questioned in view of their limited usefulness in predicting performance beyond the next year of schooling.

Returning to our example of the apprenticeship, it would make little sense to question the validity of the judgments by the master. He is so intimately associated with his novice that he can probably predict his behaviors with a high degree of accuracy. When such prediction does not occur reliably, trouble lies ahead. I believe that current assessments have moved too far away from the territory that they are supposed to cover. When individuals are assessed in situations which more closely resemble "actual working conditions," it is possible to make much better predictions about their ultimate performance. It is odd that most American schoolchildren spend hundreds of hours engaged in a single exercise—the formal test—when few if any of them will ever encounter a similar instrument once they have left school.

### Instruments which Are "Intelligence-Fair"

As already noted, most testing instruments are biased heavily in favor of two varieties of intelligence—linguistic and logical-mathematical. Individuals blessed with this particular combination are likely to do well on most kinds of formal tests, even if they are not particularly adept in the domain actually under investigation. By the same token, individuals with problems in either or both linguistic and logical-mathematical intelligence may fail at measures of other domains, just because they cannot master the particular format of most standard instruments.

The solution—easier to describe than to realize—is to devise instruments which are "intelligence-fair," which peer directly at the intelligence-in-operation rather than proceed via the detour of language and logical faculties. Spatial intelligence can be assessed by having an individual navigate around an unfamiliar territory; bodily intelligence by seeing how a person learns and remembers a new dance or physical exercise; interpersonal intelligence by watching an individual handle a dispute with a sales clerk or navigate a way through a difficult committee meeting. These homely instances indicate that "intelligence-fairer" measures could be devised, though they cannot necessarily be implemented in the psychological laboratory or the testing hall.

### Uses of Multiple Measures

Few practices are more nefarious in education than the drawing of widespread educational implications from the composite score of a single test—like the Weschsler Intelligence Scale for Children. Even intelligence tests contain subtests and, at the very least, recommendations ought to take into account the "scatter" on these tests and the strategies for approaching particular items (Kaplan 1983).

Attention to a range of measures designed specifically to tap different facets of the capacity in question is even more desirable. Consider, for example, the admission standards of a program for gifted children. Conservatively speaking, 75 percent of the programs in the country simply admit on the basis of IQ—a score of 129, and you are out, 131, and you are in. How unfortunate! I have no objection to IQ as one consideration, but why not attend as well to the products which a child has already fashioned, the child's goals and desire for a program, performance during a trial period with "gifted" children, and other unobtrusive measures? I often feel that enormous educational progress would be made simply if the Secretary of Education appeared in front of the television cameras, not accompanied by a single "one-dimensional" wall chart, but against the backdrop of a half-dozen disparate graphic displays, each monitoring a distinctly different aspect of learning and productivity.

*Sensitivites to individual differences can become part of the teacher's competence.*

### Sensitivity to Individual Differences, Developmental Levels, and Forms of Expertise

Assessment programs which fail to take into account the vast differences among individuals, developmental levels, and varieties of expertise are increasingly anachronistic. Formal testing could, in principle, be adjusted to take these documented variations into account. But it would require a suspension of some of the key assumptions of standardized testing, such as uniformity of individuals in key respects and the penchant for cost-efficient instruments.

Individual differences should also be highlighted when educating teachers and assessors. Those charged with the responsibility of assessing youngsters need to be introduced formally to such distinctions; one cannot expect teachers to arrive at empirically valid taxonomies of individual differences on their own. Such an introduction should occur in education courses or during teaching apprenticeships. Once introduced to these distinctions, and given the opportunity to observe and to work with children who exhibit different profiles, these distinctions come to life for teachers.

It then becomes possible to take these differences into account in a tacit way. Good teachers—whether they teach second grade, piano to toddlers, or research design to graduate students—have always realized that different approaches will be effective with different kinds of students. Such sensitivities to individual differences can become part of the teacher's competence and can be drawn upon in the course of regular instruction as well as during assessment. It is also possible—and perhaps optimal—for teachers to season their own intuitive sense of individual differences with judicious occasions of assessment, crafted with the particular domain of practice in mind.

### Use of Intrinsically Interesting and Motivating Materials

One of the most objectionable, though seldom remarked upon, features of formal testing is the intrinsic dullness of the materials. How often does *anyone* get excited about a test or a particular item on a test? It was probably only when, as a result of "sunshine" legislation, it became possible for test takers to challenge the answer keys used by testing organizations, that discussion of individual test items ever occupied space in a publication which anyone would voluntarily read.

It does not have to be that way. A good assessment instrument can be a learning experience. But more to the point, it is extremely desirable to have assessment occur in a context of students working on problems, projects, or products which genuinely engage them, which hold their interest and motivate them to do well. Such exercises may not be as easy to design as the standard multiple-choice entry; but they are far more likely to elicit a student's full repertoire of skills and to yield information that is useful for subsequent advice and placement.

### Application of Assessment for the Student's Benefit

An equally lamentable aspect of formal testing is the use made of scores. Individuals receive the scores, see their percentile ranks, and draw a conclusion about their scholastic, if not their overall, merit. In my own view, psychologists spend far too much time ranking individuals and not nearly enough time helping them. All assessment should be undertaken primarily to aid students. It is incumbent upon the assessor to provide feedback to the student that will be helpful at the present time—identifying areas of strength as well as weakness, giving suggestions of what to study or work on, pointing out which habits are productive and which are not, indicating what can be expected in the way of future assessments, and the like. It is especially important that some of the feedback take the form of con-

# Table 1
# Dimensions Examined in Project Spectrum

## Activities which Sample Different Cognitive Strengths:

| | | |
|---|---|---|
| Music | Production Measures: | Happy Birthday<br>New Songs—Up in the Air<br>—Animal Song |
| | Perception Measures: | Montessori Bells<br>Incidental Music Task |
| Language | Narrative Measure: | Storytelling Board |
| | Descriptive Measure: | Reporter Task |
| Numbers | Counting Measure: | Dinosaur Game |
| | Calculating Measure: | Bus Game |
| Science | Hypothesis-Testing Measure: | Water Table Activity |
| | Logical Inference Measure: | Treasure Hunt Game |
| | Mechanical Measure: | Assembly Task |
| | Naturalist Measure: | Discovery Area |
| Visual Arts | Drawing Measures: | Art Portfolios<br>Farm Animal, person,<br>imaginary animal |
| | 3-D Measure: | (Clay Activity) |
| Movement | Creative Movement Measure: | Biweekly Movement<br>Curriculum |
| | Athletics Measure: | Obstacle Course |
| Social | Social Analysis Measure: | Classroom Model |
| | Social Roles Measure: | Observations of children's<br>interactive styles |

## Measures of Working Styles:

Child is   easily engaged/reluctant to engage in activity
confident/tentative
playful/serious
focused/distractible
persistent/frustrated by task
reflects on own work/impulsive
apt to work slowly/apt to work quickly
conversational/quiet

---

### Table 1 cont.

Child    responds to visual/auditory/kinesthetic cues
                  demonstrates planful approach
                  brings personal agenda/strength to task
                  finds humor in content area
                  uses materials in unexpected ways
                  shows pride in accomplishment
                  shows attention to detail/is observant
                  is curious about materials
                  shows concern over "correct" answer
                  focuses on interaction with adult
                  transforms task/material

---

crete suggestions and indicate relative strengths to build upon, independent of rank within a comparable group of students.

Armed with findings about human cognition and development, and in light of these desiderata for a new approach to assessment, it should be possible to begin to design programs which are more adequate than those which exist today. Without having any grand design to create a "new alternative to formal testing,'" my colleagues and I at Harvard Project Zero have become engaged in a number of projects over the last several years which feature new approaches to assessment. In the following sections of this chapter, I describe our two principal efforts at the present time. I then attempt to place these efforts within a broader picture of assessment in the schools and in society as a whole.

## PROJECT SPECTRUM—ASSESSMENT AT THE PRESCHOOL LEVEL

Project Spectrum is a collaborative project undertaken by several researchers at Harvard Project Zero in conjunction with our colleague David Feldman at Tufts University and the staff and students of the Eliot-Pearson Children's School in Medford, Massachusetts. The project was originally designed to assess the different intellectual strengths or "intelligences" in a representative group of three- and four-year-old children. As I will indicate, however, it has evolved over its four-year history into a preschool curriculum, with assessment aspects folded in at various points (see Hatch and Gardner

1986; Malkus, Feldman, and Gardner 1988; Sherman, Gardner, and Feldman 1988 for further details).

When we first undertook Project Spectrum, we were interested in whether the cognitive profiles of children three or four years old could be distinguished from one another. Stated differently, we were searching for early indices of the seven intelligences identified in *Frames of Mind*. It soon became apparent, however, that far more than seven intellectual capacities wanted examination; moreover, it was also clear, at least for that age group, that it is important to examine cognitive or working styles (such as attention, planfulness, ability to reflect upon a task) as well as "sheer" cognitive strengths. Thus, at the present time, we monitor in our population approximately fifteen different cognitive strengths as well as a dozen stylistic features (see table 1).

> If one is assessing the domain of interest, it is advisable to present individuals with an ample set of experiences in that domain.

Even as we had to broaden the ensemble of skills at which we were looking, we also came to reconceptualize the nature of our assessment project. Like many others in the assessment field, we had initially assumed that one could assess "potential" or "gifts" directly, without the need for involvement in curriculum or teaching. We have come to believe, however, that this assumption is flawed. There is no "pure potential" apart from some experience in working with a domain or symbol system. As soon as one assesses, one is assessing some form of prior learning, whether or not it has been deemed relevant to the particular target domain. And so, if one wants any assurance that one is assessing the domain of interest, it is advisable to present individuals with an ample set of experiences in that domain.

Let me use an example. Suppose that one is interested in assessing talent at chess. One could see how quickly the person can respond to a light bulb, or one might examine the size of the person's vocabulary. It is conceivable that these two measures might correlate with chess talent, though I would not be surprised if neither did. One could also try to break down chess into its components and assess an individual's spatial imagery or logical reasoning skills or interpersonal skill in outwitting an opponent. Conceivably one or more of these measures might foretell chess wit or wisdom.

What is clear is that, in both of these examples, one is assessing something, whether or not it turns out to be related to facility in chess. One could simply give a chess board to children and see how well they play; but in the absence of knowing the rules of chess, the children are as likely to play chess as the proverbial monkeys are likely to pen the plays of Shakespeare.

This presentation of the chessboard does, however, point to the path that I would endorse. If you want to assess chess potential, you should teach your subjects the rules of the game and let them play chess with one another over a period of months. I have little doubt that the students would sort themselves quite reliably in terms of "chess aptitude" and that the distribution of chess talent in this population would emerge after thirty or forty games.

My colleagues and I have followed this line of thinking in surveying a variety of intellectual domains, including those which utilize linguistic, musical, and/or bodily intelligences. In each case our approach has been to expose students to experiences in the particular domain of interest and to observe the way in which they become engaged in that domain. The ensuing record provides a powerful indication of how much talent or potential the students exhibit in the domain of interest.

Having said a bit about the general philosophy and approach of Project Spectrum, let me indicate how it operates in practice. A Spectrum classroom is equipped with a rich set of materials. There are musical instruments, a fantasy play area, puzzles and games which stimulate numerical and logical thinking, a naturalist area in which students can examine different kinds of biological preparations, and the like, all of which are designed to engage the interest of students and to encourage them to play with these materials. There are also regular activities—like "Weekend News"—which give observers the opportunity to observe the child's oral language skills. A careful observer, watching children interact with these materials and participate in the activities over a semester or a year, gains consideration information about the profile of interests of each child and should also be able to perceive the degree of sophistication with which the materials have been plumbed.

Complementing these enriched classroom materials and activities is a set of tasks and measures which we have designed to look specifically at different intellectual spheres. These tasks are engaging to children and can be introduced in the course of a natural classroom interchange. In the area of number, for example, we feature two games. The dinosaur game pits the child against the experimenter in a race to escape from the dinosaur's mouth to his tail. The number and direction of moves is determined by two dice: one bearing numbers, the second featuring plus and minus signs. The players shake their dice and, at times, the child is allowed to "fix" his or her own or the experimenter's dice. The child's success at this game can be fully quantified, and the score provides a "user-friendly" index of the child's numerical sophistication.

For children who "ceiling" on the dinosaur game, there is the bus task. In this game the child plays the role of bus driver while the experimenter is "the boss." The bus proceeds on its route and, at each stop, some children and adults mount the bus and some depart. Every once in a while "the boss" telephones and asks the driver for a count of how many adults and children are currently on the bus. Tokens are available to aid in the counting. Children at this age do not ordinarily have written numbers or other tally systems at their disposal, but sheer involvement in this game stimulates the most able among them to develop "on-line" a system where they are better able to keep track of the comings and goings on the bus.

> While we wish for scoring systems to be precise and reliable, we recognize that rough-and-ready measures can be useful as well.

In other areas analogous games and exercises have been devised (see Table 1). Some of these exercises feature a fully quantifiable scoring system; others include more holistic and subjective scoring, as appropriate. In certain areas, it is not necessary to devise special exercises: for example, we evaluate talent in the visual arts by rating a collection of "spontaneous" drawings made by the child; and we evaluate social strengths through a checklist which probes how children respond to certain "charged" situations which arise in the ordinary course of events (for example, a new child coming to school, a fight breaking out, a bossy child throwing his weight around). While we wish for our scoring systems to be as precise and reliable as possible, we recognize that rough-and-ready measures can be useful as well.

The school year is divided into biweekly intervals during which a particular set of measures is taken of the children. When the classroom is an experimental one, the exercises are administered and assessed by the experimenter; in an ordinary classroom each teacher decides how to approach the targeted assessments. It is our expectation that most teachers will not wish to administer most tasks formally, nor will they generally assess them using our score sheets. Instead, they will monitor children's activities in an informal way, using our tests and sheets chiefly in instances where there is uncertainty about the child's competence. (I believe that the same philosophy should be followed in the case of standardized instruments, such as intelligence tests, which can be helpful when children appear to be "at-risk.")

By the end of the year, the teachers or experimenters will have amassed a great deal of information about the intellectual strengths and working styles of all the children in the classroom. This material becomes the basis of Spectrum Reports, brief essays which describe the particular pattern exhibited by the child: strengths, weaknesses, stylistic features, and the like. This information is presented relativistically; that is, each child's strengths are described with reference to the child's other strengths and weaknesses. In the less frequent case in which the child stands out in comparison to the entire population of preschoolers, an "absolute" strength or weakness is indicated.

As important as the trajectory of strengths illustrated in the Spectrum Report is the list of recommendations which are offered. Consistent with our belief that psychologists should help rather than rank students, we include in the report concrete suggestions about what might be done at home, in school, and/or in the community, in light of a particular profile of competences and proclivities.

With its detailed assessments and its year-end reports, Project Spectrum raises a number of questions, including the advisability of such an undertaking. Is such detailed assessment really necessary and might it in some way be injurious? Recall that our initial goal was to find out whether individual differences do exist and can be documented at this early age. However, we posed this question not only out of curiosity but because of our belief that such information can be educationally beneficial. The mind of the preschooler is both flexible and trainable; thus, if difficulties can be identified at an early age, they are much more likely to be remediable. By the same token, if our scales identify unusual strengths that have somehow been missed before, the parents or teachers gain the option of seeking special help or training.

However, there is a clear risk to the early labeling by Spectrum, particularly in view of our current practice of describing child abilities in terms of readily recognizable adult "end-states" (for example, dancer, naturalist, mediator). The danger is of premature billeting, by which an early attempt at description ends up by engendering a self-fulfilling prophecy. This risk is best mitigated by two procedures. The first is to stress to consumers of Spectrum Reports that these are descriptions at a particular historical moment; especially when children are young and active, the profile of abilities and disabilities can change dramatically from one year to the next. The second is to maintain Spectrum-like procedures each year. So long as students continue to be exposed to a variety of inviting materials and exercises, and so long as assessment is not a one-shot affair, there is every reason to believe that the cognitive profile will evolve—not remain static—and that subsequent reports will capture the new profile accurately.

> When children are young and active, the profile of abilities and disabilities can change dramatically from one year to the next.

Another question concerns the ultimate purpose of Project Spectrum. Is it simply an assessment program, or can it fulfill a broader and more integrative function? The explicit purpose of Project Spectrum has always been assessment, and the bulk of our efforts have been directed at the production of tasks and instruments which are reliable and which can be used by classroom teachers. For these reasons we are both adapting the instruments to varying degrees of fitness and planning a set of handbooks with varying degrees of detail. Note, however, that Spectrum can constitute a valuable intervention even apart from any formal assessment. That is, the range of exercises provided and the number of intellectual spheres touched upon compare favorably with offerings in most preschool programs. Even if teachers were to decide that they were not primarily interested in the Spectrum assessment materials but simply in the games, or if they used the assessment tools only in cases of children with special problems, these materials could still fulfill an important educational goal.

Indeed, this potential for curricular as well as assessment use is consistent with our belief that the line between curriculum and assessment ought ordinarily to be blurred, particularly at the younger age levels. Moreover, it is our expectation that teachers who regularly use the Spectrum materials would develop that "sixth sense" of individual differences which would allow them to make on-line assessments without necessarily having to use our formal procedures. Thus the Spectrum materials can be seen as potentially shaping teacher understandings and consequently affecting teacher practices in ways that we hope will foster the development of individual potential.

In the current political climate in America, there is tremendous pressure for good programs for preschool children. Most programs either serve as extensions upward from homecare (attachment and social ties) or as extensions downward from school (pre-literate skills). Only a few programs, like the Montessori approach, seem to be fashioned with the particular strengths and needs of the "typical" preschooler in mind. Thus another potential purpose of the Spectrum materials may be to aid in the development of innovative, developmentally sensitive, and student-centered preschool curricula. We feel that our program speaks to the wide range of potentials in the preschool child and fosters creative growth and imaginativeness without constraining development in artificial ways. No matter how well conceived, however, our program is unlikely to be adopted if its efficacy cannot be demonstrated. The existence of an extensive battery which assesses student growth in several areas of competence can document whether a Spectrum program achieves its stated goals.

Even if the majority of teachers do not employ our full paraphernalia, we feel that is it important to have developed these materials for research purposes. Indeed, we are currently carrying out a longitudinal study with Marc Bornstein which examines the relationship between standard measures of infant cognition and attainment and the results of assessment at age four with our array of instruments. This study should broaden our knowledge of the relationship between early measures of infant competence and the range of skills exhibited by preschool children.

## ARTS PROPEL: ASSESSMENT AT THE MIDDLE AND HIGH SCHOOL LEVELS

Like Project Spectrum, ARTS PROPEL is a collaborative project. The partners are Harvard Project Zero, the Educational Testing Service, and the Pittsburgh public school system. As with Project Spectrum, the original aim was to develop new means of assessing intellectual competences, particularly in the arts; over the years there has been a gradual evolution toward curriculum, so that the line between assessment and curriculum has become almost invisible (see Gardner 1989b; Zessoules, Wolf, and Gardner 1988 for further details).

The initial impetus that brought the partners together was the desire to identify youngsters who possessed intellectual strengths which are not detected by standard scholastic aptitude tests. Because the arts are an area of intellect not usually or readily tapped through standard instruments, they were selected as the arena for the collaboration.

> Traditionally, arts education has focused on artistic production. . . . Our desire [is] . . . to tie it closely to other forms of artistic knowledge.

Traditionally, arts education in our country has focused almost exclusively on artistic production. When students are assessed at all, the assessment takes place as a holistic, and often subjective, judgment about the merits of student work. Occasional objective tests sample knowledge of art history or criticism, but these are unusual.

Our desire to keep production central in arts education but to tie it more closely to other forms of artistic knowledge has colored our approach to this project. The name ARTS PROPEL captures the thinking which underlies our approach. Artistic education ought to feature at least three activities: *Artistic Production*—the creation of art objects and the gaining of facility in "thinking in" particular artistic symbol systems; *Artistic Perception*—the ability to make fine and appropriate discriminations in one's own art works and in art works produced by others, including artistic masters; and *Artistic Reflection*—the capacity to step back from works of art, to think about their purpose, the extent to which and the manner in which they have been achieved, and to clarify the nature of one's own productions and perceptions.

In embracing this trio of goals, our ARTS PROPEL team is possibly at odds with the approach called Discipline-Based-Arts Education (DBAE). The DBAE perspective, developed by the Getty Center for Education in the Arts, calls for a kindergarten through twelfth grade sequential curriculum in art history, art production, art criticism, and aesthetics (Eisner 1987; Getty Center 1985). While we share the Getty belief that arts education should not be limited to artistic production, we believe that artistic production ought to remain central in arts education at the pre-collegiate level. In effective arts education, perceptual and reflective activities ought to be ubiquitous; but they should grow naturally out of one's own productions, particularly during the early years of formal education. Historical, critical, and analytic work ought to be directly tied to one's own art work and should not ordinarily be presented as separate disciplines.

> *Domain-projects* are sets of exercises designed to present an idea, concept, or practice central within a particular domain.

As in Project Spectrum, we initially hoped to devise a battery of assessment instruments which would bring to the fore those students possessing talents or potentials in a number of art forms—specifically, creative writing, graphic arts, and musical performance. We wanted these instruments to be useful for all students in an ordinary school system, not just for those who were members of an elite school population or had special training in the arts.

We soon discovered, however, that the likelihood of assessing potential, in the absence of previous training, is as remote in high school art programs as in the preschool classes in which we are working. And so we found ourselves working directly in the region of curriculum development—not in the sense of developing a full-scale curriculum, but rather becoming deeply involved in the curricular concerns which daily preoccupy teachers. Also, our desire to pick out "stars" gave way gradually to wish to develop means of assessing growth and learning in all students.

Our approach in the curricular area is worth chronicling. We develop our materials through an extensive and intensive collaboration among a large number of individuals: skilled artists, dedicated classroom teachers, researchers in developmental psychology, experts in testing and assessment, and arts supervisors and students. Each of our exercises and concepts is reviewed by these various individuals; those which cannot be justified are revised or dropped. At the end of this extensive collaborative process, we expect to have materials that satisfy each of the partners in our project.

The core of our program is the devising of two kinds of instruments, both of which span the region between curriculum and assessment in a way that makes sense to us.

*Domain-projects* are sets of exercises designed to present an idea, concept, or practice which is central within a particular artistic domain. Thus, a specimen domain-project in the visual arts presents the notion of graphic composition, while such a project in imaginative writing deals with character and dialogue in the crafting of a play, and a sample project in music involves the learning which accrues from rehearsing a section of a piece. Each domain-project can be carried out in a few sessions. It is deliberately designed to be flexible: flexible in that it can be fit in different junctures of the standard curriculum and flexible in that teachers can substitute their own examples or questions for those in our specimen projects. We speak of the domain-projects as being curriculum-compatible—capable of being slipped into a variety of standardized (or tailor-made) curricula in a number of ways. The domain-projects each feature several assessment components, some to be used by the students themselves, some by teachers or others charged with assessing student learning.

As an example, let me describe in more detail the current version, the aforementioned domain-project in graphic composition in the visual arts. In an initial session, each student is given a piece of white paper and ten oddly shaped block cutouts. The opening assignment is to drop these cutouts randomly on the background paper and then glue them on—a so-called random composition. Next, the students are given identical sets of the same materials, but this time they are asked to put together a composition to their liking—a deliberate composition. Then they are given work sheets on which they compare the properties of the two compositions. It should be noted that this domain-project, like most others, begins with production but contains sample opportunities for perception (comparing the two compositions) and reflection (articulating the reasons for the differing impact of the two compositions). In a second session, most likely to occur the following week, students are introduced to sets of paintings executed by well-regarded artists. They are asked to describe in their own words the different compositional patterns which they see—balanced, lop-sided, symmetrical, dynamic, and so on. Literal as well as metaphoric descriptions are welcome. The teachers are provided with a discussion of compositional facets of these paintings prepared by an artist consultant. The teachers can make as much use as they like of this accessory material, adapting it to introduce ways of discussing composition, balance, and harmony.

At the conclusion of the session, students are shown some additional pairs of slides and asked to contrast them using the concepts and vocabulary which have been introduced. They are also asked to be on the lookout during the next week for examples of interesting compositions—instances in art work which come to their attention as well as instances in their natural environment which they may have to "crop" on their own. These observations can become the basis for future discussions and can be included in the students' notebooks or portfolios (see below).

In the third session, attempts are made to build upon and integrate the lessons of the first two sessions. There is discussion of what students have collected during the previous week. Then students are asked to plan a second *deliberate composition* and to anticipate what it will look like. They are asked to make the composition which they planned and are allowed to move the cutouts around. Their final assignment is to evaluate their new deliberate composition along the same lines as the earlier compositions but also in light of their newly acquired vocabulary and conceptual understanding. The teacher then fills out score sheets; these evaluate the different compositions produced by the students as well as any enhancement of the students' perceptual and reflective capacities over the course of the exercise.

It is our goal to produce a set of domain-projects for each of the artistic areas in which we are working. Taken together, an ensemble of domain-projects should survey important concepts (for example, style, composition, expressiveness), techniques, procedures, and background knowledge. These allow students to appreciate the full context of a work. The domain-projects are so devised that they can be used more than once a year and also carried over from one year to the next. And of course teachers are encouraged to alter them in whatever way makes sense to them.

Student performance can also be assessed in a developmental scheme. That is, for each domain-project we are defining levels which span the range of performances from novice to student-expert. All teachers will be exposed, during the period of their training, to this full gamut of possible responses and conceptualizations. Scoring then places the students somewhere along this continuum on as many dimensions as are being assessed. Some of the scoring focuses on explicit dimensions which are readily quantified (for example, correct notes in a performance), while some of the scoring calls on more holistic or subjective judgments (the quality of the interpretation in a performance).

Special attention is paid in the assessments to individuating features of students' productions. Thus in domain-projects of poetry writing, it is possible to secure measures of each student's command of imagery, figurative language, rhythmic sensitivity, thematic development, and other aspects of poetic skill. By the same token, in musical performance, the scales which accompany domain-projects are sensitive to technical mastery, fingering, pitch control, rhythmic expertise, interpretive skills, and so on. In reviewing the assessment with students, the teachers can assess more than overall improvement in developmental level; in addition, both students and teachers can discuss the students' progress with reference to particular features of the artistic medium.

The second curriculum-cum-assessment device with which we have been working is called a *portfolio* (or, perhaps more accurately, a *process-folio*). Portfolios are familiar in the arts as repositories of the best works fashioned by a student. Portfolios are the basis of decisions made regarding admission to art school, prizes in a competition, or display in an art gallery.

> **Our process-folios are instruments of learning rather than showpieces of final accomplishment.**

Our process-folios, however, are instruments of learning rather than showpieces of final accomplishment. A PROPEL process-folio contains full process-tracing records of a student's involvement in one or more art works. A typical process-folio contains initial plans, drafts, early self-evaluations; feedback on the part of peers, teachers, and other experts; collections of works which students like or dislike, together with comments on the reasons for the reaction; a record of the final work, together with any relevant comments; and plans for subsequent projects, whether or not these are ever carried out.

Process-folios can fulfill several purposes. They serve as convenient means of collecting information which may be relevant to the growth of individual students over a significant period of time. Process-folios can document the biography of a specific work or domain-project but can also span much longer periods of time and document growth over a year or more. Process-folios focus on students' artistic productions, where they are free to go in a direction which has meaning to them; these stand in contrast to classroom assignments, which may (however unintentionally) be confining.

Process-folios can be extremely valuable to present as well as future teachers, for they serve as complete records of the students' growth. Teachers can assess process-folios on a variety of dimensions: number of entries, richness of entry, degree of reflection shown, improvement in technical skill, achievement of one's goals, interplay of production, perception, and reflection, use of art-historical and art-critical materials, responsiveness to internal and external feedback, development of themes, and the like. Though the PROPEL team has yet to develop prototype scoring mechanisms for the process-folios, such scoring procedures are likely to include some of the dimensions that I have just listed. We are planning to produce specimen process-folios for use and study by both students and teachers.

> While our research goals center on the development of assessment tools, the procedures may prove useful to individuals whose interest is remote from assessment.

But, in my view, the process-folio is most important as an aid and even "silent mentor" to the students. Productive individuals in any domain must go through—at least tacitly—a process of self-monitoring: observing their skills, reassessing their missions, noting their growth or regression. Ultimately, these processes can take place implicitly, but in early education it is advisable to assemble a tangible record in a notebook or some other convenient format. By asking students to keep and review process-folios regularly, we hope to involve them in constant reflection on their activities and to allow them the opportunity to monitor and to learn from their own growth and even their own setbacks. Ultimately, we hope that these process-folios can become rewards in themselves as well as a tangible record of an artistic apprenticeship.

In this way, too, PROPEL parallels our experience with Spectrum. While our own research goals center on the development of powerful and valid assessment tools, the procedures and techniques may prove useful to individuals whose interest is remote from assessment. The domain-projects can be viable classroom exercises, independent of their utility in assessment. By the same token, the process-folios can serve an important educational goal, irrespective of whether they are explicitly tied to assessment by the students, their teachers, or their school districts.

In my view, process-folios have a special role to play in the educational environment of today. At the time of apprenticeships in artistic ateliers, a portfolio or process-folio was perhaps less necessary; after all, the involvement of the master in his own work was completely evident, and students soon became at least accessories to the master's current project. But in the contemporary educational environment, where so much attention is directed toward the inculcation and the testing of particulate knowledge, students may have a pressing (though often unrealized) need: to become involved in significant, long-term projects, where they can reflect upon their development and use their skills in productive ways. As I have noted, such a course has often been the choice of individuals who have become established creative masters; it is only proper to expose young students to this way of thinking, acting, and being.

As currently devised, PROPEL is a pilot project in the area of artistic education for children from ages eleven to seventeen. The required assessment tools are still in the stage of development and formative evaluation; we cannot yet say how successful they will be. It is our belief, however, that our orientation might prove valuable beyond the particular bounds of our current assignment. The completion of domain-projects and the keeping of process-folios could be extended both to younger pupils and to students who are already in college. By the same token, while these procedures have been developed for use in the arts, they may well prove adaptable and welcome in other areas of the curriculum. Some of the critiques which have been leveled at standard teaching and assessment in the arts can be extended to other areas of the curriculum as well, ranging from science and social studies to mathematics.

The projects which we feature in the arts may be applicable across the full high school curriculum. Such is the belief of Theodore Sizer who, as part of his Coalition of Essential Schools, calls for more intensive involvement in a few basic areas of the curriculum and recommends that graduation occur, not upon achievement of sufficiently high test scores or sufficiently numerous Carnegie units, but rather when students can "exhibit" their accomplishments at a satisfactory level of expertise (Sizer 1984). It may seem ironic that two projects which began with narrow assessment goals at opposite ends of the age spectrum now "have designs" across the curriculum and at all ages. I hope that this growth in aspirations is not merely a reflection of arrogance or grandiosity. I prefer to think that educational problems and opportunities extend across the curriculum and that effective pedagogical ideas might be useful across different ages.

There is another, more pragmatic reason for assuming this active stance. In America, the current modes of assessment cast a powerful shadow on what goes on in the classroom and have motivated the large-scale study of which this chapter is part. If the "assessment tail" is going to wag the "curricular dog," it is important for those who are interested in the school curriculum to become involved in assessment issues and to join forces with those whose primary expertise lies in assessment and testing.

As should be evident, our assessment experiments are designed largely as a means of improving the quality of education in America (and possibly elsewhere). The use of these instruments for purposes of selection has been a secondary consideration. In principle, of course, the materials developed for Spectrum and for ARTS PROPEL could be employed by elementary or high school teachers for placement purposes, and in the case of PROPEL process-folios, for college admissions. I am comfortable with such usages because I think

> It is important for those interested in the school curriculum to become involved in assessment issues.

that these forms of information could usefully supplement—and perhaps even replace—the more common standardized testing instruments. In addition, and not incidentally, the assessment techniques on which we are working can provide useful feedback to students, independent of their selection or non-selection. They have valuable educational purpose in themselves.

## ASSESSMENT AT OTHER AGES

Our major research efforts have been devoted to the two projects which I have just described. It is certainly feasible to envision parallel assessment projects for other ages and in other subject domains. Here I would like to mention briefly a number of related assessment efforts, focusing on those in which our research group has had some involvement. I will organize the discussion around the areas of assessment not explored above. Of course, the entire program of research and implementation sketched in this chapter is not comprehensive; we have, however, set down some of the major issues that must be explored further in a wide range of teaching and assessment contexts.

### Early Childhood

In my view there is no pragmatic reason to assess the intellectual proclivities or styles of infants or young toddlers. Children at that age have little experience with most materials used in assessment, and the results of such assessments could well be misused or over-interpreted.

> There is no pragmatic reason to assess the intellectual proclivities or styles of infants or young toddlers.

For research reasons, however, it could be extremely instructive to sample a broader survey of human abilities than are tapped by standard psychological or psychometric measures. One could examine the capacities of one- and two-year-olds to habituate to (or to distinguish among) different kinds of sensory information—linguistic sounds, musical sounds, musical rhythms, abstract pictorial patterns, numerical configurations, and so on. Skill at learning various kinds of motor or sensori-motor substances could also be assayed. While one should guard against attaching undue significance to such early cognitive markers, it would be informative to trace continuities, or lack thereof, between such early signs and the later profile of abilities detected in Project Spectrum. Indeed, in addition to the work mentioned above, the Project Spectrum team is hoping to undertake just such a set of studies with our collaborator Marc Bornstein.

### The Early Elementary Years

The methods used with three- and four-year-olds in Project Spectrum might well be extended upward to kindergarten and to the early years of school. Providing environments for rich exploration, offering tasks with which children can become engaged, devising unobtrusive means of assessing growth, and preparing detailed Spectrum-style reports for parents are all activities which could easily be implemented at the older levels and which might well provide information of use to parents and teachers. Indeed, a chief value of the Spectrum approach is the possibility that it can be carried over from one year, or perhaps even from one quinquennium, to another.

Just as the Project Spectrum ideas could "trickle up" to the primary grades, the ARTS PROPEL approach might profitably "trickle down" to elementary school. Domain-projects, process-folios, and other kinds of reflective activities might be useful tools for teachers working with students aged eight to twelve. A record of student growth extending across annual boundaries is as valuable for older children as it is for younger ones (Carini 1987).

In Indianapolis there is a Key School which is based in significant part on the Theory of Multiple Intelligences. Planned by Patricia Bolanos and seven other teachers and underwritten in the early stages by the Indianapolis public schools and the Lilly Endowment, the school is now functioning as an inner city "option" school, with racially balanced enrollment and an active parent support group (Olson 1988).

The goal of the Key School is to nourish the whole spectrum of human intelligences. To this end, teachers offer regular instruction in such areas as music, dance, visual arts, computing, and Spanish, as well as the "basic" subjects of reading, math, and social studies. But what distinguishes the school as well are a number of special offerings and organizing schemes.

To begin with, each child participates in the "flow area," a rich Spectrum-like corner of the school, where youngsters can play with games and engage in activities appealing to their specific profile of intelligences and interests. Students also participate on a daily basis in small cross-age groups called "pods," in which they have the opportunity to carry out an apprenticeship in an area of special interest, ranging from architecture to astronomy to Hispanic culture. To help tie together the disparate strands of the school, there is also a school-wide theme which changes every nine weeks—initial themes have included "connections" and "changes in time and space."

Thus far, the kinds of assessment which take place in the Key School occur chiefly during the course of regular class activities. As in other elementary schools, the teachers intervene when a problem or difficulty arises. One special feature of the school, however, is the involvement of all children in an individual project during each nine-week period. These projects give the children a chance to mobilize their abilities in the service of the "school theme." Children then present, and record on videotape, the results of their project. The videotape becomes part of the archival material maintained by the school; these visual records should prove of use to future teachers and of considerable interest to the students themselves at a subsequent time.

Other schools, like the Putney School in Vermont, have featured major student projects over the years; and a few selected schools, like the Prospect School (also in Vermont), have maintained student portfolios indefinitely. There is little question that this activity has intrinsic value for the school and the students, emphasizing as it does that learning is intensive as well as extensive, and it accrues gradually over long periods of time. The portfolios at the Prospect School also help teachers to think about student work and about the special characteristics of individual students.

Surprisingly, little assessment of these records themselves, or of their use by students and teachers, has taken place, to my knowledge, probably due to the considerable expense of such assessing activities and the other competing interests of the school staffs. However, these already assembled materials provide a repository of invaluable information which could be drawn on for many purposes and which might be assessed by techniques now being developed in ARTS PRO-PEL. The utility of such methods of learning and documentation was demonstrated in the 1930s by the Eight Year Study, a blue-ribbon investigation undertaken to determine the efficacy of nontraditional methods of education (Aiken 1942). I suspect that if this study were replicated today, these educational procedures would once again be vindicated.

### Computer Support for Domain-Projects

At Project Zero, we are developing an additional set of domain-projects for use with computer software. According to our analysis, there is much powerful software available for use by individuals with pre-existing expertise in a domain. Just to mention a few instances, there is software which allows musicians to compose, artists and architects to draft, programmers to solve problems, and the like.

We have found that novices are typically unable to make use of this software, even if they are motivated to engage in the activities for which the software has been designed. The novices lack the prerequisite skills and concepts, while the software itself does not provide sufficient clues as to its possible uses. We are therefore devising "computer domain-projects"—sample problems and solutions which are provided as databases accompanying the software, as well as manuals which instruct the novices in how to use these problem sets to "educate themselves."

The computer domain-projects have been used only on a pilot basis, but the results are encouraging. Individuals with a moderate amount of musical knowledge and with the desire to compose music have been able to compose and "orchestrate" limericks after just a few hours at the computer terminal. The computer domain-projects provide enough support so that the novice can perform at a journeyman, if not a master, level. Similar domain-projects are being created in the areas of computer programming (aiding students in learning to use PASCAL) and social studies (allowing students to recreate and solve the problems faced by Boston immigrants in the mid-nineteenth century).

Once again, we find that an ingenious curriculum approach can engage students and bring them directly into contact with the "stuff" of a culturally valued domain. And once again, the border between curriculum and assessment becomes blurred, if not irrelevant. In the case of the computer domain-projects, there is no need for extensive separate assessment. Assessment of progress and evaluation of products can be built directly into the use of the domain-project itself. The research can therefore focus directly on the questions of which factors allow some domain-projects to operate successfully and how the domain-projects, as a class of educational vehicles, can be improved.

> We find that an ingenious curriculum can engage students and bring them into contact with the "stuff" of a culturally valued domain.

### College Admissions

A final area of interest to our group is the process of college admissions, particularly as it is practiced at selective colleges. At present there is a disjunction between the actual practices of these schools and the public perception of how one gains admission to them. Most students and parents place undue emphasis on the scores received on college admissions tests. This emphasis is unwarranted because (1) so few colleges are actually selective enough to call for the use of the tests, (2) the tests have little predictive value beyond freshman year, and (3) selective colleges now recognize the importance of extracurricular activities and long-term engagement and follow-through as powerful predictors of success in and beyond college (Willingham 1985).

I sense a shift from the apparent reliance on the results of formal testing to a greater concern with student involvement in long-term projects and to a willingness to consider the kind of record which can be presented in effective portfolios or process-folios. Now what is needed are two coordinated events. First, students and guidance counselors must be apprised of the potential importance of submitting such ancillary materials as part of the college admissions packet. Second, individuals interested in rounded assessment must develop economical means for assessing such projects and process-folios; after all, with thousands of students competing for spaces at selective colleges, it is not practical to devote many hours to each dossier. We hope that the procedures being devised by ARTS PROPEL can be streamlined for such purposes.

> When less was known about individual differences in human beings, the uniform school might have made sense.

## AN INDIVIDUAL-CENTERED SCHOOL

Earlier in this chapter I outlined the assumptions of the "uniform school" where students encounter an identical curriculum, all subjects are taught according to the same procedures, and students are evaluated according to the same formal "standard" instruments. Even though current research throws each of these assumptions into question, they still constitute an ideal in our society.

At one time when the amount of formal knowledge to be conveyed was considerably smaller and when less was known about individual differences in human beings, the uniform school might have made sense. Nowadays, however, it is evident that no individual can learn even an infinitesimal percentage of extant knowledge; choice is inevitable and it might as well be informed. Moreover, now that we know something of the many differences among individuals, it is increasingly indefensible to treat them (to treat ourselves) as if no such differences exist.

On the basis of our foregoing analysis, it is possible to imagine a different school—one which I have termed the "individual-centered school." Such a school recognizes the need for certain basic skills and certain bodies of common knowledge for all students. At the same time, however, this school takes seriously the need for choices in education and the documentable differences among students and strives to make these factors central to the educational process (see Gardner 1987b, 1988b, 1989a, 1991).

In implementing such a school, one would be advised to delineate three distinct roles which can be realized in a number of ways:

(1) the assessment specialist, (2) the student-curriculum broker, and
(3) the school-community broker.

### The Assessment Specialist

It is the job of this individual to carry out regular and appropriate
forms of assessment of the children in the school, to document these
assessments, and to make the results available in appropriate form to
teachers, to parents, and (eventually) to students themselves. The assessments would cover a range of materials, procedures, and instruments. Because assessments would be regular and ongoing in such a
school, the descriptive reports should be constantly updated to provide current information. Of course, in cases where there are special
problems, needs, or skills, a more aggressive intervention may be
necessary.

Our projects have suggested a number of forms that assessment
might take in an individual-centered school. But even when "formal
standard assessment techniques" are utilized, the emphasis should
always fall on making the results of the assessment useful to the consumers—in other words, on the formulation of concrete suggestions
about what the student ought to do next.

### The Student-Curriculum Broker

The student-curriculum broker takes the results of the observations
and analyses carried out by the assessment specialist and translates
them into concrete suggestions for students. These suggestions include courses and electives which the student might take, given his
or her particular strengths and weaknesses, as well as which versions
(or sections) of a course the student ought to take, in light of his or
her particular style of learning.

I am sympathetic to the idea of course electives. These choices
might as well be informed ones, and the student-curriculum broker
is in an excellent position to guide students to courses that they
would find interesting and from which they might profit. However, I
would certainly not endorse the *assignment* of students to particular
electives—in fact, this would be a contradictory notion. Students
should be given options and allowed to make their own choices. If
students bypass courses which ought to be of interest to them or
elect courses for which they apparently have little aptitude, this practice is perfectly acceptable. Indeed, many individuals—myself included—are energized by the challenge of studying areas for which

they apparently have little natural talent. Obstinacy is fine so long as it has been properly put "on notice."

Of course in any school, including this "idealized" one, there will be required courses. The issue is whether these required courses need to be taught in the same manner to all students. To the extent that there are teachers who favor different teaching styles or who themselves can offer instruction in more than one way, information about these options ought to be used to guide students to the appropriate "section." Most subjects in a core curriculum can be presented in a variety of ways, and there is no reason why this should not happen.

Even where "custom-teaching" cannot take place, it is still possible to help individual students learn in the most effective way.

> Even where "custom-teaching" cannot take place, it is still possible to help individual students learn in the most effective way.

Many educational and technological inventions can aid students who exhibit a characteristic learning style to deal with information or to carry out analyses which might otherwise cause difficulties. To take just one example, students with deficient or limited spatial imagery have often encountered difficulties with geometry and physics. Now the existence of software which can supplement imagery by providing it "on-line" should make these subjects easier and far more palatable to these students. The task of the student-curriculum broker is to increase the chances that such salubrious student software matches can be effected.

### The School-Community Broker

Even though it would be optimal if all educational needs could be met within the walls of each school, it is not feasible. Schools can do a good job in covering the traditional curriculum and in developing some of the intelligences, but it is unrealistic to expect them to meet all needs and to cover all subjects.

Here the school-community broker comes in. It is this person's job to survey the educational opportunities which are available in the community—apprenticeships, mentorships, clubs, professions, art forms, big sisters, big brothers, and so on—and to organize them in a database. Information about print and media resources ought to be incorporated as well. This information can then be made available to students who will have the option of broadening their learning in after-school programs or, perhaps, during the school day itself. If the broker is successful, the students are more likely to develop a range of intelligences and to find an appropriate vocational and avocational niche within their community.

In truth, I do not worry about those students who are excellent in linguistic and logical pursuits. They will likely find their rewards within the school, in standard gifted programs, or in special advanced sections or honors groups. The educational challenge is to provide comparable opportunities for students who have cognitive and personal strengths which are not well-addressed by the standard school curriculum.

In the past, these students "found themselves"—if they did at all!—by accident or happenstance. The crystallizing experiences which can be so crucial in helping an individual to discover a lifelong vocation or avocation were rarely brought about through planning (Walters and Gardner 1986). To my mind, the most important educational event in a student's life is the discovery of some situation or material which excites and motivates the student to make a commitment to master the materials necessary for a deeper grasp of this area. It is the job of the school-community broker to engender more frequent crystallizations in more different fields, and most especially those crystallizations which are valued in the community-at-large but are often invisible in the school.

The question may be raised about the advisability of promoting matches in domains which do not appear to be viable vocational options for students. Certainly, efforts should be made to locate options which are both compatible with the student's proclivities and relevant for careers. Yet, I do not feel that the danger of "useless" matches need concern us much. First of all, it is better for a student to have some kind of engagement than none at all; the very feelings of competence and experience of mastering a domain may turn out to have considerable transfer value. Second, the scholastic matches which are currently valued in school do not necessarily forecast vocational success in later life; the personal intelligences may well be more important for such success. Third, it is short-sighted to try to calculate in advance just which combinations of intelligences will be valued in the future or which amalgam can be drawn upon profitably by a specific individual. Finally, even if a match cannot point the way directly to a career choice, it can at least delineate an area in which the individual can expect to gain satisfaction of a personal or avocational sort in the future.

I have described these curricular, assessment, and educational opportunities in terms of individual roles only as a convenience. School systems can evolve comfortable means of realizing these roles, perhaps by drawing on guidance counselors or other existing personnel or by creating centralized sources of information.

Implementing these roles, however, is of little avail if the school and the surrounding community are not dedicated to education across a broad spectrum of areas and abilities. Taken in combination with a supportive educational community, these roles ought to aid in the realization of a school in which individual differences are taken seriously, cherished, fostered, and mobilized to worthwhile personal and community ends.

My description of one school of the future should lay to rest any lurking fears that I am out to abolish the role of testing and assessment in the schools. If anything, the program I have laid out would call for the development of a cadre of specialists that does not now exist and that would be called on to carry out work which is even more pivotal than that now being carried out by psychologists, guidance counselors, and testing experts. I am not lobbying for the decimation of testing but for a broadening and a deepening of the assessment roles.

At the same time, I have no aim to minimize the role of teachers. Indeed, it is my hope that this scheme will free teachers to teach as expertly as possible in the ways that they find comfortable. This kind of education can only take place if teachers are highly professionalized and have responsibility for planning their curricula and for running their classes. (The model of the Indianapolis Key School is relevant here.) The improvement of teaching conditions and the upgrading of the quality of teacher-training programs central to this enterprise are topics of signal importance in our society but fall beyond the scope of this chapter.

## TOWARD THE ASSESSING SOCIETY

This chapter has been an extended essay in favor of regular assessment occurring in a natural fashion throughout the educational system and across the trajectory of life-long learning. I have reviewed a sizable body of theoretical innovations and experimental evidence, which, by and large, points up problems with standard formal testing as an exclusive mode of assessment. Many of these findings suggest that it would be more fruitful to create environments in which assessments occur naturally and to devise curriculum entities, like domain-projects and process-folios, which lend themselves to assessment within the context of their production. It would be an exaggeration to say that I have called for a reintroduction of the apprentice method. Yet I do claim that we have moved too far from that mode of assessment; contemporary assessment might well be informed by some of the concepts and assumptions associated with traditional apprenticeships.

> America has veered in the direction of formal testing without adequate consideration of the limitations of an emphasis on that approach.

Indeed, if one considers "formal testing" and "apprentice-style assessment" as two poles of assessment, it could be said that America today has veered too far in the direction of formal testing without adequate consideration of the costs and limitations of an exclusive emphasis on that approach. Even outside the realm of physics, an excessive action calls for a reaction—one reason why this chapter stresses the advantages of more naturalistic, context-sensitive, and ecologically valid modes of assessment. Standard formal tests have their place—for example, in initial screening of certain "at-risk" populations—but users should know their limitations as well.

Some objections to the perspective introduced here can be anticipated. One is the claim that formal testing is, as advertised, objective and that I am calling for a regression to subjective forms of evaluation. I reject this characterization for two reasons. First of all, there is no reason in principle to regard the assessment of domain-projects, process-folios, or Spectrum-style measures as intrinsically less objective than other forms. Reliability can be achieved in these domains as well. The establishment of reliability has not been a focus of these projects; however, the conceptual and psychometric tools exist to investigate reliability in these cases. Moreover, these assessment measures are more likely to possess "ecological" validity.

A second retort to this characterization has to do with the alleged objectivity or non-bias of standard formal tests. In a technical sense, it is true that the best of these instruments avoid the dangers of subjectivity and statistical bias. However, any kind of instrument is necessarily skewed toward one kind (or a few kinds) of individual and one (or a few) intellectual and cognitive styles. Formal tests are especially friendly to those individuals who possess a certain blend of linguistic and logical intelligences and who are comfortable in being assessed in a decontextualized setting under timed and impersonal conditions. Correlatively, such tests are biased against individuals who do not exhibit that blend of intelligences, those whose strengths show up better in sustained projects or when they are examined in situ.

I believe that, especially when resources are scarce, every individual ought to have the opportunity to show her or his strength. There is no objection to a "high scorer" being able to show off a string of eight hundreds to a college admissions staff; by the same token, individuals with other cognitive or stylistic strengths ought to have their day as well.

There are those who might be in sympathy with the line of analysis pursued here and yet would reject its implications because of considerations of cost or efficiency. According to this argument, it is simply too inefficient or expensive to mobilize the country around more sustained forms of assessment; and so, even if formal testing is imperfect, we will have to settle for it and simply try to improve it as much as possible.

This line of argument has a surface plausibility, but I reject it as well. To be sure, formal testing is now cost-effective, but it has taken millions, perhaps billions of dollars expended over many decades to bring it to its current far-from-perfect state. Nor do I think that more money spent on current testing would improve it more than marginally. (I do believe that it is worthwhile to spend money on diagnostic and interactive forms of testing, but those are not topics which I am treating in the present chapter.)

Our current pilot projects, while dependent on research funds, are modest by any standard. In each instance we believe that the main points of the approach can be taught readily to teachers and made available to interested schools or school districts. We subscribe to Theodore Sizer's estimate that a move toward more qualitative forms of education (and perhaps also to higher-quality education) might increase costs by ten to fifteen percent but probably not more.

The major obstacle I see to assessment-in-context is not availability of resources but rather lack of will. There is in the country today an enormous desire to make education uniform, to treat all students in the same way, and to apply the same kind of one-dimensional metrics to all. This trend is inappropriate on specific grounds and distasteful on ethical grounds. The current sentiment is based in part on an understandable disaffection with some of the excesses of earlier educational experiments but, to a disturbing degree, it is also based on a general hostility to students, teachers, and the learning process. In other countries, where the educational process is held in higher regard, it has proved possible to have higher-quality education without subscribing to some of the worst features of one-dimensional educational thinking and assessment.

> The major obstacle I see to assessment-in-context is not availability of resources but rather lack of will.

It is not difficult to sketch out the reasons for the tentative national consensus on the need for more testing and more uniform schools. Understandable uneasiness with poor student performance in the early 1980s resulted in a general indictment of contemporary education, which was blamed for a multitude of societal sins. Government officials, especially state administrators and legislators, entered the fray; the price paid for increased financial support was simple—more testing and more accountability based on testing. The fact that few students of education were entirely comfortable with the diagnosis or the purported cure was not relevant. After all, political officials rarely pore over the relevant literature; they almost reflexively "search for scapegoats" and call for the "quick fix."

It is unfortunate that few public officials or societal leaders have put forth an alternative point of view on these issues. If significant forces or interest groups in this country were to dedicate themselves to a different model of education, which subscribes to the assessment-and-schooling philosophy outlined here, I have every confidence that they could implement it without breaking the bank. It would be necessary for a wider gamut of individuals to "pitch in"; for college faculty to examine the process-folios that are submitted; for community members to offer mentorships, apprenticeships, or "special pods"; for parents to find out what their children are doing in school and to work with them (or at least encourage them) on their projects. These suggestions may sound revolutionary, but they are daily occurrences in excellent educational settings in the United States and abroad. Indeed, it is hard to imagine quality education in the absence of such a cooperative ambiance (Grant 1978, Grant 1988).

To my way of thinking, the ultimate policy debate is—or at least should be—centered on competing concepts of the purposes and aims of education. As I have intimated above, the "formal standard testing" view harbors a concept of education as a collection of individual elements of information which are to be mastered and then spewed back in a decontextualized setting. On this "bucket view" it is expected that individuals who acquire a sufficient amount of such knowledge will be effective members of the society.

The "assessment view" values the development with the vision of individual-centered schooling that I have outlined above. Some individuals sympathetic to a focus on assessment might still object to the individual-centered view, seeing it as an impractical or romantic view of education; they would prefer more naturalistic modes of assessment in the service of a rigorous curriculum. To these individuals I would respond, perhaps surprisingly, by unequivocally endorsing the importance of rigor. There is nothing in an "individual-centered" approach which questions rigor; in any decent apprenticeship, rigor is assumed. If anything, it is the sophomoric "multiple-choice-cum-isolated-fact" mentality that sacrifices genuine rigor for superficial conformity. I fully embrace rigorous curricula in an individual-based school; I simply call for a broader menu of curricular options.

I obviously think that the assessment approach and the individual-centered school constitute a more noble educational vision. Both are more in keeping with American democratic and pluralistic values (Dewey 1938). I also think that this vision is more consistent with what has been established in recent decades by scientific study of human growth and learning. Schools in the future ought to be so crafted that they are consistent with this vision. In the end, whatever the forms and the incidence of "official assessments," the actual daily learning in schools, as well as the learning stimulated long after "formal" school has been completed, should be its own reward.

# REFERENCES

Aiken, W. 1942. *The story of the Eight Year Study.* New York: Harper and Brothers.

Anderson, M. 1987. Inspection time and the development of intelligence. Paper delivered to the British Psychological Society Conference, Sussex University.

Bamberger, J. 1982. Revisiting children's drawings of simple rhythms: A function for reflection-in-action. In *U-shaped behavioral growth,* ed. S. Strauss. New York: Academic Press.

Bijou, S., and D. Baer. 1965. *Child development.* New York: Appleton Century Crofts.

Binet, A., and T. Simon. 1905. Méthodes nouvelles pour le diagnostique du niveau intellectuel des anormaux. *L'année psychologique II:* 245–336.

Block, N., and G. Dworkin. 1976. *The IQ controversy.* New York: Pantheon.

Bloom, A. 1987. *The closing of the American mind.* New York: Simon and Schuster.

Brainerd, C. 1978. The stage question in cognitive-developmental theory. *The Behavioral and Brain Sciences* 2:173–213.

Brown, R., and R. Herrnstein. 1975. *Psychology.* Boston: Little Brown.

Buros, O. 1978. *The eighth mental measurements yearbook.* Highland Park, NJ: Gryphon Press.

Carini, P. 1987. Another way of looking. Paper presented at the Cambridge School Conference, Weston, Massachusetts, October.

Case, R. 1985. *Intellectual development: Birth to adolescence.* New York: Academic Press.

Collins, A., J. S. Brown, and S. E. Newman. 1989. Cognitive apprenticeship: Teaching the craft of reading, writing, and mathematics. In *Cognition and instruction: issues and agendas,* ed. L. Resnick. Hillsdale, NJ: Lawrence Erlbaum.

Cronbach, L. 1984. *Essentials of psychological testing.* New York: Harper and Row.

Cronbach, L., and R. Snow. 1977. *Aptitudes and instructional methods.* New York: Irvington.

Cross, K. P., and T. Angelo. 1988. *Classroom assessment techniques: A handbook for faculty.* Ann Arbor: National Center for Research to Improve Postsecondary Teaching and Learning (NCRIPTL).

Csikszentmihalyi, M. 1988. Society, culture, and persons: A systems view of creativity. In *The nature of creativity,* ed. R. Sternberg. New York: Cambridge University Press.

Csikszentmihalyi, M., and R. Robinson. 1986. Culture, time, and the development of talent. In *Conceptions of giftedness,* ed. R. Sternberg and J. Davidson. New York: Cambridge Press.

Dewey, J. 1938. *Experience and education.* New York: Collier.

Eisner, E. 1987. Structure and magic in discipline-based arts education. In *Proceedings of a National Invitational Conference,* Los Angeles: The Getty Center for Education in the Arts.

Eysenck, H. J. 1967. Intelligence assessment A theoretical and experimental approach. *British Journal of Educational Psychology* 37:81–98.

―――. 1979. *The nature and measurement of intelligence.* New York: Springer-Verlag.

Feldman, D. 1980. *Beyond universals in cognitive development.* Norwood, NJ: Ablex.

Fischer, K. W. 1980. A theory of cognitive development. *Psychological Review* 87:477–531.

Fodor, J. 1983. *The modularity of mind.* Cambridge: MIT Press.

Gardner, H. 1975. *The shattered mind.* New York: Knopf.

―――. 1982. *Art, mind, and brain.* New York: Basic Books.

―――. 1983. *Frames of mind.* New York: Basic Books.

―――. 1985. *The mind's new science.* New York: Basic Books.

―――. 1986. The development of symbolic literacy. In *Toward a greater understanding of literacy,* ed. M. Wrolstad and D. Fisher. New York: Praeger.

―――. 1987a. Developing the spectrum of human intelligence. *Harvard Education Review* 57:187–93.

―――. 1987b. An individual-centered curriculum. In *The schools we've got, the schools we need.* Washington, DC: Council of Chief State School Officers and the American Association of Colleges of Teacher Education.

―――. 1988a. Creative lives and creative works: A synthetic scientific approach. In *The nature of creativity,* ed. R. J. Sternberg. New York: Cambridge University Press.

―――. 1988b. Mobilizing resources for individual-centered education. In *Technology in education: Looking toward 2020,* ed. R. Nickerson. Hillsdale, NJ: Lawrence Erlbaum.

―――. 1989a. Balancing specialized and comprehensive knowledge. In *Schooling for tomorrow: Directing reforms to issues that count,* ed. T. Sergiovanni. Boston: Allyn and Bacon.

————. 1989b. Zero-based arts education: An introduction to ARTS PROPEL. *Studies in Education,* 30(2), 71–83.

————. 1991. The school of the future. In *Ways of Knowing,* ed. J. Brockman. Englewood Cliffs, NJ: Prentice Hall.

Gardner, H., and C. Wolf. 1988. The fruits of asynchrony: Creativity from a psychological point of view. *Adolescent psychiatry* 15:106–23.

Gardner, H., V. Howard, and D. Perkins. 1974. Symbol systems: A philosophical, psychological and educational investigation. In *Media and symbols,* ed. D. Olson. Chicago: University of Chicago Press.

Gelman, R. 1978. Cognitive development. *Annual Review of Psychology* 29:297–332.

Getty Center for Education in the Arts. 1985. *Beyond creating: The place for art in American schools.* Los Angeles: J. Paul Getty Trust.

Goodman, N. 1976. *Languages of art.* Indianapolis: Hackett.

Gould, S. J. 1981. *The mismeasure of man.* New York: Norton.

Grant, D., ed. 1978. *On competence.* San Francisco: Jossey-Bass.

Grant, G. 1988. *The world we created at Hamilton High.* Cambridge: Harvard University Press.

Gruber, H. 1981. *Darwin on man.* 2d ed. Chicago: University of Chicago Press.

————. 1985. Giftedness and moral responsibility: Creative thinking and human survival. In *The gifted and talented: Developmental perspectives,* ed. F. Horowitz and M. O'Brien. Washington: American Psychological Association.

Guilford, J. P. 1950. Creativity. *American Psychologist* 5:444–54.

————. 1967. *The nature of human intelligence.* New York: McGraw Hill.

Hatch, T., and H. Gardner. 1986. From testing intelligence to assessing competences: A pluralistic view of intellect. *The Roeper Review* 8:147–50.

Hirsch, E. D. 1987. *Cultural literacy.* Boston: Houghton Mifflin.

Hoffmann, B. 1962. *The tyranny of testing.* New York: Crowel-Collier Press.

Jencks, C. 1972. *Inequality.* New York: Basic Books.

Jensen, A. R. 1980. *Bias in mental testing.* New York: Free Press.

————. 1987. Individual differences in the Hick paradigm. In *Speed of information processing and intelligence,* ed. P. Vernon. Norwood, NJ: Ablex.

Kagan, J., and N. Kogan. 1970. Individual variation in cognitive processing. In *Handbook of child psychology*, ed. P. Mussen. New York: Wiley.

Kaplan, E. 1983. Process and achievement revisited. In *Toward a holistic developmental psychology*, ed. S. Wapner and B. Kaplan. Hillsdale, NJ: Lawrence Erlbaum.

Laboratory of Comparative Human Cognition. 1982. Culture and intelligence. In *Handbook of human intelligence*, ed. R. J. Sternberg. New York: Cambridge University Press.

Langer, S. K. 1942. *Philosophy in a new key*. Cambridge: Harvard University Press.

Lave, J. 1980. What's special about experiments as contexts for thinking? *Quarterly Newsletter of the Laboratory of Comparative Human Cognition* 2: 86–91.

Malkus, U., D. Feldman, and H. Gardner. 1988. Dimensions of mind in early childhood. In *The psychological bases of early childhood*, ed. A. D. Pelligrini. Chichester, UK: Wiley.

Messick, S. 1988. Validity. In *Educational measurement*. 3d ed., ed. R. Linn. New York: Macmillan.

Newell, A., and H. A. Simon. 1972. *Human problem-solving*. Englewood Cliffs, NJ: Prentice-Hall.

Olson, L. 1988. Children flourish here: 8 teachers and a theory changed a school world. *Education Week* 7 (18): 1, 18–19.

Perkins, D. 1981. *The mind's best work*. Cambridge: Harvard University Press.

Piaget, J. 1983. Piaget's theory. In *Manual of child psychology*, ed. P. Mussen. New York: Wiley.

Polanyi, M. 1958. *Personal knowledge*. Chicago: University of Chicago Press.

Ravitch, D., and C. Finn. 1987. *What do our seventeen-year-olds know?* New York: Harper and Row.

Resnick, L. 1987. The 1987 presidential address: Learning in school and out. *Educational Researcher* 16(9): 13–20.

Rogoff, B. 1982. Integrating context and cognitive development. In *Advances in developmental psychology*, vol. 2, ed. M. Lamb and A. Brown. Hillsdale, NJ: Lawrence Erlbaum.

Scribner, S. 1986. Thinking in action: Some characteristics of practical thought. In *Practical Intelligence*, ed. R. Sternberg and R. K. Wagner. New York: Cambridge University Press.

Sizer, T. 1984. *Horace's compromise*. Boston: Houghton Mifflin.

Squire, L. 1986. Mechanisms of memory. *Science* 232: 1612–19.

Sternberg, R. 1977. *Intelligence, information processing, and analogical reasoning.* Hillsdale, NJ: Lawrence Erlbaum.

———. 1985. *Beyond IQ.* New York: Cambridge University Press.

Sternberg, R., ed. 1988. *The nature of creativity.* New York: Cambridge University Press.

Strauss, S. 1982. *U-shaped behavioral growth.* New York: Academic Press.

Thurstone, L. 1938. *Primary mental abilities.* Chicago: University of Chicago Press.

Uzgiris, I., and J. McV. Hunt. 1966. *An instrument for assessing infant intellectual development.* Urbana, IL: University of Illinois Press.

Wallach, M. 1971. *The intelligence/creativity distinction.* Morristown, NJ: General Learning Press.

———. 1985. Creativity testing and giftedness. In *The gifted and talented: Developmental perspectives,* ed. F. Horowitz and M. O'Brien. Washington, DC: American Psychological Association.

Walters, J., and H. Gardner, 1986. *The crystallizing experience. In Conceptions of giftedness,* ed. R. Sternberg and J. Davidson. New York: Cambridge University Press.

Wexler-Sherman, C., H. Gardner, and D. H. Feldman. 1988. A pluralistic view of early assessment: The Project Spectrum approach. *Theory into Practice* 27(1): 77–83.

Willingham, W. 1985. *Success in college.* New York: College Entrance Examination Board (CEEB).

Zessoules, R., D. Wolf, and H. Gardner. 1988. A better balance: ARTS PROPEL as an alternative to discipline-based art education. In *Beyond discipline-based art education,* ed. J. Burton, A. Lederman, and P. London. North Dartmouth, MA: University Council on Art Education.

# Authors

**Jie-Qi Chen** is a professor at the Erikson Institute for Advanced Studies in Child Development and co-director for Erikson's Schools Project. A former researcher at the Harvard Graduate School of Education's Project Zero, she edited the multiple intelligences-based curriculum book *Early Learning Activities Guide.*

**Howard Gardner** is a psychologist specializing in developmental psychology and neuropsychology. He is co-director of Project Zero, an educational research organization at the Harvard Graduate School of Education. His 1983 book *Frames of Mind* presented his theory of multiple intelligences.

**Thomas Hatch** is a research associate at the Harvard Graduate School of Education's Project Zero.

**Elizabeth A. Hebert** is principal of Crow Island Elementary School in Winnetka, Illinois. She lectures and writes extensively about the uses of student portfolios and is a frequent contributor to *Educational Leadership.*

**C. June Maker** is a professor at the University of Arizona. She is the author or coauthor of numerous articles, chapters, and books on the education of gifted learners.

**Aleene B. Nielson** is an adjunct assistant professor at the University of Arizona and one of three developers of the DISCOVER Assessment Process and the DISCOVER Curriculum Model. She coauthored *Teaching Models in Education of the Gifted* and *Curriculum Development and Teaching Strategies for Gifted Learners.*

**Judith A. Rogers** is coordinator of DISCOVER III, a Jacob Javits Gifted and Talented Act Program at the University of Arizona College of Education. She collaborates with practitioners to improve learning environments for all learners.

**Evangeline Harris Stefanakis** is a research assistant at Harvard's Project Zero and an assistant professor at Lesley College in Cambridge, Massachusetts. She has taught bilingual, early childhood, and special education. Her current research focuses on assessing and teaching children from diverse language and cultural backgrounds.

**Bruce Torff** is a researcher in the fields of education and cognitive psychology. As project director at Harvard Project Zero, he conducts research on implicit learning, symbolic development, professional development, multiple intelligences, and the role of the arts in the basic curriculum. Bruce is also a piano performer and composer.

**Joseph M. Walters** is a senior scientist at TERC, a research and development company in Cambridge, Massachusetts, that specializes in mathematics, science, and technology education. He is the coauthor of the computer programs *Just Enough Pascal* and *Immigrant 1850.*

# Acknowledgments

Grateful acknowledgment is made to the following authors and agents for their permission to reprint copyrighted materials.

## SECTION 1

Thomas Hatch and Howard Gardner for "If Binet Had Looked Beyond the Classroom: The Assessment of Multiple Intelligences" by Thomas Hatch and Howard Gardner. From *International Journal of Educational Research*, vol. 14, no. 5, 415–29. Copyright © 1990 by Thomas Hatch and Howard Gardner. Reprinted with permission. All rights reserved.

Jie-Qi Chen and Howard Gardner for "Alternative Assessment from a Multiple Intelligences Perspective" by Jie-Qi Chen and Howard Gardner. A paper prepared for *Beyond Traditional Intellectual Assessment: Contemporary and Emerging Theories, Tests, and Issues*, edited by D. F. Flanagan, J. L. Genshaft, and P. L. Harrison, published by Guilford Publications. Copyright © 1994 by Guilford Publications. Reprinted with permission. All rights reserved.

Thomas Hatch for "From Research to Reform: Finding Better Ways to Put Theory into Practice" by Thomas Hatch. From *educational HORIZONS*, vol. 72, summer 1993, 197–202. Copyright © 1993 by Thomas Hatch. Reprinted with permission. All rights reserved.

## SECTION 2

Association for Supervision and Curriculum Development (ASCD) for "Portfolios Invite Reflection—From Students *and* Staff" by Elizabeth A. Hebert. From *Educational Leadership,* vol. 49, no. 8, 58–61, May 1992. Copyright © 1992 by ASCD. Reprinted with permission. All rights reserved.

Evangeline Harris Stefanakis for "The Power in Portfolios: 'A Way for Sitting Beside' Each Learner" by Evangeline Harris Stefanakis. A paper prepared in May 1995. Copyright © 1995 by Evangeline Harris Stefanakis. Reprinted with permission. All rights reserved.

Officers and Fellows of Harvard University, Cambridge, Massachusetts, and Howard Gardner for "Domain Projects as Assessment Vehicles in a Computer-Rich Environment" by Joseph Walters and Howard Gardner. A technical report for the Center for Technology in Education, August 1990. Copyright © 1990 by Officers and Fellows of Harvard University and Howard Gardner. Reprinted with permission. All rights reserved.

## SECTION 3

The Council for Exceptional Children (CEC) for "Giftedness, Diversity, and Problem Solving" by C. June Maker, Aleene B. Nielson, and Judith A. Rogers. From *Teaching Exceptional Children,* Fall 1994, 4–19. Copyright © 1994 by CEC. Reprinted with permission. All rights reserved.

C. June Maker for "Authentic Assessment of Problem Solving and Giftedness in Secondary School Students" by C. June Maker. From *Journal of Secondary Gifted Education,* Fall 1994, 19–29. Copyright © 1994 by C. June Maker. Reprinted with permission. All rights reserved.

Howard Gardner for "Assessment in Context: The Alternative to Standardized Testing" by Howard Gardner. From *Multiple Intelligences: The Theory in Practice,* edited by Howard Gardner, 161–83 (New York: Basic Books). Copyright © 1993 by Howard Gardner. Reprinted with permission. All rights reserved.

# Index

Achievement, culture implications of, 8–9
Adams, M., 31, 39, 45, 47–49
Aiken, W., 192
Alvino, J. J., 112
Anderson, Michael, 157
Angelo, T., 169
Apprenticeships
  assessment of, 14–15, 170–71
  choice of formal testing as opposed to, 154–55
Army Alpha, 156
Arts PROPEL, 1, 85, 89, 190–92
  assessment in, 15–16, 181–89
  domain projects in, 89–93
Assessment
  alternative models of, 15–18
  in apprenticeships, 14–15, 170–71
  in context, 12–13
  as alternative to standardized testing, 153–202
  definition of, 169
  designing projects that combine technology and, 98–106
  domain projects as vehicle for, 85–107
  domain-specific, 38–46

intelligence-fair, 2–3, 11–12, 17, 139–42, 164, 171
  need for emphasis on, 169
  as ongoing process, 37
  proper place for, 13–15
  purpose of, 37–38
  as simple, natural, and occurring on reliable schedule, 170
Assessment specialist, 195
ATLAS Communities, 61–63
ATLAS project, 2
Authentic, definition of, 134
Authentic assessment of problem solving and giftedness in secondary school students, 133–49

Baer, D., 157
Baird, L. L., 136
Bamberger, J., 161
Behavior checklist, 146–49
Bibby, J. M., 48
Bijou, S., 157
Binet, Alfred, 5, 155–56
Bixby, J., 69–70
Block, N., 6, 155

There are
one-story intellects,
two-story intellects, and three-story
intellects with skylights. All fact collectors, who
have no aim beyond their facts, are one-story men. Two-story men
compare, reason, generalize, using the labors of the fact collectors as
well as their own. Three-story men idealize, imagine,
predict—their best illumination comes from
above, through the skylight.
—*Oliver Wendell*
*Holmes*

SkyLight
Training and Publishing Inc.